A Playful Panther

By the same author

When London Walked in Terror
The Empress Brown

A Playful Panther

THE STORY OF
J. MAUNDY GREGORY,
CON-MAN

Tom Cullen

Illustrated with Photographs

Houghton Mifflin Company Boston

1975

To Dan and Barbara Stowens

FIRST PRINTING   C

FIRST AMERICAN EDITION 1975

ISBN: 0-395-19410-5

Printed in the United States of America

CONTENTS

"It was like feasting with panthers; the danger
was half the excitement."

OSCAR WILDE

The Owl of Minerva

J. Maundy Gregory is in the direct line of English con-men that descends from the promoters of the South Sea Bubble to today's pyramid sales racketeers, by way of Arthur Orton, the Wapping butcher turned Tichborne claimant, and Horatio Bottomley, who not only looked like John Bull but founded a periodical by that name in order to promote his lotteries.[1] Moreover, Maundy Gregory's niche in the valhalla of con-men is unique. He was not the first Englishman to sell royal honours, but he was by all odds the most successful—he sold more knighthoods and baronetcies than any other, and he got away with it for a longer period of time. It may not be true that the Honours (Prevention of Abuses) Act of 1925 was passed by Parliament for the express purpose of stopping Gregory in his tracks, but in nearly half a century no other person has ever been prosecuted and punished under this Act. Needless to say Gregory could not have operated long as a peddler of honours without the connivance of what are known as 'the powers that be', meaning that he was the friend of politicians, including those of Cabinet rank, police officials, generals, admirals, and senior civil servants. 'He was on intimate terms with men whose names have become household words,' as one Fleet Street journalist rather grandly put it. In time he came to be feared by the very men who had befriended him as 'The Man Who Knew Too Many Secrets', and the same Establishment that had offered him its protection vowed his destruction, which was duly carried out. But

[1] South Sea Bubble was the name given to an early eighteenth-century swindle that centred on the slave trade with Spanish America, and that involved government ministers, including a Chancellor of the Exchequer. Orton posed as 'Sir Roger Tichborne, 11th baronet', in order to lay claim to the latter's estate, and was eventually convicted of perjury. As for Bottomley, sentenced to seven years' imprisonment for fraudulent conversion, he was making a mailbag when a prison visitor came upon him. 'Sewing, Bottomley?' the visitor enquired. 'No, reaping,' the unabashed Bottomley replied.

before that time Arthur John Peter Michael Maundy Gregory, to give him his complete handle, streaked across the sky of Whitehall politics and high finance like 'an incandescent meteor', in the words of his friend A. J. A. Symons.

Curiously, it was not in Whitehall, nor indeed in any part of the British Isles that my quest for Gregory began. It began in the French market town of Châteauneuf-du-Faou in that part of Brittany known as the Finisterre, to which I journeyed one frosty morning in February, 1972, in order to identify a man. Châteauneuf (3,929 souls) lies only some three hundred miles from the Gare Montparnasse in Paris, but it was like journeying to a different planet, I reflected as I regarded the melancholy landscape from the train window. The sensation of other-worldliness if anything became more pronounced after I had left the Paris–Brest Express at Carhaix and had boarded a rickety bus of the S.N.C.F. for the remainder of my journey. The country through which the bus jolted, winding its way along a sunken road topped by scrub oak and gorse, had nothing in common with the gaily coloured travel posters of Brittany which featured lobster pots and beach umbrellas and fishing smacks pulled up on to the white sands of Quiberon and Beg-Meil. It was wooded, gloomy, steeped in legend. One does not have to tarry here long before succumbing to the Celtic twilight and imagining that every clump of trees is Brocéliande where Merlin the enchanter dwells, and that every boulder is a menhir behind which a druid is hiding.

Neither menhirs nor druids nor Arthurian legends were the objects of my visit to the Finisterre, however. I had come there in an effort to establish the identity of an Englishman with the improbable name of 'Monsieur de Grégoire'. I had learned of the existence of this mysterious Englishman just before leaving for Paris, and had heard how he had hidden out from the Germans at Châteauneuf during the early days of the Nazi occupation. Acting on a hunch that 'Monsieur de Grégoire' and Maundy Gregory were one and the same person I had decided to break my holiday in Paris with a trip to the Finisterre to carry out an on-the-spot investigation. I had no idea then that it would lead to a prolonged pursuit of the truth concerning Gregory, though the man had always fascinated me as one of the greatest rogues of his time (I was, of course, familiar with the facts of his life in broad outline).

The bus stopped to deliver parcels at hamlets with names like

Cléden-Poher and Spézet-Landeleau, then on again it went past wayside calvaries dripping with grotesque statuary. Finally, spluttering and wheezing, it climbed the hill on which Châteauneuf-du-Faou is located, and deposited me in front of a white stucco building, three storeys high, with 'Hôtel Belle-Vue' lettered in gold on its front. Mme Anne Yvinec, the *patronne*, to whom I had telegraphed the hour of my arrival, was waiting for me in the entrance, completely dwarfed by its massive doors.

Mme Yvinec, who was in her seventies, was not at all as I had imagined her to be judging from her letter to me. She was short and plump, whereas I had pictured her as tall and angular. She was friendly and forthcoming whereas I, basing myself on previous experiences with concierges, had feared that she might be spikey and taciturn. At first sight she reminded me of nothing so much as a barn owl, an impression heightened by the thick lenses of the glasses she wore which made her eyes appear big and sightless. Her cheeks were faded, but in her youth they would have been pink and firm, *pommes saillantes*, the French call them. She wore a white nylon *tablier* over her dress, and a dark blue knitted shawl over that, and she carried a cane because of her lameness. This was no ordinary owl, I soon discovered. Mme Yvinec was more like that downy creature whom the Etruscans depicted perched on the hand of Minerva as a symbol of wisdom.

There was no porter to help me with my luggage. With a rueful expression on her face, Madame explained about her game knee, asked me to show myself to Room Number 5 on the second floor, where she had made up a bed for me at my request. (There was a Monsieur Yvinec, I should add at this point, but he made an appearance only on the last day of my stay at the Belle-Vue, and then only long enough to shake my hand.) No doubt I would like to freshen up after such a fatiguing journey from Paris, Madame suggested, adding that supper would be served in a quarter of an hour.

Number 5 differed in no respect from the other rooms in this auberge, its floor being uncarpeted, though spotlessly clean, and its furniture being of the sparsest, consisting of bed, armoire, table and chair, and washstand. Yet it held a special fascination for me, for in this tiny room, which all but an anchorite would have scorned, 'Monsieur de Grégoire' had hidden out for four months in the summer of 1940 while German troops had occupied the rest of the hotel. During this time he had taken all of his meals in his room, venturing out only to use the toilet at the end of the hall. The Germans may not have been aware of the English cuckoo in their nest, but the four thousand inhabitants of Châteauneuf knew about him. Soon Gregory's fame had spread to the surrounding countryside, where he was known simply as 'l'anglais du Belle-Vue.'

My hunch, which amounted almost to a certainty, was that 'l'anglais du Belle-Vue,' alias 'Monsieur de Grégoire,' was in reality J. Maundy Gregory, an Englishman who had been in France at the time of the German invasion, but who had disappeared from sight at about the time 'de Grégoire' surfaced in Châteauneuf. Arthur John Peter Michael Maundy Gregory, to give him his full name, was enough of a ham actor to attempt an impersonation of a Frenchman, I reflected. Moreover, having lived by his wits as a con-man all of his life, he had the requisite coolness and daring to carry off such an impersonation successfully.

All doubt concerning 'Monsieur de Grégoire's' identity vanished when I went down to supper bearing with me a photograph of J. Maundy Gregory taken in his prime. It showed him with his hair parted neatly in the middle, the beginning of bags beneath his eyes, jowls sagging gently over his Gladstone collar, his cravat of a rich foulard, and a monocle dangling carelessly from a black cord around his neck. '*Mais si, c'est Monsieur de Grégoire,*' my hostess chirped when I showed her the photograph. '*On ne se trompe jamais sur un visage pareille. Pourtant quand il est venu ici il avait beaucoup amaigri,*' she added.

* * *

Mme Yvinec remembered perfectly the date of Gregory's arrival, because it was 'le samedi du panique', panic Saturday, when a large number of Parisians, fearing that the capital was about to be bombed, lost their heads and fled to the countryside.

The supper things cleared away, we were seated in Madame's parlour, a room heavy with oaken chests carved with Breton designs (there were enough chests and armoires in the hotel to hide a whole army of fugitives, I reflected) and with a few landscapes on the wall by a painter of the Pont-Aven school named Serusier. Madame crocheted as she described the events of panic

Saturday, June 9, 1940, when the Belle-Vue suddenly filled with frightened strangers. Evidently none was as strange as the English apparition that materialized on Madame's doorsill. Although it was a scorcher of a day Maundy Gregory wore a fur coat of a shaggy variety that reached down nearly to his ankles, and that was wrapped around him and tied as though it were a bathrobe. With this he wore a shapeless felt hat with the brim turned down, from beneath which peeped a nose that was '*rouge comme une framboise*', to use Madame's vivid phrase. Tucked under one arm was a Pomeranian that answered to the name of Monsieur le Beau.

Maundy Gregory had not come on his own, but had hitched a ride from Le Mans with a Parisian dentist and his family named Fevrier, who had made a reservation at the Belle-Vue for themselves. Screwing a monocle into his right eye, this bizarre hitchhiker explained that owing to the rapid German advance he had found himself stranded at Le Mans when 'these kind people', meaning the Fevriers, had picked him up in their Renault. Could Madame put him up? Although the Belle-Vue was full, Madame could and would put him up. It wasn't every day that an apparition turned up in Châteauneuf-du-Faou. '*On l'aura donné le bon Dieu sans confession*' (One would have given him Holy Communion without asking him to confess his sins) is the way Madame described the impression this English 'milord' had made upon her.

It was Mme Yvinec herself who supplied the alias under which Maundy Gregory hid so successfully from the Germans. 'Grégoire' was easier to pronounce than 'Gregory', and her nimble brain added the preposition 'de', for obviously the Englishman was of the noblesse. 'De Grégoire', at any rate, was the name she filled in on the form sent to the Préfecture, as required by law. Thus, almost unknowingly, she had taken the first step towards becoming Gregory's accomplice. The serpent had charmed the little bird.

The Parisians, having learned that they were to be spared in their beds, cleared out in the next few days leaving Madame with more time to devote to her English guest. Gregory, in turn, dazzled her with stories of his exploits in the British Secret Service. For her benefit too he trotted out the con-man's usual box of tawdry toys—the jewelled cuff-links and gold cigarette cases given to him by various royalties, his insignia as Knight Grand Cross of the Equestrian Order of the Holy Sepulchre (good Catholic that she was, Madame was most impressed when Gregory told her that he had been on friendly terms with the late Pope Pius XI). While exerting his charm Gregory managed to insinuate the fact that he was broke, or 'temporarily short of funds', as he put it, though expecting a large remittance to arrive from England. In the meanwhile, if Madame could see her way clear to extending him credit during his stay at her hotel she would be handsomely rewarded, he hinted.

The typical Breton is like the land he inhabits, 'more nerves than flesh', if his chroniclers are to be believed. Highly strung, impressionable, he is a dreamer given to jettisoning reality if it interferes with his dreams. Mme Yvinec would seem to be a case in point. How money was to be transmitted from England to 'M. de Grégoire' in the wilds of the Finisterre, moreover a Finisterre that was overrun by the *Boches*, was a question which never even entered Madame's head. Nor did she stop to think of the risk she took in sheltering the Englishman, of the penalty she would incur if caught. How the two conspirators managed to communicate was even a mystery, for Gregory spoke only that variety of French known as '*petit nègre*'. One thing was certain: Madame's faith in Gregory was total.

*　　*　　*

Ironically, many of the things Maundy Gregory had told Madame were true. Gregory had been a secret service agent employed in cloak-and-dagger work, but it had occurred in the First World War, and not shortly before the outbreak of the Second, as he had told Madame. And he had been received by Pope Pius XI at a private audience during which he had been given the Apostolic Blessing, though whether this qualified Maundy to look upon His Holiness as a personal friend was another matter. As for the gold cigarette cases, they too were genuine. One, a present from King George II of Greece, had the royal arms picked out in diamonds.

The thing about Gregory was not so much that he lied but that he bent the truth. He regarded truth as something infrangible that could be twisted and contorted out of all recognition. 'Maundy missed his calling, which was that of a Jesuit priest,' a close friend of his had told me. I refrained from repeating this judgment to Madame however, having no desire to give offence to her religious susceptibilities.

Under her prompting I told Mme Yvinec all that I knew about Maundy Gregory, she listening attentively as she crocheted. Although he claimed to have royal blood, there was very little evidence to support this, I explained. Gregory came from a long line of clergymen, his father having been vicar of St Michael's, Southampton. His mother, as a Wynell-Mayow, had aristocratic connections, but Maundy had allowed her to die neglected in an almshouse at Winchester. From this rather humble background Maundy Gregory had conned his way to the top where he was courted by royalty, as well as by ministers of Cabinet rank, and by young men aspiring to Parliament. All of this Mme Yvinec took in readily, though I had some difficulty when it came to explaining Gregory's speciality, which was the sale of royal honours.

Maundy Gregory was an honours broker, I told her, dealing in those esoteric handles of 'Sir' and 'Bart', which precede or follow one's name, and which make it easier to obtain credit from one's tradesmen. Gregory was not the first, but he was by all odds the most successful honours broker in recent times, more often than not delivering the knighthoods and baronetcies for which he had been paid. It was only in the early 1930s when he began to run out of steam that Gregory had resorted to outright fraud, selling 'non-existent' honours, as it were. (At my use of the word *'escroc'* Madame's eyes lit up, and she nodded vigorously. Gregory in the role of con-man, she understood very well indeed.) His swindles had finally caught up with him, and Gregory had found himself standing trial at the Bow Street Magistrates Court, where he was sentenced to imprisonment at Wormwood Scrubs.

When I told her that Maundy Gregory had been suspected of murder Madame's eyes opened very wide, and she even stopped crocheting. Gregory's name had been linked with the death in September, 1932, of a middle-aged, red-headed actress named Edith Marion Rosse with whom he had shared a flat in London at 10 Hyde Park Terrace. There was no question of them having been lovers, as Gregory was not attracted to women. He was in fact a homosexual, though I spared Mme Yvinec this detail.[1] There was no lack of circumstances to cause the finger of suspicion

[1] Lest the above statement sound self-serving, it is based on the testimony of those who either have known Gregory, or who have had opportunity to observe him at close quarters; notably, Inspector Arthur Askew, John Baker White, Mrs Maisie Saunders, and Ronald Russell.

to be pointed at Gregory. Mrs Rosse's will, for example. Written on the back of a hotel menu in Gregory's handwriting, the will named him as sole beneficiary of her £18,000 estate. Then there were Gregory's bizarre burial instructions. Mrs Rosse was buried in an unsealed coffin in a riverside cemetery that was known to flood in the winter. But thinking I had burdened her mind enough for one evening, I did not tell Madame these grisly details. Instead I bid her good-night and went upstairs.

*　　*　　*

Alone in my room, I fell to pondering the strange fate that had blown Maundy Gregory like a tumbleweed to this out-of-the-way place (not for nothing did the word Finisterre signify 'Land's End'). Who would ever have suspected that Maundy the Magnificent, who loved luxury and the company of his fellow men, would end up in a monk's cell, measuring 10 feet by 10 feet, with only an ill-tempered Pomeranian for companion? I had journeyed to Châteauneuf-du-Faou in the hopes of tracking Gregory to earth, of capturing that part of his personality which so far had eluded me. Perhaps something of his essence still clung to these walls, I thought as I looked around me—but no, the room was completely impersonal. It gave off no clues as to what made Gregory run, or, more accurately, stop running.

'Maundy was obsessed with power,' his friends had told me. But this was no answer at all. Everyone wanted power over someone or something. The exercise of power in the abstract held no meaning for me. Gregory was skilled at role-playing, I was told. He got his enjoyment from manipulating people, from the feeling that he was the grand panjandrum. With his genius for bending truth he had justified his wheeling and dealing in the honours racket as performing a public service. In a bullish market he was merely supplying a demand, he had argued. Through the procurement of baronetcies and knighthoods, had he not brought happiness to many successful businessmen, helped them to realize their dreams?

The trouble with Gregory was that he was so pompous, so devoid of any sense of humour, I reflected as I undressed for bed. 'I have always endeavoured never to give way to what is commonly called "wind up",' he had told a reporter shortly after his release from Wormwood Scrubs prison, adding, 'There seldom was a truer phrase than "Fear and be slain".' Whatever did he mean by these bromides? 'I have steeled myself during these recent and surprising experiences to say over to myself daily, "They say. What say they? Let them say".' Did people really talk like this, outside the novels of Henry James? More to the point, did Gregory as he shaved in the morning look into this very mirror and tell himself, 'Now Maundy, steady old fellow—mustn't get the wind up—remember, if you allow fear to conquer you, you're as good as done for'?

Notwithstanding the ordeal Maundy Gregory endured in this room there was no doubt that he had for company a magnificent view, I conceded as I pushed open the shutters. Châteauneuf-du-Faou is situated on the side of a hill overlooking the river Aulne, which the moon had turned into a trickle of quicksilver. In the distance the jagged peaks of the Montagnes Noires, so called because they are covered with fir trees, looked curiously unreal in the moonlight, like a cardboard cut-out pasted on to the sky. Off to the left the steeple of Notre Dame des Portes shone like a silver splinter. That night I had a dream which was remarkable in that Maundy Gregory, the subject of the dream, was felt as a presence rather than seen. I dreamt that the bus from Carhaix pulled up in front of the Hôtel Belle-Vue and out stepped a bowler-hatted detective from Scotland Yard, who rapped smartly on the hotel door, demanded of Mme Yvinec when she answered to see Mr Maundy Gregory. 'We think that he may be able to help us with our enquiries,' the detective explained, but as he spoke, in one of those metamorphoses that are common to dreams, he was transformed into a Gestapo official complete with swastika armband. 'Madame Yvinec, we have reason to believe that you are harbouring an enemy of the Third Reich,' the Nazi harshly accused. Madame appeared frightened. There must be some mistake, she protested. There was no one in the hotel but herself, her husband, and a paying guest named 'Monsieur de Grégoire'. But even as she pleaded I was aware that Maundy Gregory was watching the scene from above, his presence betrayed by the twitch of a curtain at an upper-storey window. The oddest part of the dream was Mme Yvinec herself. She had a tiny barn owl perched on her shoulder.

PART ONE

'You should study the peerage, Gerald . . . It is the best
thing in fiction the English have ever done.'
OSCAR WILDE

'It is really very difficult to say why anybody does get
Honours. Why is F. E. Smith made a Baronet? . . . Why
are any of us made anything?'
LORD CURZON OF KEDLESTON

'The voracity for these things quite surprises me.
I wonder people do not begin to feel the distinction
of an unadorned name.'
SIR ROBERT PEEL

'. . . members rise from C.M.G. (known sometimes in
Whitehall as "Call Me God") to the K.C.M.G. ("Kindly
Call Me God") to . . . the G.C.M.G. ("God
Calls Me God").'
ANTHONY SAMPSON

'. . . if I were Chancellor of the Exchequer I would
create new Honours . . . I would give Garters
on both legs.'
J. G. S. MACNEILL, MP for South Donegal

I

The Red Light in
the Window

Maundy Gregory had the blood of eight English kings, starting
with William the Conqueror, flowing through his veins, or so he
claimed. With the slightest encouragement Gregory would produce
a 4 ft. long pedigree compiled for him by the College of Heralds
and signed by the Garter King of Arms which suggested that on
his mother's side Gregory was indeed of the royal blood. This
remarkable document showed that Gregory could number among
his forebears John of Gaunt, 'time-honoured Lancaster', Henry
Percy, otherwise known as 'Hotspur', who was slain at the Battle
of Shrewsbury in 1403, and the Black Prince. Edward III was the
last of Gregory's kingly ancestors, after which his pedigree shuttled
between princes, dukes, and earls. Of course it was all a lot of
nonsense, or rather another example of Gregory's proclivity for
bending truth. By a judicious selection in each generation between
the male and female branches of his family, which is what Gregory
did, almost any gentle-born Englishman could claim kinship with
the illustrious.

Where does the myth leave off and the man begin? With Maundy
Gregory, publisher, titles broker, influence peddler, and general
'Mr Fix-it', one can never be certain. His capacity for myth-
making, for creating an atmosphere of mysterioso concerning
himself and his surroundings was such that one is never sure what
is make-believe and what is real. Take such a simple matter as
Gregory's mode of travelling from point A to point B. Most men
of Gregory's wealth and social standing were content to be driven
around London in a Rolls-Royce. But not Maundy. He had himself driven in an Austin taxicab of a distinctive yellow-and-brown
wickerwork pattern and fitted out with a dummy taximeter whose
flag was for ever down, moreover a taxicab which he claimed that
he kept on permanent hire (actually he owned it and paid its
driver, Tom Bramley, a salary).

Why a taxi, his friends would ask, whereupon Gregory would launch into a long and involved explanation. As 'principal co-organizer of the great secret anti-Bolshevist movement', which was one of the descriptive tags he gave himself, he, Maundy Gregory, was a marked man, he would assure his friends. His name stood high on the list of those whom Joseph Stalin wanted out of the way, and even at that moment Comintern agents might well be looking for him with orders to kill. But what did this have to do with his mode of travel, the more disingenuous of his friends would persist? Ah, a taxicab could shake off pursuers by snaking in and out of traffic (Gregory had had a special peephole cut in the back of the cab, the better to observe whether or not he was being followed). Besides, a cab waiting outside a door passed unnoticed, whereas a car would be remarked. But if Gregory sincerely believed this why had he chosen a taxi with such distinctive bodywork? Bramley's cab stood out in traffic like a hornet in a stream of black beetles. Even to pose the question was to betray total ignorance of the irrational workings of Gregory's mind.

And so with the phantom Comintern agents in pursuit, Gregory took evasive action. Every morning he had himself driven to work from his house at 10 Hyde Park Terrace by a different route. Sometimes the tell-tale cab went via Park Lane to Constitution Hill, then past Buckingham Palace into Birdcage Walk and so to Parliament Square. At other times it took a longer, more circuitous route via The Mall, turning right at Admiralty Gate into Whitehall. Once arrived, Gregory had himself driven to the mews at the rear of 38 Parliament Street, where his offices were. Here he alighted and hurried into the building. Maundy Gregory made it a rule never to use a front door if there was a rear entrance available.

How much of this was play-acting? Did Gregory deliberately cultivate eccentricity in order to get himself talked about? There is no doubt that he was paranoid when it came to the Bolshevists and their works, just as his great idol, Frederick Rolfe, alias Baron Corvo, had been paranoid about the Jesuits. (Rolfe wore a ring set with a revolving spur-rowel with which he threatened to attack any Jesuit who got in his way.) At the same time Gregory's anti-Red phobia served to strengthen the belief which he carefully fostered that he was in reality a high-level secret agent engaged in cloak-and-dagger work.

Another of Gregory's eccentricities was his studied carelessness when it came to money or objects of value. For example, he carried in his waistcoat pocket a heart-shaped, rose-coloured diamond that had once belonged to Catherine the Great of Russia, and during conversation he would take this diamond out and play with it, much as Humphrey Bogart toyed with a couple of steel ball-bearings in *The Caine Mutiny*. Did the feel of this expensive worry-bead in his hand give Gregory reassurance? Or was he merely showing off? 'He loved visible things, and the physical results of wealth, with something between the zest of the parvenu and the joy of the artist,' writes A. J. A. Symons of Gregory in *The Quest for Corvo*.

This same source is authority for another strange Gregorian quirk, his insistence on conducting business transactions wherever possible in cash. (Gregory accepted other people's cheques, but he was chary about putting his own signature to paper.) Describing one such transaction, the sale to Gregory of some of Frederick Rolfe's letters for £150, Symons writes that Gregory 'opened a drawer in his desk and from a thick packet handed me fifteen £10 notes'. 'The packet was not noticeably diminished by the transfer,' Symons adds; 'there must have been at least £5,000 on that table.' Lest it be thought that Symons exaggerated, another of Gregory's friends assured me, 'Maundy habitually carried around with him a wad of notes the size of a newly born baby's head.'

*　　*　　*

Gregory's offices at 38 Parliament Street were as bogus as his personality. Pushing through swing doors lettered in gold 'The Whitehall Gazette', the visitor barely had time to note that the page boys' uniforms were identical with those worn by government messengers (it was Gregory's idea to have tiny crowns stitched in gold on their lapels) before being whisked into an ante-chamber which was more like a gothic folly, with tinted glass in its pointed windows. Gregory facetiously referred to this ante-chamber as his 'Chapel', but its missals were copies of the *Tatler* and *Country Life*.

38 Parliament Street was the centre of an isosceles triangle formed by the Houses of Parliament, the Prime Minister's residence in Downing Street, and Scotland Yard, which abutted on Cannon Row. This was Gregory heartland, the precinct over which

he exercised a territorial prerogative. The Prime Minister, the Police Commissioner, who happened to be a retired General in the British Army, the Chief Whip in the House of Commons, who also served as Patronage Secretary to the Treasury, these archetypal figures who might have strayed from a Jean Genet black comedy were the ones from whom Maundy Gregory derived his influence and power. All that was lacking to complete the Establishment line-up was the Archbishop of Canterbury, but then Gregory enjoyed excellent relations with Bishop Ryle, the Dean of Westminster, on whose behalf Gregory had raised money to gild the choir stalls of Westminster Abbey (not surprisingly the water gilt soon wore off and had to be replaced eventually by gold leaf).

After a suitable wait in this gothic purgatory the visitor was shown into Gregory's own office which, in contrast, was almost sybaritic in its splendour. 'A cross between Downing Street and MI-5,' is the way Sir Colin Coote describes Gregory's inner sanctum. But surely the Prime Minister's office could not boast a carpet of deeper pile, nor the head of British counter-intelligence more gadgets on his desk. On a side table in silver frames were signed photographs of various celebrities, including the Duke of York (later King George VI), Major-General Sir John Hanbury-Williams, Marshal of the Diplomatic Corps, and Lord Birkenhead, one-time Lord Chancellor, whose pet name for Gregory was 'The Cheerful Giver'. On another table were ranged red dispatch boxes similar to those used by the Foreign Office.

Gregory's own desk was cluttered with telephones, indicators which buzzed, coloured lights which flashed, and a Morse 'tapper' key for summoning his secretary. Each of these stage props had been chosen with the care that the proprietor of a well-ordered brothel might lavish in furnishing a room for a favoured client. (To what Genet-like power fantasy did the portrait of the notorious hanging Judge Jeffreys, of the 'Bloody Assizes', which hung on the wall opposite Gregory's desk, cater?)

Through this *maison de tolérance*, which Gregory with some justification called his 'Chancellery',[1] passed a steady stream of clients in the 1920s, particularly in the years immediately following the First World War. Most of them were industrialists, 'hard-faced

[1] Gregory's offices were used as a Chancellery by the Equestrian Order of the Holy Sepulchre of Jerusalem, a Papal Order of which he was Knight Grand Cross.

men who looked as though they had done very well out of the war', in Stanley Baldwin's phrase. And so they had. One was a Midlands shoe manufacturer, who had made a fortune selling boots to the Army under contract. Another had invented a new type of trench mortar. A third was the father of a fragmentation grenade of which 75 million were supplied to Allied troops during the war. ('Those miniature metal pineapples were the deadliest military fruit that ever dropped into the maw of the Teuton monster,' exulted Gregory in a profile of the inventor in the *Whitehall Gazette*.) These were men who went around with slide-rules in their back pockets, who felt more at home in a workshop or a laboratory than in a drawing-room. As Gregory coyly observed of the hand grenade manufacturer, 'No Mrs Leo Hunter has ever secured him for one of those social functions in which celebrities are fed and exhibited to inquisitive society.' If the First World War had not intervened these men would have made a comfortable living turning out the nuts and bolts which had made Britain the machine shop of the world. The war had bumped them up to millionaires, and now with the return of peace they were anxious to acquire all the perks that money could buy, including titles.

Maundy Gregory understood these backroom boffins and their needs perfectly. Did not he, too, have a deep craving for respectability? He not only spoke their language, but shared their essentially philistine outlook on life. Forgetting momentarily that he had the blood of eight English kings in his veins he would on occasion go so far as to describe himself as a 'self-made' man. Looking like a rather dissolute Cardinal, Gregory, in his scarlet-upholstered chair, would listen to the backroom boys pouring out their dream fantasies and their ambitions. None would ever admit that it was he who sought the knighthood or the baronetcy. No, it was always his wife, 'the little woman', who sought it. 'The missus thinks that the title "Sir" would look nice on the firm's letterhead,' the industrialist would explain apologetically. 'Help business along, you know,' he would add. And Gregory, in his role of brothel-keeper-cum-confessor, would nod sympathetically.

*   *   *

Not all of the industrialists who were in need of a leg-up socially sought out Gregory. When business was slack Gregory had to rustle up clients, and he employed touts for this purpose, touts who acted as beaters in driving the game over the butts. Doyen of these touts was J. Douglas Moffatt, who, in another age, might have been classified as genus Begging-Letter Writer, species Decayed Gentleman, as depicted in Mayhew's *London's Underworld*. The Begging-Letter Writer was 'the connecting link between mendacity and the observance of external respectability,' Mayhew writes. 'He affects white cravats, soft hands, and filbert nails. He oils his hair, cleans his boots, and wears a portentous stick-up collar.' His outward appearance of pious resignation is at variance, however, with 'restless, bloodshot eyes, that flash from side to side, quick to perceive the approach of a compassionate-looking clergyman, a female devotee, or a keen-scented member of the Society for the Suppression of Mendacity'.

Moffatt had begun his political apprenticeship under impeccable auspices when in 1905 he was adopted by the Tories as their candidate for Parliament for the Barnard Castle division of Durham, a working-class stronghold. But in December, 1905, a begging-letter episode from Moffatt's past caught up with him, and he was forced to resign, pleading that he had been 'unexpectedly called abroad on urgent business'. When next heard of Moffatt had set up in business as an honours tout and was thriving.

Moffatt's method was to dig up a lively prospect, then to approach the Whips' Office of whichever political party—Conservatives or Liberals—happened to be in power, his proposition being, 'I've got a client who is willing to pay such-and-such for a knighthood, are we in business?' much as Harry-the-Horse might urge, 'I gotta horse right here. His name is Paul Revere.' Moffatt would then give his client's 'racing form', such particulars as whether he was a Justice of the Peace, a Master of Fox Hounds, the Deputy Lieutenant of a County, a donor to local charities.

Curiously, it was Maundy Gregory who put Moffatt out of business, for under the brokerage system which Gregory instituted there was no room for independent operators like Moffatt. The latter had, in fact, been 'taken over' by Gregory whom he bore no grudge even though Moffatt now worked for a smaller commission than before.

*   *   *

If Maundy Gregory had not existed Lloyd George would have had to invent him. As it was, Gregory became closely identified with that peculiar 'wide boy' brand of corruption that the Welshman introduced during the six years he was Prime Minister.

'You and I know that the sale of honours is the cleanest way of raising money for a political party,' Lloyd George once confided to J. C. C. Davidson (later Viscount Davidson). 'The worst of it,' he added, 'is you cannot defend it in public.'[1] Lloyd George went on to make a shrewd comparison of his method of filling the party coffers with the method then in vogue in the United States. 'In America,' he said, 'the steel trusts support one political party, and the cotton people support another. This places political parties under the domination of great financial interests and trusts.' 'Here,' Britain's wartime Prime Minister concluded, 'a man gives £40,000 to the party and gets a baronetcy. If he comes to the leader of the party and says, I subscribe largely to the party funds, you must do this or that, we can tell him to go to the devil.'

Lloyd George's analysis was correct as far as it went.[2] He overlooked one factor, however, and that is that a bought peerage entitled the purchaser to a seat in the House of Lords, and thus to a voice in the running of the nation's affairs; whereas in America a candidate supported by the steel trusts or the cotton interests still had to present himself to the voters and to convince a majority of them that he was the man for the job.

Although the traffic in honours did not originate with him, Lloyd George was the first Prime Minister to establish a tariff for the sale of honours, a price scale which Maundy Gregory was authorized to enforce. At the bottom of the scale were knighthoods which, because they were not hereditary, went for £10,000 to £12,000. These were 'bread and butter' honours, so-called because they kept the touts supplied with those staples of life. At £40,000 apiece, baronetcies were dearer because they could be handed on from father to son. These were the high-stakes honours on which Maundy Gregory concentrated, his commission on a baronetcy being handsome. Above the baronets stretched the glittering realm

[1] Robert Rhodes James. *Memoirs of a Conservative: J. C. C. Davidson's Memoirs and Papers, 1910–37*. London: Weidenfeld and Nicolson, 1969.
[2] Nearly fifty years later it has received brilliant confirmation in the political scandals which have plagued President Nixon in his second term in office.

of peers, a peerage being not only hereditary, but carrying with it, as already stated, a seat in the House of Lords. The peerage was a sort of Jacob's ladder the lowest rung of which were the barons, followed in ascending order by viscounts, earls, marquesses, and dukes. No one has ever suggested that under Lloyd George dukedoms were for sale (only one dukedom has been offered this century, and that was to Winston Churchill, who turned it down), nor even earldoms or marquisates. But quite a few of the seventy-three baronies Lloyd George created are suspect, as are some of the Lloyd George viscountcies.

Lloyd George also broke new ground by distributing titles to ex-convicts, including at least one man convicted of trading with the enemy in the 1914–18 war.[1] Likewise he became the first British Prime Minister to honour undischarged bankrupts and guilty parties in divorce proceedings, and to use titles to bribe the press on a wholesale scale. No fewer than forty-nine honours were bestowed by Lloyd George upon proprietors, principal shareholders, editors, and managing directors of newspapers. Thus were 'whole groups of newspapers . . . deprived of any real independence', according to the Duke of Northumberland.[2] Meanwhile, the Prime Minister showered so many honours on his compatriots that Cardiff became known as 'the city of dreadful knights'.

'My father has an artful bank of thirty-six ribands to supply a fund of favours,' Horace Walpole wrote of Sir Robert Walpole's use of patronage in the early 18th century to keep his Whig supporters sweetened. Thirty-six ribands were paltry compared to the artful bank Lloyd George had at his disposal two and a half centuries later, including the Orders of the Garter, the Thistle, St Patrick, the Bath, the Star of India, St Michael and St George, the Indian Empire, and the Royal Victorian Order. Each had its price tag. Not content with the existing orders Lloyd George persuaded King George V in 1917 to create the Order of the British Empire in order to reward those whose wartime service in the factory or on the battlefield merited some distinction. By 1919 there were 22,000 O.B.E. members and medallists, which works out at a decoration for every man, woman, and child in Lloyd George's

---

[1] Duke of Northumberland's speech in the House of Lords, July 17, 1922 (Hansard, Lords, v. 51, col. 505).
[2] *Ibid.*

Caernarvon constituency.[1] In fact the O.B.E. became so common that music hall comedians joked about it as the 'Order of the Bad Egg'. One such egg, Richard Williamson, a Glasgow bookmaker with a police record, was made Commander of the British Empire for his 'untiring work in connection with various charities', according to the citation.[2]

The situation became so bad that in certain clubs in Pall Mall younger members took to chanting under their breath 'Lloyd George knows my father, Father knows Lloyd George' to the tune of 'Onward Christian Soldiers' whenever some newly invested parvenu came into the room.

'I have a couple of deaneries vacant that you might like,' Lloyd George remarked to Viscount Rothermere, in enquiring whether Rothermere had any relatives in the Church of England.[3] In fact, his last day in office as Prime Minister found Lloyd George still frantically distributing ribands. 'I had the honour to recommend your name to His Majesty the King for the vacant Thistle,' he wrote to the Marquess of Bute the day he left 10 Downing Street for good. In the same honours list Lloyd George recommended for an earldom an undischarged bankrupt who had misappropriated £200,000 from Tory party funds.[4]

Lloyd George's greed was such as to cause a sharp outcry from *The Banker*, a financial journal not ordinarily given to driving the money-changers from the temple. In castigating Lloyd George's peerages as being 'blatant unto notoriety', *The Banker* had this to say: 'Many are gross illiterate profiteers, doubtful in their reputations, vulgar in their lives, who, to the shame of honour and decency, were shovelled into the House of Lords, created baronets and knights, merely upon the strength of the money they had obtained in preying upon England in the most awful crisis of her affairs.'[5]

*　　*　　*

[1] James Macmillan. *The Honours Game*. London: Leslie Frewin, 1969.
[2] LG Papers, F/6/4/10.
[3] Cecil King. *Strictly Personal*. London: Weidenfeld and Nicolson, 1969.
[4] Lord Beaverbrook. *The Decline and Fall of Lloyd George*. London: Collins, 1963.
[5] *The Banker*. September, 1927.

What was Maundy Gregory's cut? What was his share of the honours spoils amassed by Lloyd George? In the absence of proof it is impossible to say with any degree of exactitude. 'If he "sold" only one title a month on the average, and received only £1,000 for each, he still made £12,000 a year,' writes Richard Aldington. But this would have been a bad year for Gregory, who would only have had to swing the sale of a baronetcy or two to swell this total considerably. There is no doubt that the immediate post-war years while Lloyd George still lingered in power were the golden years for Maundy. It was then that he laid the foundation for the various business interests he was to pursue. I estimate that during this harvest time Gregory cleared at least £30,000 a year, which made him a wealthy man, indeed.

Lloyd George's fall from power in October, 1922 by no means put an end to Gregory as titles broker. Although his views were right-wing Tory, Gregory was truly impartial where business was concerned, operating with equal ease under Conservative, Liberal, or coalition-type National governments. The sale of honours was one of the few means open to all parties to attract large political contributions, which, in turn, were their life blood. Even the Labour party did not have clean hands as far as honours were concerned. One of Ramsay MacDonald's first acts after becoming Britain's first Labour Prime Minister was to bestow a baronetcy on a biscuit manufacturer in exchange for £30,000 worth of shares in his company and a Daimler motor-car. (Thereafter MacDonald was heckled at meetings with cries of 'Biscuits!')

After August, 1925 the situation changed, however. For in that month an act of Parliament known as the Honours (Prevention of Abuses) Act (15 & 16 Geo. 5, c. 72) received the Royal Assent and became law. Section One of this Act made it an offence to accept 'any gift, money, or valuable consideration as an inducement or reward for procuring . . . the grant of a dignity or title of honour'. Persons convicted of this offence on indictment could be sentenced to a maximum of two years imprisonment and fined £500, or, if the conviction was a summary one, to three months imprisonment plus a £50 fine. A unique feature of this legislation was that the person who paid money for an honour was just as liable to prosecution as the tout who sold the honour.

Although it cramped his style, the 1925 Honours Act did not put Gregory out of business. What it did was to force him to diversify. The well-to-do continued to queue at the door of the strange Chancellery at 38 Parliament Street, seeking everything from an introduction to Lady Londonderry to Gregory's intervention with the Vatican to obtain a marriage annulment.

But how was it that Gregory could mingle in high society? Wasn't he held in ill-repute by those who knew the chief source of his income? I posed these questions to Mrs Maisie Saunders (she and her late husband Eric Saunders had been frequent guests at the Ambassador Club which Gregory owned). 'Not at all,' she replied. 'Gregory's reputation as an honours peddler was an asset, if anything.' 'Everyone wanted honours in those days,' Mrs Saunders explained, 'and Gregory was the man who could get them for you. He had connections with Buckingham Palace, or so it was believed. Consequently he was invited to all the smartest parties.'

But it was not all party-going. Gregory frequently worked until late at night at the Chancellery in order to satisfy the whims and social ambitions of his varied clientele. And because he was paranoid, and disliked being taken by surprise, he had a system of coloured light signals installed in his window which served much the same purpose as the phallic symbols cut into the paving-stones of Pompeii. Whereas the phalli guided the footsteps of drunken sailors to the crib-houses of the lupinari, the light signals were used to warn off Gregory's confederates when he was occupied with a client. They could be seen from a vantage point in Parliament Square which was known only to his closest associates. A red light in the window meant that Gregory was in conference with a client and must not on any account be disturbed. Seeing the red light winking lewdly in the window, the associate, who might have pressing business with Gregory, would have to prowl Parliament Square until the signal turned white signifying that the coast was clear.

This make-believe world where a phoney Cardinal received suppliants in an equally phoney Chancellery; this dream factory where nothing, from the red dispatch boxes to the signed photographs of royalty, was what it seemed; this gigantic pinball machine of flashing lights and buzzing indicators—all of it came crashing down on Friday, February 3, 1933. On that date the Assistant Police Commissioner, Norman (later Sir Norman) Kendall sent for Chief Inspector Arthur Askew and told him that

[31]

proceedings were to be instituted against Maundy Gregory at once. Accordingly, Askew, armed with the Attorney-General's fiat, proceeded to the Bow Street police court to apply for a summons against Gregory for an offence under the Honours (Prevention of Abuses) Act of 1925.

II

A Summons is Served

'I have met many villains in my lifetime,' ex-Superintendent Arthur Askew told me, 'but none whom I distrusted more than Maundy Gregory. There was an air of the bogus about him. He was too well-dressed, used too much oil on his hair, wore too many rings—one, a green scarab ring, had belonged to Oscar Wilde, or so he said. I said to myself, "Hello, here's a crook, if ever I saw one."' Ex-Superintendent Askew (this was the grade in which he retired from Scotland Yard) and I discussed Gregory at Askew's home at Kemsing, near Sevenoaks, Kent, where he lives with his son and daughter-in-law. A big man, now in his early nineties, Askew still smokes a pipe, and goes bowling at a nearby bowling green. His father was a policeman, as were various uncles and cousins, the family between them having chalked up a total of 130 years of service with the men in blue. Before his retirement Askew was one of the 'Big Five' at Scotland Yard, his responsibility being the Central Division. Askew was in charge of the security arrangements at King George VI's Coronation, the high point of his career.

But on Friday, February 3, 1933, when Askew went to the Bow Street police court to obtain a summons against Maundy Gregory his rank was that of Detective Chief Inspector. That same night Askew, accompanied by a police sergeant, called at 10 Hyde Park Terrace; but Gregory, whose jungle telegraph operated very efficiently, apparently had got wind of the summons and was lying low. At least the housekeeper, Mrs Kate Wells, claimed that Gregory was not at home. Nor could she say when he would return. 'Mr Maundy Gregory is a very busy man indeed,' the housekeeper stated. 'His hours are most irregular.' When Askew pressed for an appointment, Mrs Wells said that she thought ten o'clock the following morning would be the best time to call.

'This time I took no chances, but showed up at eight o'clock with my police sergeant in tow,' the Scotland Yard chief recalled as he filled his pipe and lit it. 'But would you believe it,' he chuckled, 'Gregory still tried to give me the run-around by having his housekeeper tell me that he had been called away unexpectedly. "Very well," I said, "I shall enter the house and wait until Mr Gregory returns." The poor housekeeper, who by this time was getting flustered, excused herself, and presently she came back with the news that Gregory would see me as soon as he had dressed.'

*   *   *

The room into which Askew was shown on the ground floor was furnished sumptuously, if in bad taste, one wall being occupied by a huge poster for Sigmund Romberg's operetta, 'The Desert Song', which showed Edith Day in jodhpurs being passionately embraced by the 'Red Shadow'. When the detective remarked on the poster, Mrs Wells volunteered the information, 'It belonged to Mrs Edith Rosse, who passed away last September. Poor dear, she was mad about "The Desert Song", must have seen it a dozen times at the Drury Lane.' At the memory of Mrs Rosse the house-keeper grew quite loquacious. 'Mrs Rosse herself had had quite a career on the stage, you know. "Vivienne Pierpont", she called herself in those days, and she toured in such musicals as *The Arcadians* and *The Quaker Girl*. Her husband was Frederick Rosse, the composer. But then I expect that Mr Gregory can tell you more about her than I can, if you are interested.'

'But I was not interested,' Askew told me, 'at least not then. I was more concerned that Gregory had kept me waiting for nearly an hour while he finished dressing.'

'Finally Gregory came bounding into the room, like an actor who expects his first entrance to be greeted by applause,' Askew declared. 'He came trailing clouds of after-shave lotion, or of some other scent, and this combined with the hair oil, and all those rings, not to mention the unctuous manner, made a bad impression on me from the start.' Gregory must have sensed this, for dropping his air of false bonhomie he came straight to the point. 'What can I do for you, Inspector?' Askew then handed Gregory the summons and cautioned him that anything he said might be used in evidence against him.

The summons alleged that on or about January 23, 1933,

Maundy Gregory had tried to obtain £10,000 from one Lt-Cmdr Edward Whaley Billyard-Leake, D.S.O., Royal Navy (Ret.) as an inducement for procuring an honour for the said Billyard-Leake. Although the summons did not mention it, the honour in question was a knighthood. The maximum penalty for such a violation of the Honours (Prevention of Abuses) Act was, as stated in the previous chapter, two years' imprisonment if the case were tried on indictment. However, neither the specific offence alleged nor its possible consequences was the overriding consideration in the mind of the Director of Public Prosecutions in instituting proceedings against Gregory. Almost any charge more serious than an ordinary traffic violation would have served his purpose equally well.

For Maundy Gregory belonged to that breed of men in public life who operate in darkness, whose need for secrecy is supreme. Once the searchlight of publicity was turned on him he was finished, his effectiveness as a political fixer being completely destroyed. Gregory was like the philanderer who goes his merry, home-wrecking way for years until suddenly he is named as co-respondent in a divorce action. After that he finds himself shouldering not only his own adulteries, but those of his neighbours and friends.

All of this did not detract from the uniqueness of the prosecution brought against Gregory, who thus became the first man to be called to account for selling, or rather attempting to sell, a Royal honour under a law that was tailored to Gregory's specification. But the honours summons was in the nature of a holding charge; it was a necessary preliminary to doing a deal. The decision to prosecute Gregory was a political one taken at a fairly high level, and it was a measure of the power that Gregory still wielded, and of the awe in which he was still held, that both the Attorney-General and his agent, the Director of Public Prosecutions, trod very warily in Gregory's regard.

*   *   *

Much nonsense has been written about the effect of Gregory's impending trial on those who had known him, or who had had dealings with him of one sort or another. Some writers claim that news of the trial precipitated an exodus from England of men who

[35]

had recently acquired titles, an exodus which, at times, took on the proportions of a stampede. Cook's and the American Express were besieged by such people clamouring to book passage on late winter cruises, one writer claimed. 'London in mid-February was as deserted as when the grouse season opens in August,' according to another observer. While it is true that during the period between February 4 and February 16, when Gregory's trial opened at the Bow Street police court, some of his friends were suddenly called away on business or found it expedient to seek their villas in the south of France, their numbers have been greatly exaggerated. And not all were persons who had recently acquired titles.

A number were innocents who had supped at Gregory's board, but had forgotten to bring a long spoon. 'Some men who had been stupid rather than criminal, and others who had no knowledge of Gregory's activities but had accepted his hospitality . . . would have been ruined by the disclosure of their association with him,' as Robert Rhodes James points out.[1] Among those who can be classified as dupes no face was redder than that of the Rt Hon Sir Alfred Frederick Lumley, K.G., G.B.E., K.C.B., 10th Earl of Scarborough. As Sub-Prior of the Order of the Hospital of St John of Jerusalem, the earl had not only approved of Maundy Gregory becoming a Commander of the Order, but had invited Gregory to become Deputy Director of the Order's £100,000 Centenary Appeal. Moreover, his lordship had been Gregory's guest at the Ambassador Club, as had Colonel (later Sir) James Sleeman, C.M.G., C.B.E., M.V.O., Director of the Centenary Appeal, who had nothing but praise for Gregory's public-spiritedness. 'Fortunately in the Order's long history,' Colonel Sleeman wrote in the Chapter-General's annual report, 'it has always been found that every emergency finds the man, and in this instance Mr A. J. Maundy-Gregory, a Commander of the Order . . .' This, of course, was before Gregory's fall from grace.

However in February, 1933, there were reasons apart from the threat of a political scandal for getting away from it all, including an influenza epidemic which was responsible for 1,911 fatalities during the week ending February 3 and which had caused their Majesties the King and Queen to cancel two investitures. That other plague, unemployment, received due attention at Hyde Park, on Sunday, February 5, when a quarter of a million jobless

[1] *Op. cit.*

[36]

workers turned up to demand an end to the means test, and to raise the hackles of the bourgeoisie by singing 'The Red Flag'. As if this were not enough, in Rome the tenth anniversary of fascism was being loudly trumpeted, while in Berlin the Reichstag had just been dissolved preparatory to Hitler coming to power. 'No one doubts Herr Hitler's sincerity . . . But nothing is known so far of his capacity for solid administration,' *The Times* commented in one of its more fatuous leaders.

At the Carlton Club on Wednesday, February 8, the day *The Times* carried an item about Gregory's summons, a curious story made the rounds. A member lunching there was told on 'unimpeachable authority' that a munitions maker, desiring a barony but distrusting Gregory, signed his cheque for £50,000 with the full title he had decided to adopt as baron. 'The day I get my peerage you can cash this cheque,' the arms manufacturer informed Gregory. Within an hour this same member had the story from the lips of two other persons, the would-be peer being transformed into (*a*) a Nottingham chemist who owned a chain of stores scattered throughout Britain; and (*b*) a whisky distiller who was a great horse fancier, and had once won the Derby.

* * *

For one person at least, 33-year-old Peter Mazzina, the impulse to bolt at the first sign that Maundy Gregory was in trouble must have been well-nigh irresistible. As managing director of the Ambassador Club which Gregory owned, Mazzina was involved in the latter's shady dealings up to the hilt; hence, Mazzina lived from day to day in the expectation that Chief Inspector Askew would walk into the Ambassador Club and hand him a summons. Despite the temptation to run, he stuck to his post, however; and in the end he was to prove his loyalty to Gregory, who was fourteen years his senior.

According to one story, Gregory's interest in Mazzina began while the latter was still a boy: Gregory is said to have put Peter through the exclusive Mercers' School (motto: 'Thynke and Thanke God'), founded by Henry VIII in 1542. Whether Gregory paid his tuition I have been unable to verify, but Peter was certainly enrolled at the Mercers' School in April, 1915, according to the school records.

What is known for certain is that Maundy Gregory plucked
Mazzina, as a 23-year-old waiter, from the dining-room of the
Carlton Hotel, and installed him as managing director of the Ambassador Club at a salary of £3,000 a year. Thus Mazzina, whose
patent leather hair and Italianate good looks gave him a superficial
resemblance to the then cinema idol Rudolph Valentino, overnight
acquired the reputation of being a Boy Wonder, a reputation
enhanced when he bought himself a Rolls-Royce. In what was
perhaps the most touching gesture of all, Maundy Gregory pro-
cured for Peter the Noble Order of the Republic of San Marino.

In view of the fuss Gregory made over him, and in view of
Gregory's known sexual deviation, most people who frequented
the Ambassador Club assumed that Mazzina was Gregory's boy-
friend. But this is not at all certain, nor even likely. At the age of
eighteen Mazzina had wed Josephina Coletta, and the couple had
three children. The middle son, Peter Mazzina, Jr, who now
manages a hotel in Leatherhead, Surrey, explained to me that his
father had introduced to Gregory many of the men to whom
Gregory sold honours. 'That was in the days before it was unlaw-
ful to sell honours,' the son maintained. 'Later when the Ambassador Club was running so successfully my father tried to
dissociate himself from the honours traffic,' he continued. 'My
father said that it was bad for business.'

*   *   *

As a friend of his youth, the Reverend Harold Davidson (he
still styled himself 'Reverend' despite the fact that he recently had
been unfrocked) no doubt read about Maundy Gregory's impending trial with mixed emotions. There were, in fact, two items in
The Times of February 8, 1933, that would have held the interest
of the Reverend Mr Davidson, M.A., late Clerk in Holy Orders,
late Rector of Stiffkey (pronounced 'Stewkey') in Norfolk. The
first related to Maundy Gregory, and the other to his, Davidson's,
own trial before a consistory court the previous summer on charges
of immorality, a trial which had swept even the Yo-Yo craze off
the front pages as the sensation of the year.

A combination of Timon of Athens and Mr Salteena ('I am
parshial to ladies if they are nice') of The Young Visiters, Davidson
suffered from what today would be diagnosed as a Lolita syndrome.

It manifested itself as an intense interest in the welfare of the waitresses, many of them in a highly nubile state, who were employed by Lyons Corner Houses and A.B.C. tea-shops. Davidson, who denied that his relations with these nymphets was other than pure, castigated his fellow clergymen as 'icebergs of the Church [who] draw their skirts away from these girls'. In a letter to the Bishop of Norwich, Davidson went further and expressed the view that if Christ were to be born again He 'would be found constantly walking in Piccadilly'. 'His attitude towards the woman taken in adultery, and still more His close personal friendship with the notorious harlot of Magdala . . . have always been my inspiration,' the Stiffkey rector concluded.

In order to raise £2,000 for an appeal against this same Bishop of Norwich, who had unfrocked him, Davidson had offered himself seated in a barrel as a sideshow freak on Blackpool's Golden Mile. Now broke and living in a cheap Blackpool boarding-house Davidson read in *The Times* that his trial before the consistory court had cost the Ecclesiastical Commissioners £8,205, which was four times what it had cost to send Dr Crippen to the gallows. But then Crippen had only poisoned his wife and buried her body in the coal cellar, Davidson could reflect with bitterness; whereas he, who gloried in the title 'The Prostitutes' Padre', had tried to do Christ's bidding.

The other item of news, that relating to Maundy Gregory's summons, could have occasioned no surprise on the part of Davidson, who had been predicting just such an ending to Gregory's career for years. Though not contemporaries, Davidson and Gregory had both attended the same school, Banister Court, at Southampton, where the former had been known as 'Jumbo' because of his diminutive size.[1] Both had fathers who were clergymen, but the thing that drew the two boys together was a passionate love of the theatre. Maundy wrote verse plays which he dragooned his two brothers, Jumbo Davidson, and any other child he could lay hands on to appear in, charging a penny admission. Jumbo, whose talents lay in comedy, hated Maundy's versifying and

[1] Another alumnus to achieve notoriety was Wilfred Macartney, who, aged 12, used to be excused classes at Banister Court to attend board meetings of his father's construction firm in London, where he threw spitballs at the office girls. Macartney later wrote for the *Sunday Worker*, fought with the British battalion during the Spanish civil war.

pageantry. Cast to play Sir Francis Drake to Maundy's Queen Bess in a red wig, Jumbo on one notable occasion rebelled. Gregory had punished such *lèse majesté* swiftly by locking Davidson in the woodshed, which the former pretended was the Tower of London; and it was only after Jumbo's screams had attracted attention that he was released. Still Davidson bore Gregory no grudge. 'Jumbo didn't have it in his heart to bear any man malice, not even the Bishop of Norwich,' a friend of his explained to me. Certainly on that grey morning in February, 1933, in reading about Gregory's misfortune, Jumbo would have felt nothing but sympathy.

*   *   *

Under the heading 'MAUNDY GREGORY'S MOTHER IN ALMSHOUSE: I WAIT AND PRAY FOR A LETTER', The *Daily Express* on February 28, 1933 ran a front-page story with a Winchester dateline which began: 'An eighty-five-year-old woman is waiting stoically each day at the window of her humble dwelling in the shadow of the ancient cathedral here for the letter from her son which never comes.' Peering through the window, the *Express* reporter described Mrs Elizabeth Ursula Wynell Gregory (*née* Maynow) 'her head, with its wealth of snow-white hair, bowed over a Prayerbook'. Again, he described her as 'this pathetic figure, whose declining years have been marred by tragedy'.

This portrait, which calls to mind Whistler's mother, does not tally at all with the description supplied to me by one who knew her well in her widowhood. In fact, Harry B. Perkis, 76, a retired blacksmith of Totton, had gone to work as a boy of twelve for Mrs Gregory while she was still living in Southampton. There was a maid-servant to do the cooking, but Perkis waited on Mrs Gregory at table. 'She used to run us off our feet,' Perkis recalled. 'Every room in the house was connected by a bell to the kitchen, and whenever Mrs Gregory rang for us, we had to run to the kitchen first to see what room she was in. I used to guess what room she was in, but woe betide me if I guessed wrong—I would get a severe wigging.'

'Mrs Gregory thought herself a cut above the generality of people,' the retired blacksmith told me. 'She used to talk about

[40]

Old Park, which was the Maynow family seat in Devizes, Wiltshire, and of the servants they had had there when she was a girl. There was royal blood in the Maynow family, she used to say, and she had had her family tree framed and hung on the wall to prove it. She never said a word about her husband's, the Reverend Francis Gregory's, family, but I remember that her own family's silver which I used to polish every Saturday had some sort of crested monogram on it.'

Mrs Gregory had a half-dozen or so Persian cats in the house, according to Perkis, and the maid-servant used to grumble because she had to sleep downstairs while the cats had a bedroom to themselves. When Mrs Gregory was given one of the eight red-brick almshouses that had been endowed in the 17th century by Bishop Morley of Winchester, she was allowed to keep only one cat, a big tabby answering to the name of 'Binnie'. That was in 1927, and by that time her eldest son Colonel E. D. W. Gregory was dead, while her youngest son Stephen had emigrated with his family to Canada to take up farming. That left only Maundy, on whom Mrs Gregory had always doted because he was the artistic one of the family. 'My son is not a criminal,' she had told the *Express* reporter. 'No, he is a gentleman. He is more sinned against than sinning.'

III

A Dragon at Bay

As February 16, the date of the Bow Street hearing, approached, Chief Inspector Askew's diligence in probing Maundy Gregory's past proved to be a source of embarrassment to Askew's superiors, notably to Sir Thomas Inskip, the Attorney-General. For one thing, Askew's digging had uncovered the startling fact that a dossier compiled on Gregory earlier was missing from the files at Scotland Yard. For another, the detective's relentless poking into the dark corners of Gregory's life had angered the latter, with the result that now Gregory was threatening to tell all he knew about the honours racket, which was the last thing in the world that the Attorney-General desired.

A lifelong evangelical, Sir Thomas Inskip (later Viscount Caldecote) had studied at Cambridge originally with the intention of becoming a missionary, later opted for a career in politics and the law. Moreover, in 1927, he had led and won the fight to reject the Revised Prayer Book as undermining the moral fibre of the nation, not to mention the foundations of the Church of England. It was therefore from the loftiest of principles that the Attorney-General viewed Maundy Gregory's activities as a wheeler-dealer. At the same time Sir Thomas was enough of a practical politician to realize that Gregory must be handled with kid gloves if a public scandal were to be avoided, a scandal that might involve his Conservative colleagues in the government.

As previously indicated, deterrence rather than punishment had been the Attorney-General's intention in prosecuting Gregory. There was no need to make an example of Gregory, since the honours traffic was no particular problem in 1933. Honours touts were, in fact, noticeably thin on the ground. As the darling dodo of the honours racket, Gregory could be put out of action by a light sentence under the 1925 Honours (Prevention of Abuses) Act, or so it was reasoned. In return for his case being heard in summary court instead of on indictment, Gregory was expected to plead Guilty, and to take his medicine like a man. That way all unpleasantness could be avoided. There would be no need to call a long string of witnesses, some of whom might prove embarrassing to the Crown.

But with the Bow Street hearing only days away Sir Thomas's sleep may well have been troubled by the nightmare of Maundy Gregory standing up in court and pleading Not Guilty. Reports had reached the Attorney-General's office that Gregory at the last minute had turned defiant. Gregory's paranoia, which was never far beneath the surface, apparently had got the better of him, and now he was convinced that he was the victim of a frame-up. Lt-Cmdr Billyard-Leake, in Gregory's tortured mind, now assumed the proportions of a decoy who had been put up by Gregory's enemies to lure him into committing a blunder. The zeal with which Chief Inspector Askew questioned Gregory's business associates merely confirmed the latter in this supposition, and now Gregory was telling friends, 'I intend to fight this case all the way.'

All of this must have saddened the Attorney-General, for if Maundy Gregory were determined to fight his case Sir Thomas would have no choice but to throw the book at him, which would be dangerous for all concerned. It would mean that the Director of Public Prosecutions would have to buttress the present charge against Gregory by bringing additional charges. This, in turn, would mean subpoenaing additional witnesses, with the risk to the high and mighty of having their names dragged into the proceedings.

*   *   *

Above all it was the prospect of playing dragon opposite Billyard-Leake in the role of St George that had made Maundy Gregory unco-operative and disinclined to listen to proposals for a deal. Lt-Cmdr Edward Whaley Billyard-Leake was as unlike the usual client with whom Gregory did business as it was possible for a man to be, which in itself should have warned Gregory off him. For one thing, the naval commander was an authentic war hero, in contrast to most of Gregory's clients, who had stayed at home and had made their piles from government contracts. Appropriately enough it was on St George's Day, April 23, 1918, that

'Billy Leake', aged 22, won his D.S.O., when he sank the H.M.S. *Iphigenia*, an over-aged cruiser, in the mouth of the Zeebrugge Canal thus blocking the use of this waterway by German submarines. His citation spoke of Billyard-Leake as having shown 'the greatest bravery'. Admiral of the Fleet Sir Roger Keyes went further, praising 'this cool-headed young officer' as 'one in a thousand'.

But it was in the matter of social distinction that Billyard-Leake differed most markedly from the tycoons who made up the bulk of Gregory's clientele. The tall naval officer, whose blue eyes and clean-cut features made him attractive to women (he married four times, one of his wives being the actress Betty Chester), was part of a highly sophisticated social set that included Lord Louis Mountbatten (Billyard-Leake was godfather to Mountbatten's daughter). Had he desired a knighthood what better means of obtaining it than through Mountbatten, who was a cousin of the Prince of Wales? But Billyard-Leake had no desire to be knighted, recognizing that his wartime services had been amply repaid by the award of the D.S.O., the Légion d'Honneur, and the Croix de Guerre with Palm. In approaching him, Gregory had been guilty of a grave error of judgment.

* * *

Meanwhile, the hush which preceded Gregory's trial was broken by the squeak of Chief Inspector Askew's galoshes as he made his rounds. Evidence against Gregory was not hard to come by, once one took the trouble to dig for it. Among the cases involving honours trafficking which Askew uncovered was one concerning an alderman of the City of London, whom Viscount Davidson refers to in his memoirs.[1] Already a knight bachelor, the alderman was recommended to Davidson for an honour by the Conservative Association in the City. Purely as a matter of routine, Davidson asked the alderman whether or not he had ever been approached by an honours tout, whereupon the alderman admitted 'rather naïvely', as Davidson writes, that he had paid a large sum to Maundy Gregory on account. 'I told him that that was not a very clever thing to have done,' Davidson records, 'because Baldwin couldn't possibly recommend to the Sovereign for an

[1] *Op. cit.*

[44]

honour a man whose name was on Maundy Gregory's list.' 'I said that it was equivalent to buying an honour through a broker. He said that he hadn't looked at it in that light, and that he had been told that it was quite a usual thing.' Davidson then made the alderman a sporting offer: 'If you can give me proof that you have got your money back and it is in your complete and sole possession, then we might consider the recommendation but it will have to be a *sine qua non*.' In due course the alderman produced for Davidson's inspection a receipt for monies paid bearing Maundy Gregory's flourishing scrawl, and in return got his baronetcy.

*   *   *

It was a composed, even a cheerful-looking dragon who stepped into the dock of the Bow Street courtroom on Thursday morning, February 16, the opening day of Gregory's hearing on the honours charge. The usual *boutonnière* was missing from his lapel. Perhaps Gregory thought it too flamboyant to wear a flower on this occasion. Glancing round, Gregory, his *pince-nez* glittering, had smiles for Peter Mazzina and one or two other friends whom he spotted in the tiny courtroom.

The hearing was presided over by Sir Rollo Frederick Graham-Campbell, Chief Magistrate of the Police Courts of the Metropolis, who had been knighted in the New Year's Honours List. Indicative of the importance which the Crown attached to the case was the presence of both the Attorney-General and the Director of Public Prosecutions, Sir E. H. Tindal Atkinson. Scotland Yard was represented by a blue serge phalanx which included Chief Inspector Askew, Chief Constable Howe, Superintendent Horwell, and Colonel Carter, Chief of the Special Branch. That Maundy Gregory's fame had spread to the continent was attested by the presence among the Fleet Street journalists of Dr Karl Abshagen, London correspondent for several German newspapers including the *Hamburger Nachtrichten* and the *Deutsche Tageszeitung*, who said that Gregory was a personality 'well known in German political and diplomatic circles'.

Briefed to defend Gregory was Norman Birkett, K.C. (later Baron Birkett of Ulverton), who would later in life represent Britain at the Nuremberg war criminal trials, and crown his career by becoming Lord Justice of Appeal. The son of a linen draper,

Birkett had been called to the Bar at the Inner Temple shortly before the outbreak of the First World War, and had taken silk eleven years later. By February, 1933, when he accepted Gregory's brief he had already earned a considerable reputation as a criminal lawyer, securing acquittals for his clients in a number of sensational murder cases. He had been less lucky in defending Clarence Hatry, who got a 14-year prison sentence in 1929 for his part in mulcting investors of millions of pounds. In February, 1933, Birkett was glad enough to take Gregory's case, but canny enough to demand that his £300 retainer be paid in advance.

After the court had been convened Birkett rose to apply for an adjournment on the grounds that, as he had only recently been instructed, he had not had time to study the case in all of its aspects. Alternatively he asked permission to reserve the cross-examination of witnesses until he had taken full instructions. In agreeing to the latter request, the Chief Magistrate asked the Attorney-General to state his views as to whether the case should be tried on indictment or summarily. Now it was the turn of Sir Thomas Inskip to appear gracious, which he did in agreeing to a summary hearing. This automatically reduced the maximum penalty on conviction from two years to three months. In consenting to this course of action, Sir Thomas, of course, was gambling that Maundy Gregory could be persuaded to plead guilty and to throw himself upon the mercy of the court. But the dragon still breathed fire when in a loud voice Gregory entered a 'Not Guilty' plea.

Although it was in the nature of a preliminary skirmish, this first day of Maundy Gregory's trial was instructive in that for the first time it revealed in some detail exactly how the honours racket worked. The description came from the lips of Lt-Cmdr Billyard-Leake, who took the stand as the prosecution's first witness.

*   *   *

It was in December, 1932, Billyard-Leake told the court, that he was first approached by J. Douglas Moffatt, that virtuoso of the Begging-Letter whom Gregory employed as a contact man. (The advantages of using a contact man were obvious in that such a system protected Gregory, whose name need never enter the negotiations if the potential client was not interested in the proposition.) Moffatt's letter to Billyard-Leake, written on the letterhead notepaper of The Sports Club, 16 St James's Square, had differed not a jot or tittle from the specimen sent out in the past, which had proved so successful in gaining entry to the socially ambitious. 'Dear Sir,' it began, 'I am requested to place before you a social matter of a very confidential nature which it is thought may be of interest to you. Will you kindly let me know whether you can suggest a meeting within the next few days in London or elsewhere. I cannot put more in a letter.' The postscript which followed added, 'In case you might care to find out who I am I am well known to ——.'

Moffatt had followed up the letter with a telephone call requesting an interview, after which Billyard-Leake had agreed to see him at the former's town house in Lowndes Square, Knightsbridge. That had been late in January, 1933. When they met Moffatt had informed the naval commander that he had been suggested for a knighthood 'by the highest authority in the land'. The honours tout then took from a brown paper parcel a copy of the *Whitehall Gazette* for June, 1932, containing an account of the Derby Dinner, which had been held at the Ambassador Club on the eve of the racing classic earlier that month, and which had been attended by a brilliant assemblage of sportsmen and politicians, including Winston Churchill and his cousin, the Duke of Marlborough. Pointing to the name 'J. Maundy Gregory, Esqr., C. St. John', which was sandwiched between Viscount Elibank and Lord Hanworth, Moffatt had announced, 'This is the man you must see.' 'But I don't even know the person you have indicated,' Billyard-Leake had protested. 'You will,' the honours tout winked knowingly, 'because Mr Gregory is the one who is going to carry this thing through.'

That same afternoon the two men drove to 10 Hyde Park Terrace where, after making the necessary introduction, Moffatt left the naval commander alone with Maundy Gregory. After a few abortive attempts at small talk, Gregory had come directly to the point, 'Commander, some of the highest authorities in the land are desirous that you should accept an honour—the suggestion was a knighthood.'

'I said it was a very great surprise to me,' Billyard-Leake testified. 'I could not understand why such a situation should arise . . .

unless it was the aftermath of my service in the war.' Predictably, Gregory had seized upon the pretext offered, saying, 'Your name, I know, has been mentioned in connection with this, and is very high on the list at the present moment.' 'I then said,' the commander related, 'that I did not quite understand why it should arise in the way it had. It seemed to be rather curious, but as it was a conversation entirely between gentlemen I would take his word for it.' (One wonders if Gregory appreciated the irony implied in the expression 'entirely between gentlemen', for Billyard-Leake could not have failed to take Gregory's measure in the first few minutes of their conversation.) 'Gregory then told me,' the commander continued, 'that these matters had to be arranged, that sinews would be necessary in order to open certain doors. In a case such as mine it could be done for £10,000, but if I could make it £12,000 it would make it easier.'

Bullyard-Leake had asked for time to think it over. Immediately afterwards he had reported his conversation with Gregory to a third party, though it is unclear from his testimony whether it was his own solicitor or a detective from Scotland Yard. Nor is it clear whether the commander was acting on advice in stringing Gregory along, which he now proceeded to do. On January 25 the two men met for lunch at the Carlton Hotel, at which time Gregory assured the commander that 'the matter was going extremely well'. On this occasion Billyard-Leake asked Gregory for his bona fides, some proof of his ability to carry the matter through.

Attorney-General: What did he say to that?
Billyard-Leake: He told me of the different orders which he held and mentioned the names of prominent people. I asked him whether he could show me something which I could show my wife in order to satisfy her. He produced from his pocket a typewritten docket of about five pages which I read.
Attorney-General: Was anything further said about money?
Billyard-Leake: Different prices of honours were discussed, ranging over the years.
Attorney-General: Was anything else said?
Billyard-Leake: Only that he had been instrumental in arranging these matters for some considerable time.
Attorney-General: Were any names mentioned as references?
Billyard-Leake: I asked permission to discuss his name with

[48]

three friends of mine, who happen to be well-known influential people. He approved of two, and asked me not to speak to the third.

The 'third man', although his name was not mentioned in court, was Vice-Admiral Sir Reginald Hall, wartime Director of Naval Intelligence, and Gregory's sworn enemy. 'Blinker' Hall (a facial tic gave him his nickname) had been in charge of Room 40 at the Admiralty where German wireless messages were decoded, and had taken part in the interrogation of such famous spy suspects as Sir Roger Casement and Margaret Zeller, the sloe-eyed Oriental dancer whom the world knows as Mata Hari. 'The man is a genius,' U.S. Ambassador Walter Hines Page had informed President Wilson. 'Hall can look through you and see the very muscular movements of your immortal soul while he is talking to you. Such eyes as the man has! My Lord!' Perhaps those X-ray eyes had penetrated to the muscular movements of Maundy Gregory's soul and had been displeased with what they saw, but 'Blinker' Hall, who became a Tory politician after the war, never missed an opportunity to put in a bad word for Gregory, or to try to thwart the latter's designs. Small wonder that Gregory objected to him as a referend.

On January 26 Maundy Gregory wrote to Billyard-Leake as follows:

My dear Commander,—I much hope to see you at luncheon tomorrow with Lord Southborough—Carlton, 1.30. Apart from this I should be glad if you would call upon me tomorrow morning in the neighbourhood of 11 o'clock, as I want just to complete data, which I have practically completed. Your great sporting effort, of which you told me, I am very interested in, and I think I have just the man to help you very materially in completing the matter. Will you 'phone me about 10 in the morning?

> Yours very sincerely,
> *J. M. Gregory*

Upon receipt of this letter Billyard-Leake took it to a Treasury Solicitor and made a full statement of his dealings with Gregory. The 72-year-old first Baron Southborough, P.C., G.C.B., G.C.M.G., G.C.V.O., K.C.B., referred to in the letter, had at one time been a Civil Lord of the Admiralty, and had excellent Court connections besides. As to the 'data', Gregory evidently was completing Billyard-Leake's *curriculum vitae* listing his achievements, including those in the field of sports. This hocus-pocus was designed to make the client feel that he was getting his honour as a result of merit, as well as for cash on the nail.

Billyard-Leake did not keep the luncheon appointment, but telephoned to apologize, whereupon Gregory wheeled out the biggest gun in his arsenal—King George II of Greece. Would the commander care to meet His Majesty the King of the Hellenes? Gregory asked. Billyard-Leake said that he would be pleased to do so, but that he was leaving for Scotland that night. Upon his return from his estate in Ayrshire, Billyard-Leake rang up Gregory in the presence of Michael Isaacs, a company director, and told Gregory that the deal was off. The conversation, which was overheard by Isaacs, ran in part:

> *Billyard-Leake*: I have discussed the matter fully with my wife, and, no bones having been broken on either side, I definitely do not wish to continue.
> *Gregory*: It is very regrettable as the matter is now practically complete. If you adhere to your decision the matter must drop, and I cannot revive it. Couldn't you give, say, £2,000 or £3,000 on account to keep the pot boiling?
> *Billyard-Leake*: I told you before that my decision would be final.

Called as a witness, Michael Isaacs, of Albert Hall Mansions, corroborated the naval officer's testimony concerning the telephone conversation. The next witness was Billyard-Leake's chauffeur, Walter Percy, who was asked if he could see J. Douglas Moffatt in the courtroom. After scanning the spectators carefully Percy's eyes lighted upon a grey-haired, nondescript-looking man with a worried expression on his face. 'That's him,' the chauffeur exclaimed, pointing to Moffatt, after which the hearing was adjourned until February 21.

*   *   *

The curtain may have been rung down on the first act, but the real drama had only just begun. For in the five days remaining

[50]

before the trial was resumed Maundy Gregory must be persuaded by those involved in his dealings to change his plea from Not Guilty to Guilty, after which the sentencing would be a mere formality. At all costs he must be stopped from going into the witness box and telling all, as he had been threatening to do in talks with friends. He must be made to listen to reason, and it was not going to be an easy task.

For as he sat there in the dock of the Bow Street police court Gregory's mood had hardened. He had become more convinced than ever that the case was a frame-up, that he was 'for the high jump', as he expressed it to friends. The shadowy figure of 'Blinker' Hall in the background did as much as anything to convince him. Maundy Gregory forgot that it was he who had approached Billyard-Leake with the offer of a knighthood for £10,000. To his paranoid way of thinking, it was 'Blinker' Hall, the former head of naval intelligence, who had put his fellow naval officer up to the plot, and Billyard-Leake had merely trailed his coat. Hall was the mastermind of the conspiracy which aimed at Gregory's ruin. 'After all,' Gregory argued with friends, 'to frame someone on a charge of this sort would be child's play for the man who, if he did not actually forge Sir Roger Casement's diary, made sure that the diary was used to hang him.'[1]

Thus those who were anxious to buy Maundy Gregory's silence had not only the delicate question of the price to consider, but his paranoia to contend with. The paranoia, in turn, had bred reck-lessness. 'My own reputation is in shreds—why should I protect the reputation of others?' he was overheard to threaten at about this time. But those who knew Gregory best suspected that there was more bluster than madness behind his threat. Maundy was merely trying to raise the price for remaining silent, they main-tained. He wanted something more than pious assurances that he would be taken care of, once he had served his prison sentence. He wanted copper-bottomed guarantees.

The five days that elapsed before the final disposition of

[1] Gregory was referring to diary extracts indicating that Casement was a homosexual. These excerpts were circulated by Hall on the eve of Casement's execution as a spy in order to prevent him being reprieved from the gallows. Hall's biographer Admiral Sir William James thinks that Hall's part in this sorry episode may explain why once the war was over he was never again employed by the Admiralty.

Gregory's case were thus a period of furious, behind-the-scenes activity of haggling and horse-trading in which offers of money and threats of blackmail mingled. They provide a fitting climax to one of the most spectacular careers in British politics between the wars.

That career began in the parish of St Michael's, Southampton, where Maundy Gregory's father was vicar, and Maundy himself the greatest disappointment that this saintly clergyman was called upon to bear.

PART TWO

'History has yet to reveal—perhaps it never will fully reveal—the measure of corruption which Lloyd George permitted to enter politics during his six years as Prime Minister.'
ROBERT BLAKE

'He [Lloyd George] detested titles. This, no doubt, is why he distributed them so lavishly.'
A. J. P. TAYLOR

'My dear fellow, I am no worse than Walpole.'
DAVID LLOYD GEORGE

'I wonder what you thought of the Honours List. I have never ceased to congratulate myself that I did not figure among that rabble.'
NEVILLE CHAMBERLAIN, in a letter dated January 12, 1918

IV

'Oh, Mabel' and Others

Maundy Gregory's first love was the theatre, which was also the source of early grief. For many years he laboured under the illusion that his father's death had been hastened by his own debut as a playwright. Yet the Reverend Francis Maundy Gregory was already dying on August 1, 1898 when he attended the opening night of his son's play at the Philharmonic Hall in Southampton. He was suffering from a malignancy that had been wrongly diagnosed as a peptic ulcer. Judging from a photograph taken earlier, the Reverend Mr Gregory had been a strikingly handsome man. There is an arrogant tilt to the head, which is wearing a biretta; the eyes are hooded, sensual; the silver beard cascades down the front of his soutane. Clearly, in his prime he had been an imposing figure. But now his flesh had wasted away. Maundy's father, as he sat in the audience at Philharmonic Hall, looked much older than his fifty-eight years.

Self-Condemned (the title could hardly have been more apposite) was the first, and as far as I have been able to discover, last full-length play that Gregory ever wrote. But it was much more than a conceited young man's initial effort in the theatre. *Self-Condemned* was a family affair. It was the continuation of a dialogue between Maundy Gregory and his father, or rather, of a duel. It was a manifesto. It was Maundy Gregory, aged 21, and studying to take Holy Orders at Oxford University, telling his father that he totally rejected the priesthood. Hamlet-like, he believed that the play was the thing wherein to catch the conscience.

The prologue takes place in the sacristy of St Mark's, Venice, where Father Lorenzo, a Roman Catholic priest, suspecting the sacristan of having seduced his (Lorenzo's) sister, strikes the wretched man what he believes is a mortal blow, then flees from the scene. Father Lorenzo takes refuge in England, where he renounces the Roman faith for no apparent reason, changes his name to Victor Austen, takes up an Anglican curacy at Winborough. This permits Gregory to introduce such social types as the Dowager Lady Barrington and the Duchess of Dent, who are clearly modelled on his friends, the Loraine family of Yew Tree Cottage, Lyndhurst. These grace notes, if one may call them that, are incidental to the real purpose of the play, which is to ridicule the High Anglican beliefs of the Reverend Mr Gregory and of all other 'high parsons [that] turns their churches inter theaters with all their ritjul and ceremonies', as Gregory has one of his characters, a Cockney, express it.

It was a *succès de scandale* on the part of the budding dramaturge, and when the curtain came down on the last act there were cries of 'Author!' from Gregory's friends in the audience. According to the *Southampton Times*, 'Gregory made the usual little speech of thanks to the audience and company, and announced that, having received an offer from a theatrical manager, he hoped that the play would be seen on a larger stage'—a typical Gregory boast. When a few weeks later *Self-Condemned* played the industrial town of Workington in Cumberland not far from the Scottish border it was booed off the boards after the second performance, and its actors were left stranded. 'None of the cast had money to get home,' I was told by Miss May Trelawny, now 87, whose sister Elma had played the part of Lady Barrington. (Both sisters were to enjoy successful stage careers under the management of Mr Seymour Hicks.) 'Mother didn't want my father to know anything about it, so she sold some of her jewellery in order to send Elma her fare home.'

Returning to the play's opening night at Southampton, it was not so much Maundy's irreverence, as his thoughtlessness, that wounded the father. 'To get costumes for the play Maundy raided the sacristy of St Michael's and helped himself to the vestments there, all without asking his father's permission,' Miss Trelawny told me. 'Not only that, but for the scenes in St Mark's, Venice he had borrowed from St Michael's such priceless church ornaments as the 16th-century chalice and paten, and the medieval brass lectern. The first the Reverend Gregory knew about it was when the curtain went up on the play.' 'I don't think he ever quite recovered from the shock,' Miss Trelawny added.

* * *

In examining the conflict between Maundy Gregory and his father, it is difficult to assess how much of it was due to the disappointments suffered by his mother. After the splendours of Old Park, the family seat near Devizes, Wiltshire, where she was brought up as a girl, the decaying parish of St Michael's must have seemed a come-down to Ursula Wynell Maynow Gregory. The living, which was in the gift of the Lord Chancellor, was in fact the poorest in the whole of Southampton, it being worth no more than £183 a year plus vicarage. At first there wasn't even a vicarage. The newly married couple were forced to live outside the parish at 9 Portland Terrace, where their three sons—Edward, Arthur John Maundy, and Stephen—were born, Maundy making his entry into the world on July 1, 1877. Later the family moved to 55 Bugle Street, opposite St Michael's church.

To make matters worse, the Reverend Francis Gregory's efforts to introduce the High Church principles of the Oxford Tractarian movement to what had been predominantly an evangelical parish had aroused fierce hostility. As late as 1850 St Michael's vestry, at a special meeting, had petitioned Queen Victoria 'to put down the pretensions of the Pope and to remove the clergy who would destroy the great principles of the Reformation'. Barely twenty years later, these Papist pretensions raised their ugly heads again as the Reverend Mr Gregory, on his very first Sunday in the pulpit, introduced changes in ritual. 'Psalms and prayers were intoned,' reported the *Southampton Times* of September 17, 1870; 'the back of the officiating priest was turned towards the congregation during the recital of the Apostle's Creed ... while in preaching the new vicar discarded the black gown for the white surplice and, contrary to all precedent here, pronounced the Benediction from the Communion.' Saints' days were to be observed throughout the year, as were Holy Days of Obligation, it was announced. Also the vicar intended to introduce *Hymns Ancient and Modern*. The new vicar announced that he was 'quite ready to give any explanation respecting these changes to all ... who came to him in a peaceable and charitable, and in some sort, a teachable spirit'. Few, however, took him up on his offer at first. Instead, there were 'whispers of disapproval', to quote the *Southampton Times*, whispers which grew in volume. 'There were times when insults were hurled at him in the streets and even physical violence was threatened,' writes Mrs Doris C. Cotton, wife of the present churchwarden of St Michael's, in her informative history of the church. Gradually the Reverend Mr Gregory, who was to remain their shepherd for thirty years, was able to win over his parishioners to the point where today his reputation at St Michael's is that of a saint (a bronze plaque dedicated to his memory is affixed to a wall in the north transept, but a more lasting memorial perhaps is the marble-topped high altar which the Reverend Mr Gregory had brought with him from St Paul's, Knightsbridge, London).

Some of the early hostility expressed towards his father rubbed off on Maundy Gregory when he enrolled at Banister Court School in 1886. Banister Court, which was founded for the sons of merchant marine officers, was no forcing shed for delicate plants. (Its most famous alumnus, Admiral Jellicoe, hero of the Battle of Jutland, was described by a contemporary as 'nervous and timid, though by no means a coward'.) The school's founders appear to have shared the conviction of Eton's famous headmaster, Dr Keate, that boys, at least lower-form boys, were fundamentally wicked. Wickedness could be exorcized only through games, or as Christopher Ellaby, the headmaster, explained in his prize-giving-day speech the year Gregory was enrolled at Banister Court, 'By a judicious use of games the spirited part of a boy's nature is turned to good, whereas it would otherwise expend itself in evil.'

As Gregory was hopeless at games he was treated roughly by his classmates, who christened him 'Bum Cheeks' in tribute to the fullness and rosiness of his face. They also mimicked his walk (he toed in), taunted him with being a 'Pope lover', claiming that the Reverend Mr Gregory rode around St Michael's church on a donkey on Palm Sunday. Even in the school debating society, which was Maundy's only outlet for self-expression, he was more often than not on the losing side, according to the school magazine. At least one sadistically minded master joined in the sport of Maundy-baiting, conditioning its victim to blubber at the command, 'Cry, Gregory, cry!'

As indicated, Maundy sought relief from his torment by retreating into the world of make-believe, the theatre. In particular, after he had passed the Oxford University entrance exam with distinction, and had gone into residence at Oxford as a non-collegiate student at the beginning of the 1895 Michaelmas term, the theatre seemed to become an obsession. This coincided with Gregory making the acquaintance of Mrs Frederick Loraine, wife of a retired Royal Artillery colonel, of Lyndhurst, Hampshire, and her daughters Ida, Vivien, and Florence, each of whom seemed to be more stagestruck than the next. It was in the amateur theatricals which the Loraines organized at Yew Tree Cottage, their Lyndhurst home, that Gregory established a small reputation as a drawing-room entertainer. Sometimes he did solo turns, appearing as 'Signor Gregorio, ventriloquist, and his talking dolls', for Maundy had sent away for a manual on ventriloquism, and had made himself quite proficient in the art. Or again, he might give a reading from Dickens—'Mrs Jarley's Waxworks' was a favourite—or recite his own comic verse. A specimen of that verse entitled 'The Artistic Temperament' was published in the *Banister Court School Magazine* for July, 1902. A lampoon on the 'greenery-yallery' school of aesthetes, the poem tells of a shipwrecked artist, modelled on the poet Bunthorne of Gilbert and Sullivan's *Patience*, who declines rescue because the colour of the lifeboat is too, too vulgar, and who later perishes in a blaze rather than descend a fireman's ladder that is painted a hideous red. It was all rather jejune, but it charmed the Loraine girls and their circle, to whom Maundy was known as 'Oh, Mabel', a nickname derived from one of his performances.

Almost nothing is known about the three years Maundy spent at Oxford for the simple reason that he was not attached to any College or Hall. One would expect him to have been active in the Oxford University Dramatic Society, but no—a search of the society's archives at the Bodleian Library discloses no trace of Gregory. Neither was he a member of the Oxford Union despite the interest he showed earlier in debate. As a non-collegiate student or 'tosher', Maundy was restricted in his choice of digs to those located within a one-and-a-half-mile radius of Carfax Tower, which serves Oxford as an umbilicus. *Self-Condemned* contains a rather amusing portrait of his Wesleyan landlady, a Mrs Johnson, who went around boasting, 'I'm not proud or puffed up, yer know.' Referring to her stagestruck boarder, Mrs Johnson remarks, 'I never knew before that a man 'ad taste . . . but I know where he gets it . . . at the thee-a-ter. That's the way they do things at the thee-a-ter.'

The death of his father in March, 1899 left Maundy free to make the 'thee-a-ter' his career. Academic life had never appealed to him to begin with, and he certainly had no desire to follow in his late father's footsteps by taking Holy Orders. So with only two terms remaining before Finals he came down from Oxford without a degree, and without regret, one might add.

The £3,374 estate left by the Reverend Mr Gregory was barely enough to provide for his widow, let alone to see his three sons launched in careers. Six months after the father's death Stephen, the youngest son, left Banister Court School for the South African War, serving first with the Natal Mounted Rifles, then, as corporal, with the Scottish Horse. ('Don't be frightened at not hearing from me as we are too busy chasing Boers,' he later wrote to his mother.) The war over, restless Stephen tried his hand first at prospecting for gold in Borneo, then at farming in British Columbia, where he married the sister of one of his Banister Court schoolmates. In the First World War Stephen was stuck, as a lieutenant in the Hampshire Regiment, in the dreary hole of Salonika and was soon invalided out with a weak heart. With only his Army pension to live on Stephen at one time was so hard up that he moved his family, which had grown to five children, in with his mother to share a large Victorian house in Portswood Road, Southampton. In 1927 the family emigrated to Canada, where Stephen's two sons, by now grown men, helped to make a go at farming.

Gerald Macmillan writes that Stephen Gregory 'attained high military rank in the Canadian Army', an error repeated by Richard Aldington in asserting that this youngest son 'became a distinguished officer in the Army of one of the great Dominions'.[1] Both writers have confused Stephen with his brother Edward, who served with distinction in both the South African War and the First World War, where he attained the rank of lieutenant-colonel. At one time the business partner of Maundy, whom he loathed, Edward's life was relatively humdrum, and he died early in Harrogate, where he had retired to take the waters.

*   *   *

Macmillan likewise appears to be in error in claiming that Maundy, when he came down from Oxford, obtained an assistant mastership at a private school in the Winchester–Southampton area, possibly Banister Court itself. I can find no record of this

[1] Richard Aldington. *Frauds*. London: William Heinemann, 1957.

employment, though it is possible that Gregory, as an under-graduate, earned money during the Long Vacation by tutoring Banister Court boys. Instead, I find in the *Banister Court School Magazine* for March, 1900 an item to the effect that 'A. Gregory is acting in one of Ben Greet's companies.' (Philip Ben Greet, a Southampton lad made good, pioneered the presentation of Shake-speare in the open air, notably in London's Botanical Gardens, and was later knighted for his services to the theatre.) Thus within a year of his father's death Maundy had already embarked upon a theatrical career. Further light on that career is shed in *The Green Room Book*, Gregory's entry in the 1907 edition of this theatrical *Who's Who* reading in part:

MAUNDY-GREGORY, J. (Arthur John Maundy-Gregory), theatrical manager and playwright . . . First appeared pro-fessionally as a drawing-room entertainer; then manager of Prince of Wales's Theatre, Southampton, and afterwards toured in a long list of dramas and farcical comedies, under some eighteen different managements, including Miss Fortes-cue, Messrs W. W. Kelly, Ben Greet, etc.

Has devoted himself to management since 1902; founded an agency for dramatists, 1903; manager for F. R. Benson's Company, 1903 to 1906; in November of that year he pre-sented 'Lights Out', from the Waldorf, on its first provincial tour, and now holds the sole rights.

Hobbies: Motoring, skating and swimming. Address: Waldorf Theatre, W.C., and 55 Bugle Street, Southampton.

Why Gregory decided to hyphenate his name is not known, any more than it is known why he continued to bill himself as 'play-wright' after his abortive attempt in this field. The Prince of Wales's Theatre (later the Hippodrome) presented burlesque, drama, and pantomime. As for Miss Fortescue (*née* Finney), she achieved fame by collecting £10,000 damages from Lord Gar-moyle for breach of promise, at that date (1884) the largest settle-ment of its kind ever recorded in England, according to the *Law Journal*.

Gregory's first sizeable role was as a comic butler in *The Brixton Burglary* with which he toured in 1902. In the next five years, if

[61]

his entry in the *Green Room Book* is correct, he appeared under eighteen different managements, which does not speak well for Gregory's staying ability. Either he was restless and changing jobs, or he was being fired with extraordinary frequency. His longest and most satisfying engagement undoubtedly was with W. W. Kelly's Company on tour in *A Royal Divorce*, a tear-jerker about Napoleon's domestic troubles. Gregory played Talleyrand, the second male lead, and managed to earn some kudos for his performance, the *Era* describing it as 'a faithful portraiture of that wily Minister of State'.

Whatever acting experience Gregory may have picked up with the company was as nothing compared to what he learned in showmanship from W. W. Kelly, a jovial Irish-American whose cable address was 'Hustler'. Kelly taught Gregory the importance of selling oneself rather than the product, a proposition which Madison Avenue was to immortalize as 'sell the sizzle not the steak'. In this case, the sizzle was Edith Cole (in real life Mrs W. W. Kelly), who had been playing Josephine for as far back as anyone could remember. To make her more palatable to the public Kelly's technique was to whip up controversy. Weeks before the show was scheduled to open in a particular town, Kelly had that town plastered with posters calling upon the public to take sides in the battle of wits between the Empress Josephine and her rival for Napoleon's affections, Marie-Louise. The result was that Miss Cole's every entrance on stage was applauded while the poor actress who played Marie-Louise was booed and hissed.

Wherever the show played, a benefit was organized for Miss Cole on Friday night (next to Monday the worst night in the week as far as the box office was concerned), the implication being that this was her farewell tour. The following year the indestructible Miss Cole would be back 'in response to public demand'.

After six months of touring with *A Royal Divorce* Gregory left the company, whether as a result of a disagreement with Kelly, or simply because he grew tired of living out of a suitcase is not known. He never forgot the lessons in showmanship he had learned from Kelly, however.

It was through his mother's cousin, Percy Vernon, the actor, that Maundy in June, 1903, secured an interview with Frank R. Benson who was then at Stratford-on-Avon appearing in *Macbeth* for the Shakespeare festival. At Oxford University Benson had

[62]

been a famous all-round athlete, excelling at football, cricket, rowing, and running (he beat Cambridge in the 3-mile race). His interest in sports scarcely waned after he had made a name for himself in the theatre, with the result that he hired actors as much for their prowess as fast bowlers and soccer forwards as for their acting ability. Upon learning from Gregory that he had failed to win a blue at Oxford in any sport, Benson lost interest in him as an actor, but told Gregory that there was an opening for stage manager with Benson North, one of three companies the Shakespearean had on the road. He did better, giving Gregory a letter of introduction to Bill Savery, the assistant general manager, with the result that Gregory got the job at £5 per week, which was about twice what he had been earning as an actor.

Probably at no other time in his life did Gregory work so hard as he did during the three years he was with Benson. For even though Benson North played mostly the cotton towns of Lancashire and Yorkshire its repertory was unrelenting: Monday night it was *Macbeth*; Tuesday, *The Merchant of Venice*; Wednesday, *The Merry Wives of Windsor*; Thursday, *Julius Caesar;* and Friday, *Twelfth Night*. On Saturday nights it was always *Hamlet* with the lovely, red-headed Dorothy Green playing Ophelia and looking startlingly like Elizabeth Siddal in the Millais painting of the same. 'The audiences Benson North played to were composed largely of semi-literate mill-hands,' George Hannam-Clark, 92, last of the Bensonians, told me when I interviewed him at a nursing home in Cheltenham. 'They flocked to see Shakespeare because the theatre had nothing else to offer them except cheap melodrama.' 'Seeing *Hamlet* for the first time, many of the spectators had no idea how the play ended, so there was tense excitement when in the third act play-within-a-play Claudius starts guiltily and calls for lights. For dramatic effect Benson used to ring the curtain down at this point, leaving the audience buzzing with anticipation.'

The transformation wrought in Gregory by the £5 per week and the title 'manager' was startling. Overnight he blossomed forth in the most literal sense of the word, for no matter where the company played Gregory had a buttonhole, usually a rose or an orchid, sent up daily from Covent Garden, and collected at the station by a cabman.[1] That evening, with the posy ostentatiously displayed

[1] For this and other information concerning Gregory as manager of Benson North I am indebted to J. C. Trewin and his entertaining and

in the lapel of his evening suit, Gregory would appear in the best box of the theatre where Benson North was playing, and proceed to scrutinize the players, a habit loathed by all. Already he showed himself adept at the type of *mise-en-scène* which later was to become his hallmark. For example, Bill Savery found when he visited Birkenhead that Gregory had rented an office next door to the theatre, and, to give the impression of himself as a busy man of affairs, had scattered wire letter baskets on every available desk and table.

Savery made another important discovery: Gregory had been dipping his hand in the till. Gregory's taking ways apparently were common knowledge to members of Benson North, which would explain the following enigmatic reference to him which appeared in 1905 in *The Flea*, a house organ circulating among members of the company:

Count Whatsthatski: No, thank you, we lost over the shoes. Why not offer it to the management for the mat in the Play scene? Or Mr Maundy Gregory might relieve you of it.

The implication was that Gregory was good at 'relieving' people of things. After a few more broad hints of this nature Bill Savery was sent to Birkenhead to investigate Gregory's financial dealings. He found that Gregory's accounts were in a mess. 'There would be plenty of opportunity for someone like Gregory to cook the books,' George Hannam-Clark told me. 'But he would have been up against a tough customer in Savery,' Hannam-Clark added. 'I acted as manager of one of the Benson companies for a short time, filling in while the real manager was sick, and I found that I had not just one set of books, but five or six sets of books to keep,' he recalled. 'Savery was always very polite and helpful, knowing that I was a greenhorn at the business, but he kept a sharp eye on what I was doing. You couldn't put much past him.'

As soon as he discovered Gregory's peculations Savery fired him. Gregory might easily have been had up in court for misappropriation of funds, but his youth perhaps predisposed Benson in his favour, or the fact that he was a fellow Oxonian. Whatever

---

informative study, *Benson and the Bensonians* (London: Barrie and Rockliff, 1960). Trewin talked to W. H. 'Bill' Savery, the assistant general manager, shortly before the latter's death, and Savery was full of stories about Maundy Gregory.

the reason, he was allowed to go free. Gregory later tried to magnify his role with Benson. Thus, in a profile of Gregory in *What's On* for September 14, 1907, there occurs this boast: 'For some years Mr Maundy Gregory was prominently associated with the Bensonian management, and was instrumental (with Mr Smyth Pigott) in developing the Benson Company into four companies.'

*　*　*

Gregory's first brush with the law came two years later, by which time he had formed the partnership of 'Messrs E. D. and J. Maundy-Gregory' with his brother Edward, who was an accountant. The partners then had three shows on the road, including Mr and Mrs Charles Sugden in a revival of *Zaza*. Far from being chastened by his experience with Benson North Gregory was more brash than ever, judging from the publicity handouts which appeared in the trade press from time to time. The image he sought to create was that of a dynamic, Broadway-style producer, 'one who combines American "slickness" and whirlwind methods with the tact and "aplomb" of an Irving,' to quote from a blurb appearing in *What's On* which bears every evidence of having been dictated by Gregory. The article went on to say: 'His well-known red carnation buttonhole, and a smile that will not wear off, are personal hallmarks, which conceal a disconcerting shrewdness . . .' (The 'smile that will not wear off' is a rather neat conceit; in later life many of Gregory's victims would have given a great deal to wipe off that smile.)

The human dynamo image is somewhat belied by the photograph which accompanies this article, and which shows a 27-year-old Gregory, in high, starched collar, looking rather dreamy-eyed as he leans his head on his hand. The face is full, unlined, babyish, like that of the early Paul McCartney of Beatles fame. The hair is parted so as to show off his widow's peak.

Gregory's debt to showman W. W. Kelly is evident in the press hand-out appearing in the *Era* for January 19, 1907. 'Mr Maundy Gregory,' it reads, 'is a firm believer in the hustling principle, and thinks nothing of dictating in the train 40 or 50 letters to his American manager, who types them all on the journey.' 'He frequently travels the length of England,' the publicity puff continues,

[65]

'for half an hour's interview with someone, and then gets straight on the train again for another journey, which may possibly last through the night.'

By far the most ambitious project undertaken by 'Messrs E. D. and J. Maundy-Gregory' was the Christmas pantomime *Little Red Riding Hood*, which began its provincial run at the Lyceum in Ipswich on December 27, 1907. Featuring a cast of sixty, it was billed as 'The Largest Pantomime Ever Travelled' and 'A West End Production in the Provinces'. The trouble was that the show was built around a 7-year-old dancer named Miss Barbara Alleyne, who was billed as 'the smallest solo dancer in Europe' and starred as Baby Innocence in a Ballet of the Clouds devised by Gregory. Barbara shouldn't have been on the stage at all, according to the Prevention of Cruelty to Children Act, which barred children below the age of eleven from appearing 'in any circus or other place of public amusement, to which the public are admitted by payment, for the purpose of singing, playing, or performing, or being exhibited for a profit'. Miss Alleyne, who is now Mrs Barbara Benjamin, a widow living in St John's Wood, London, recalls very well the contretemps to which this led. 'Maundy Gregory,' she told me, 'knew the law as well as anyone, but he assured my parents that everything would be all right. When the panto opened in Ipswich on Boxing Night I was the hit of the show and got rave notices in the local papers. Unfortunately, this brought my tender years to the notice of the police.'

Acting on instructions of the Chief Constable, a Detective Sergeant Firman was dispatched to the Lyceum to witness a performance of *Little Red Riding Hood*, and as a result Gregory was haled before the Ipswich Police Court and fined £5, which his manager paid in his absence. The *East Anglian Times* described the courtroom scene, reporting: 'Winsome Barbara with the golden hair . . . cried rather bitterly, it is true, but not because she was afraid of the Magistrates or the people in the court. Not a bit of it. She . . . shed tears of anger and disappointment at the prospect of having to wait three or four years before she can go on the stage again.'

Gregory had spent too much money in advertising Barbara's charms to be put off easily. 'When the show opened in Peterborough the following week,' Mrs Benjamin recalled, 'Gregory put me in a stage box and had me singing "By the Side of the

Zuyder Zee" in Dutch costume with a baby-blue spotlight trained on me. I guess he thought that if I were not actually dancing on the stage he was not breaking the law. But the Peterborough police thought otherwise, and my mother, who by this time had had enough of Gregory, took me out of the show.' In later life Barbara was to appear under the management of Mr George Edwardes at the Daly in such successes as *The Marriage Contract*, which starred Gertie Millar.

But the 'Red Riding Hood' episode had an ugly sequel. Far from waiting for three or four years before appearing again on the stage, as the Ipswich reporter had predicted would be the case, Barbara was engaged within a year by Beerbohm Tree to appear in *Pinkie and the Fairies*, starring Ellen Terry which opened at His Majesty's Theatre on December 19, 1908. 'What happened,' Mrs Benjamin explained, 'was that I used my sister's birth certificate, which made it appear that I was ten years old, and I changed my name to Ellise Craven, hoping that the Ipswich episode would not catch up with me.' Predictably Barbara/Ellise was an immediate hit, the *Era* praising her as 'a marvel of Terpsichorean training and cool self-possession'. One newspaper headlined her as 'The child who earns £100 a week', which was enough to attract the attention of Maundy Gregory, who of course knew her real identity.

Mrs Benjamin described to me what happened: 'One day Gregory's secretary, a young woman named Audrey Jekyll, called on my mother, pretending to be concerned about my welfare. Then she revealed the true purpose of her visit, which was black-mail. For a certain consideration—I don't recall what the exact amount was—she was prepared to forget that I was under-age and using a forged birth certificate. After a stormy passage Miss Jekyll left the house empty-handed, for my mother was a very astute woman. What she did was to threaten to expose Maundy Gregory if anything were said about my age. There was no doubt in her mind that the blackmail scheme had originated with Gregory, who had put Miss Jekyll up to the whole unsavoury business.'

*   *   *

By March, 1908, Gregory had run out of steam. *Little Red Riding Hood* had long since concluded its ten weeks' tour, and *Lights Out* and *Zaza*, the two other shows under Gregory's management, were getting only sporadic bookings. By April, 1908 Gregory was reduced to organizing Pierrot shows to play the end of the pier in various seaside resorts.

The late J. Rowland Sales, who was then a lad of 19 from Whitstable, went to work for Gregory at about this time as his secretary–manager. Mr Sales, who died in August 1972, had a tiny flat in the Haymarket above Fribourg & Treyer, the tobacconists, who supplied snuff to Beau Brummel, and it was there that I talked to him, finding him a charming, urbane man. 'My mother paid my fare to come to London in answer to Maundy's advertisement for a manager in the *Era*,' Sales recalled. 'Maundy was living at 18 Burleigh Mansions in St Martin's Lane, and I remember thinking to myself, "Oh dear, this is rather dingy for a man of such importance." But Maundy, himself, was very cordial. He wanted someone with enthusiasm and love of the theatre, he explained, rather than someone who was acquainted only with the business side. Evidently I filled the bill, for I was hired at the princely sum of £5 a week. Theoretically, that is, for I seldom got more than £3, and sometimes not even that. But I was young and eager to break into West End theatre management, so I didn't care.' (On the wall of Sales' flat was a framed playbill of George Formby Senior appearing at the Granville Music Hall in Fulham, which Sales managed in later life.)

'Maundy used his flat as his office,' Sales explained, 'and whenever he was expecting important visitors—potential angels to back his shows, or actors whom he was considering for parts—the stage had to be set to impress them, with cut flowers on the table, and so forth. Maundy couldn't afford a typewriter that was in working order, but he had acquired a battered old Underwood. And so while Maundy entertained his distinguished visitors I would be in the bedroom with the connecting door ajar banging away on the broken-down Underwood in order to create the impression that the office was a bee-hive of activity.'

Sales' duties included not only those of secretary-manager, but of valet as well. 'Maundy was so hard up on one occasion,' he reminisced, 'that he didn't have a shirt to wear to the theatre. I had to attach the collar to his torn shirt-front by means of bent pins, and then to tie the bow so as to hold it together.'[1] This was Gregory's situation in April, 1908, when good fortune smiled on

[1] Gregory must have found this particularly galling, as he was inclined

him in the person of his Southampton chum Harold 'Jumbo' Davidson who had blossomed into the Reverend Harold David-son, M.A., Clerk in Holy Orders, and rector of the parish church of St John with St Mary, Stiffkey, Norfolk. A more unlikely fairy godfather it would be difficult to imagine.

to equate immaculate linen with affluence. A few years after the episode related by Sales, Gregory suddenly turned up at the home of the Loraines in Lyndhurst, having motored there by taxi.When his friends remonstrated with him at this extravagance, Gregory tut-tutted, 'Money's no object now. Clean shirt every day!'

V

Jumbo to the Rescue

'Maundy's debt to Harold Davidson was an enormous one,' J. Rowland Sales told me during one of our chats at his Haymarket flat. 'Without Davidson's help Maundy would never have got anywhere in the theatre, in my opinion,' Sales declared. 'It was Davidson who introduced him to influential people. It was Davidson who rustled up the money. It was Davidson who nerved Maundy to audacious undertakings.' 'Of course, in doing these things the rector of Stiffkey was not altogether motivated by love for Gregory,' Sales added. 'He had his own fish to fry.'

Davidson was, in fact, motivated by two passions: the theatre and everything that pertained to it (the play-acting he and Maundy had indulged in as boys had marked him for life), and missionary work among nymphets. Concerning his first passion, Jumbo Davidson is probably the first Clerk in Holy Orders ever to finance his studies at Oxford University by appearing on the stage as a comic recitalist. This he did with the special permission of the Rector of Exeter College, taking five years to obtain his B.A. degree instead of the customary three. Moreover, he was enormously successful as a comic, earning as much as £1,000 a year by giving humorous recitals in the manner of George Grossmith Senior, Clifford Harrison and Corney Grain. After ordination Davidson may have intended to turn his back on the stage for ever in order to devote himself to pastoral duties; if so, his resolve was speedily dissipated when, in August, 1905, he was sent to London to become assistant curate at St Martin-in-the-Fields. It was like asking an alcoholic to do occupational therapy in a brewery.

In London Davidson lost no time in renewing old stage acquaintances. In February, 1906, he became a chaplain of the Actors' Church Union, which brought him into contact with the Lord Bishop of London; the bishop, in turn, officiated at Davidson's wedding to an Irish girl in 1906. Davidson also met a number of titled people. It was the period when London society, taking its cue from King Edward VII, had begun to patronize the stage. Actresses married into the peerage, while peeresses like the Duchess of Rutland attended dress rehearsals at His Majesty's Theatre, and their daughters, notably Lady Diana Manners, planned careers on the stage. It was through his friendship with the 6th Marquess Townshend, a nobleman whose ancestor had sailed against the Spanish Armada, that Davidson became rector of Stiffkey (pop. 502), whose handsome living of £800 per annum was in the gift of the marquess. It was a mistake, as it happened, for Jumbo Davidson was never meant for the quiet, rural life.

Davidson, in fact, suffered from hypomania, an abnormal mental state in which thought processes are, like film, speeded up. Its symptoms are insomnia—Davidson never slept more than two or three hours a night, often didn't bother to go to bed at all; euphoria which reveals itself in unjustified optimism and grandiose plans; and compulsive chatter, the hypomaniac switching from one subject to another so rapidly that his listener has difficulty in following his train of thought. 'Davidson was always in a hurry,' Sales claimed. 'He would rush in crying, "Hello, old chap, haven't got a minute—must be off to see Gladys, the Marchioness Townshend—how are you getting on?" and away he would go.' Finding Stiffkey devoid of any challenge to his restless energy, Davidson spent five days a week in London. Usually he took the last train home on Saturday nights, but sometimes he cut it fine, catching the 5.5 a.m. train on Sunday and arriving in Stiffkey with barely time to don a surplice before hurrying into the pulpit of St John's with St Mary's.

As to the second of his passions, Davidson was attracted not just to one or two nymphets, nor even to a dozen; he was attracted to the whole world of girls between the ages of 14 and 21. At his trial before the Norwich Consistory Court the following exchange took place:

Ryder Richardson (for the defence): How many girls have you spoken to in tearooms in the past decade?
Davidson: I have a list of over 500.
Richardson: How many have you helped?
Davidson: Perhaps 200.
Richardson: Not only financially, but with advice?

[71]

Davidson: Oh, with advice between 500 and 1,000.
Richardson: Have you ever spoken to any of these 1,000 for an immoral purpose?
Davidson: Never.

The truth of this last assertion is vouched for by J. Rowland Sales, who in June, 1932, booked Davidson on a lecture tour. 'I knew Davidson very, very well,' Sales told me, 'and believe me he was entirely innocent of any immorality with those girls he was accused of consorting with. He only wanted to help them. He was the most generous and kind-hearted man I have ever met.'

Innocent or not, Davidson's behaviour was highly eccentric. 'We would walk into the Lyons Corner House in the Strand,' Sales recalled, 'and right away Davidson would accost some pretty waitress with, "What is a lovely girl like you doing here? With your looks you should be on the stage." It sounds corny, but Davidson meant it. He got many of these girls walk-on parts by badgering the theatrical producers. It got so that at the mere sight of Davidson standing at the stage-door, Beerbohm Tree would clutch his head and groan, "Oh, no, not you again." ' 'No,' Sales concluded, 'Davidson's interest in these girls was not sexual, the proof of it being that he used to take them home to his wife.'[1]

*   *   *

When Davidson and Gregory, these two stage-struck boyhood chums, met again after an absence of years there was a subtle reversal of roles. In Southampton it had always been Maundy who called the tune, pre-empting for himself the star parts in the verse playlets he wrote. Now it was Jumbo who was the preceptor, and Maundy, for the moment at least, was content to listen and learn. J. Rowland Sales described to me how Jumbo with his usual euphoria took Maundy's affairs in hand. Their conversation

[1] Shades of W. E. Gladstone who, at the age of 80, was still picking up prostitutes on the Duke of York Steps, and bringing them home to Mrs Gladstone, much to the horror of his sovereign, Queen Victoria. In his musical *The Vicar of Soho*, which is based on the life of Harold Davidson, Stuart Douglass agrees about Davidson's innocence, suggests that he was sexually under-developed. But this latter suggestion is rather hard to square with the fact that Davidson's wife bore him two daughters and two sons.

at that initial meeting went something like this, according to Sales:

> *Davidson* (after surveying Gregory's financial position): So you're broke, down on your luck, reduced to sending out Pierrots to play at the end of the pier—very good, we'll soon put matters right. (He picks up the telephone, calls Wyndham's Theatre, asks that a box for that evening's performance be placed at the disposal of 'J. Maundy-Gregory, the well-known theatrical producer', who will be entertaining the Duchess of Somerset.)
> *Gregory* (protesting): But I don't even know the Duchess of Somerset.
> *Davidson:* You will, my boy, you will. Like all the aristocracy, she's simply mad about the theatre.
> *Gregory:* But why should I entertain a duchess I don't even know in a box I can't pay for?
> *Davidson* (pityingly): If you want to attract investors it's important that you be seen in such company.

The fruit of this reunion was 'Combine Attractions Syndicate, Ltd', launched with Gregory as managing director, and a nominal share capital of £5,000, its ostensible purpose being to import stage hits from America to tour the English provinces. The division of labour was sharply demarcated. Davidson's role in this promotion was to shoo customers in the direction of Gregory, who persuaded them to buy shares. Among others who, thanks to Jumbo, invested in the syndicate were Lord Howard de Walden and Baron Carl von Buch, who agreed to become chairman of 'Combine Attractions'.

It was through Jumbo that Gregory met the playwright Reginald Kennedy-Cox, who had just written *Cleopatra*, a 4-act play based on a Rider Haggard story. Gregory was looking for something for 'Combine Attractions' to back in order to give the shareholders a return on their investment. After reading *Cleopatra* he took an option on it, with Ruby Miller in mind for the title role.[1] In ex-

[1] Miss Miller, who at 83 is probably the last of the Gaiety Girls, wrote me from Bognor Regis where she now lives that she met Gregory while she was playing in *The Dust of Egypt* produced by Gerald du Maurier at Wyndham's. 'Gregory,' she explained, 'saw me in the costume of an Egyptian mummy come to life, and decided then and there that I would

change for a bloc of 'B' shares worth £966 15s. Gregory then assigned the production rights to 'Combine Attractions'.

A number of events conspired to focus Gregory's attention on a revival of *Dorothy*, a 3-act comic opera by B. C. Stephenson and Alfred Cellier. In the first place, a provincial production of *Dorothy* had just concluded a successful tour. Then again Hayden Coffin, the star of the original production, was available for a limited engagement. Finally, 'Combine Attractions' had an option on the New Theatre, where it had been intended that *Cleopatra* should open.

On December 8 Gregory wrote to Sales, who was ill at his parents' home at Whitstable, that *Dorothy* was in production. 'Everything is going wonderfully,' Gregory claimed, adding, 'I've engaged the Gaiety orchestra.' Director of the Gaiety Theatre orchestra was Frederick Rosse, a composer of note (he wrote the incidental music for *Monsieur Beaucaire* and *The Merchant of Venice*), who was to play an important part in Gregory's life; or rather, it was his wife Edith who was to become Gregory's close friend.

It was while *Dorothy* was in rehearsal that Rosse married Edith Marion Sheppard who, under the name of Vivienne Pierpont, had had a successful stage career. A good figure, an abundance of auburn hair, and a strong contralto voice had fitted her admirably to tour in such musicals as *The Arcadians* and *The Quaker Girl*. Arthur Machen, the writer, fell madly in love with Edith, whom he called 'the Shepherdess', later recalled that 'she twined dark violets in my hair' at the Café de l'Europe in Leicester Square. But Edith Rosse had a tragic side to her as well. Before marrying Frederick Rosse she had been very happily married to Harry Sheppard, a purser on the *Arundel Castle*, who, during one of that ship's voyages, had disappeared at sea. Edith never recovered from this blow, which left her crippled emotionally.

*   *   *

At his trial on charges of immorality the Reverend Harold Davidson was questioned concerning Miss Barbara Harris, a 16-year-old nymphet whom he had befriended. Was it true that he

---

make the perfect Cleopatra. We discussed it many times. We even got to the stage of designing the sets when the scheme fell through.'

called Miss Harris 'Queen of My Heart'? he was asked. 'I often call people "Queen of My Heart",' the unabashed preacher rejoined. 'I even call my landlady that. It comes from a song "You are Queen of My Heart tonight", which in turn comes from a comic opera entitled *Dorothy*,' he added by way of explanation. Originally the song was not part of the libretto of *Dorothy* when that show, starring Marie Tempest, opened at the Gaiety Theatre in 1886. It was added later in order to give Hayden Coffin, the leading tenor, a solo worthy of his talents, and it saved *Dorothy* from being a certain flop. Soon milkmen sang 'Queen of My Heart' as they made their rounds. So did omnibus drivers, chimney sweeps, shop girls, and men-about-town. Thanks largely to this song hit the original production of *Dorothy* ran for 931 performances.

Such miracles do not repeat themselves, as Maundy Gregory discovered when *Dorothy* was revived at the New Theatre in December, 1908. On the surface Gregory seemed to have everything working for him. Hayden Coffin, whom *The Times* described as a 'sweet singer and gallant actor', was supported by a strong cast which included Constance Drever, Louie Pounds, and Arthur Williams, plus a chorus of sixty. The comic opera, itself, whose plot was reminiscent of Sheridan's *The Rivals*, was given an elaborate production from the opening scene, which was laid in the hop gardens of Kent, to the final curtain. In between there was a 'Tallyho' number during which a pack of foxhounds was brought on stage. On opening night the audience insisted upon double encores of several of the songs. Even the critics were kind. In spite of all these favourable signs *Dorothy* turned out to be an unmitigated disaster.

What went wrong? In the first place Gregory misjudged his timing and opened *Dorothy* at the height of the Christmas holiday season. Thus it had to compete with no fewer than twenty-four pantomimes then occupying the London stage. Then Hayden Coffin was free for only a limited engagement, after which he was booked to appear opposite Miss Ellaline Terriss in *The Dashing Little Duke* at the Hicks Theatre. With a suitable replacement for Coffin, Gregory might still have surmounted his difficulties had the lease at the New Theatre not expired at the end of a fortnight. As it was, no sooner had *Dorothy* broken in at the New Theatre than the show had to transfer to the Waldorf Theatre, which was known as a 'jinx' house.

As a portent of disaster Gregory burnt his coat-tails on the opening night at the Waldorf. 'Actually, they were my coat-tails,' J. Rowland Sales explained to me. 'Maundy had borrowed my swallowtail coat, which fitted him perfectly. During the intermission, while holding court in the foyer, he backed too close to an open fire with instant combustion resulting. Anyone else would have been overcome with mortification, but not Maundy. He quickly beat out the flames, borrowed someone's overcoat, and went on talking as though nothing had happened. He never replaced the dress coat he had ruined, nor did he offer to reimburse me for it.'

* * *

Dorothy had been playing to full houses at the New Theatre. After the transfer to the Waldorf box office receipts took a spectacular nose-dive. Again Davidson came to the rescue. Nothing, it seemed, could quench the Micawber-like optimism of Stiffkey's rector. His line of reasoning paraphrased that of Maréchal Foch, according to Sales: 'Your centre is giving way? Your right is in retreat? Very well, old chap, the thing to do is to give a charity performance, for the benefit of' (snatching up a copy of *The Times* and glancing at the headlines)—'of the Messina earthquake victims!' (Messina and Reggio di Calabria had just been devastated by what *The Times* called 'the most appalling disaster of modern times', with an estimated 200,000 persons either dead or missing.) 'The way to do it is to get the Lord Mayor of London to attend in state, and to charge ten quid a head. This will create good will for *Dorothy*, and get people talking about it again.'

The resultant Messina benefit was, in fact, one of the most brilliant social events of the season. Headed by the American and Russian ambassadors, Prince Alexander of Teck, and Princess Lowenstein Wertheim, the list of patrons included the Lord Chancellor, the Lord Mayor of London, the Lord Bishop of London, and a cross-section of Debrett. 'The fire from the diamond tiaras in the boxes was enough to put your eyes out,' Sales recalled. After the performance, Maundy Gregory presented members of the cast to Prince Alexander, the actresses curtseying prettily to His Highness.

To Gregory the benefit performance was a revelation, one of the most important in his life until then. Charity, he realized, could un-pick the locks of doors which otherwise would remain for ever closed to persons like himself who had neither wealth nor family connections. With the ermine-and-coronet crowd as bait, wealthy but untitled persons could be induced to pay handsomely for the privilege of sitting in the stalls and gazing upwards at the boxes. But this was only the minor premise of the syllogism. The major one was: If the well-to-do were eager to pay for mere propinquity to the titled, they could be persuaded to shell out infinitely more for the thing they coveted, the title itself. Maundy Gregory's educa-tion as a con-man which had been begun by showman W. W. Kelly was now well on its way towards completion.

*　　*　　*

As for *Dorothy*, the end came with dramatic swiftness on Satur-day, February 6, when the musicians, who had not been paid, went on strike after the matinee performance. Sales is of the opinion that had the orchestra waited until the evening's box office receipts had been counted there would have been enough in the till to cover the musicians' wages. Instead of explaining this to the musicians Gregory lost his head. Like the madman in *The Phantom of the Opera*, Gregory rushed to the basement of the Waldorf Theatre and pulled the mains switch, thereby plunging the audi-torium into darkness. To theatre-goers who were queuing outside for the evening performance he gave it out that there had been an 'electricity failure', and that the performance therefore would have to be cancelled. In his autobiography Hayden Coffin told what happened when the cast arrived to find the theatre dark. 'All they could do was to light the candles, which were stage property for the second act of *Dorothy*, and grope their way in semi-darkness to collect their belongings from the dressing-rooms. They, too, had not received any salary.' As an aftermath the Charing Cross Electricity Supply Company indignantly denied that there had been a power failure. Trade papers did not hesitate to place the blame for the fiasco where it belonged, squarely on Gregory's shoulders. In an editorial headed 'West End Gambles', the *Stage* condemned what it called 'speculative and insolvent management', specifically citing *Dorothy* as an example. Conditions in the theatre were such as to 'help the adventurer and the swindler, and collapse and scandal are inevitable in their wake', the theatrical weekly lamented. What was needed was a law 'to prevent irresponsible persons from renting theatres'. 'As it is, speculative management has ... so much in its favour,' the editorial pointed out. 'If the piece makes a hit with the public all will be well: money will roll in. If it fails—well, the rehearsals have not been paid for, the engagements are subject to the run, and the artists have dressed their parts. The losses can in any case be cut ...' Seldom can a theatrical manager have received a more stinging rebuke.

This marked the end of 'Combine Attractions Syndicate Ltd', whose affairs were hastily wound up at an ' extraordinary general meeting' held on February 12, 1909, with Gregory's brother Edward being appointed liquidator. But where was Gregory himself during this crisis? He was nowhere to be seen, according to Sales, who added, 'It was entirely characteristic of Maundy to walk away from the scene of the crash leaving someone else to pick up the pieces.' The 'someone else' in this case was Hayden Coffin, who, moved no doubt by the plight of the unpaid chorus girls, borrowed enough money from George Edwardes' business manager at the Gaiety, Gorrett Todd, to pay off the company. 'Personally,' Coffin wrote, 'I was a heavy loser.' Nor was he the only loser. In the stunned silence that followed the *Dorothy* crash Jumbo Davidson could be heard moaning, 'Ruined, ruined—I shall be ruined.' The rector of Stiffkey had sunk £2,000 of his savings into the ill-fated operetta. All that he managed to salvage from the wreckage was the 'Queen of My Heart' refrain with which he beguiled landladies.

VI

Maundy's
Finishing School

After the *Dorothy* fiasco Maundy Gregory dropped completely
from sight so far as the theatrical world was concerned. Nor was he
to be found in such West End London haunts as the Café Royal,
which he had frequented in the past. 'I tried to maintain contact
with him, but my letters went unanswered,' J. Rowland Sales recalled. 'It was as though the earth had opened and swallowed him
whole.' Gregory, of course, was hiding out from theatrical suppliers
and from angry investors who had put money into 'Combine
Attractions'. But the collapse of *Dorothy* had also had a traumatic
effect upon him. Thereafter he would be at pains to obliterate from
his life all traces of his ten years in the theatre. For example, there
is not so much as a mention of his stage experience in the 'confidential' memorandum which he gave to clients in order to establish
his bona fides. When he did emerge from hiding, it was with the
brand-new persona of 'J. M. Gregory, journalist'. It will be noted
that even his name had undergone a subtle change.

Where and how Gregory met the brothers Keen-Hargreaves is
not known; though in view of their interest in actresses, it is possible that the two brothers were among the backers of the ill-
fated *Dorothy*. But when Gregory surfaced again in 1910 it was as
business partner of the Baron J. C. (Jack) Keen-Hargreaves and his
brother Harry (a third brother, Arthur, bowed out of the picture
early) in a publishing venture known as *Mayfair & Town Topics*,
The Society Journal (the 'Town Topics' was later dropped from the
masthead). The brothers Keen-Hargreaves were if anything more
bogus than Gregory himself, though they lacked his cunning. They
were adventurers living from hand to mouth, spending money
lavishly when they had it, running up debts when they did not,
until the 'baron' eventually went bankrupt. They were products of
Edwardian society which, one is apt to forget, was as corrupt as
that which flourished in the 1920s. As George Dangerfield points
out in his study of Asquithian England, 'That extravagant

behaviour of the post-war decade . . . had really begun before the War. The War hastened everything—in politics, in economics, in behaviour—but it started nothing.'[1]

The noble 'baron' (his claim to that title is examined further on) and his brothers came from a very humble background indeed, their father John William Keen being a merchant seaman who shipped out of Liverpool. In 1860 Keen, aged twenty, and stirred no doubt by the prospect of adventure, joined the so-called 'British Legion' to fight alongside Garibaldi and his Red Shirts. The legionnaires, 600-strong, were recruited almost entirely from the slums of London, Glasgow, and Liverpool. They arrived in Naples too late for the fighting, but in time to parade with flowers stuffed into the muzzles of their Enfield rifles by the admiring populace. Neapolitans soon had cause to regret this exuberant welcome, for the legionnaires proceeded to 'distinguish themselves in a truly national manner', in the words of the resident British Minister, 'by getting drunk and disorderly, and in sleeping on and under the tables in the principal café in Naples'. The party over, Keen had his fare paid home by the Sicilian government, resumed his life as a mariner, and in due course married and begot sons, the eldest of whom was Jack Keen (the mother's maiden name of 'Hargreaves' was added by deed poll much later). In May, 1905 the father died in the Sick Asylum at Poplar, the death certificate listing him as a 'ship clerk'.

So much for the facts, but in the hands of a skilful publicist such as Jack Keen-Hargreaves these self-same facts were embroidered into an amazing fiction. In the first place, the father was promoted to 'lieutenant-colonel' and referred to as 'one of Garibaldi's principal lieutenants', and as having 'raised the famous "British Legion" which went to Garibaldi's aid', and again, as having 'commanded the famous thousand of Marsilia'. Neither G. M. Trevelyan nor any other English historian of the Garibaldi movement makes mention of a 'Lt-Col J. W. Keen.' The same is true of the Italian experts in this field. The definitive word comes from Professor Emilio Morelli, secretary-general of the *Istituto per la Storia del Risorgimento Italiano* specializing in Garibaldi studies, who writes me that it is 'utterly impossible' that Keen could have held the rank assigned to him by his son.

[1] George Dangerfield. *The Strange Death of Liberal England*. London: Constable and Co, 1936.

But the inventive son did not stop there. Having given his father a field commission he now proceeded to ennoble him by means of a barony allegedly bestowed upon the 'lieutenant-colonel' by King Victor Emmanuel in grateful recognition of his services as a mercenary. (In fairness it must be stated that the father was never a party to such bogus pretensions, so far as I have been able to ascertain.) When the father died in 1905 the title 'baron' (in strict accuracy it should have been 'barone') devolved to Jack Keen-Hargreaves, who apparently could not be bothered to obtain permission from his sovereign before using it. His right to the title, however, was challenged in an article entitled 'Bold, Bad Baron' which appeared in *John Bull* magazine, and which referred to Jack as 'the most barren baron' the writer had ever met. To settle this question it should be noted that the *Consulta Araldica* in Rome, which corresponds to the College of Heralds in London, has no record of any barony ever having been conferred upon J. W. Keen.

Of the two brothers Harry Keen-Hargreaves was by far the more sympathetic. A *bon vivant*, Harry had exquisite taste so far as wine, motor cars, and women were concerned (Lily Langtry is said to have been his mistress at one time). He married money, which did not prevent him from being perennially broke. As his nephew J. W. R. Keen-Hargreaves told me, 'Uncle Harry would give you anything he had, the trouble being that he never had anything.' During the period when Gregory knew him, Harry was to be found most of the time at the gaming tables at Monte Carlo with Anna Held, the French–Polish star of the Folies Bergère, who was later to become famous for her milk baths.

*   *   *

Like water seeking its level Maundy Gregory sought out the two brothers early in 1910 with a magazine dummy and a business proposition. 'I have been studying the magazine market,' Gregory told the brothers, 'and my research indicates that there is room for a weekly where business and society can rub shoulders. Not to put too fine a point on it, there are no end of industrialists who will pay handsomely to have their portraits sandwiched between gossip paragraphs about duchesses.' 'My idea,' Gregory expanded, 'is to call the magazine *Mayfair*, and to build it around a regular feature

[81]

with some such title as "Man of the Day". This would consist of a colour portrait of the chosen subject by "Spy", or some other outstanding cartoonist, together with a few paragraphs about the man's career, the balance of the magazine to be made up of snippets of society gossip plus Court news.'

Mayfair's cover for the greater part of its existence was graced by the figure of a woman in a rose-coloured gown with an aigrette in her hair who appears to be doing the Maxixe—or is it the Hesitation Waltz?—as a solo. Her presence on the cover gave some indication of the sprightliness of the magazine's contents inside, which set *Mayfair* apart from such staid competitors as the *Tatler* and the *Sketch*. Although its first issue appeared in November, 1910, it was not until January, 1913 that *Mayfair* got around to defining its purposes as 'to provide sound, reliable, and exclusive society news', dealing with 'questions of real and live interest to the upper classes'. 'It will make no bow to sensationalism and will be free from scandal in any shape or form,' its editor promised. Of live interest to the upper classes, to judge from the rubrics which appeared regularly in *Mayfair*, were such topics as 'The Court and Its Train', 'Gossip in Mayfair', 'Cupid's Diary', 'Turf Jottings', and 'Throgmorton Street', this latter being financial news.

But all of this was mere window-dressing for *Mayfair*'s reason for being, which was the feature entitled 'Man of the Day'. Gregory had shrewdly gauged the temper of the times. The number of social-climbers who were willing to pay cash to have their names bracketed with those of duchesses in an obscure magazine with no circulation was seemingly limitless. Soon they were queuing to have their portraits done by artists with such fanciful names as 'Pip', 'Elf', and 'Quip' (a portrait by the inimitable Leslie Ward, who signed his work 'Spy', cost extra). Gregory slyly changed the heading from 'Man of the Day' to 'Men of the Twentieth Century', and ran them off in batches of four or five each week. The duchesses, of course, were given a free ride, full-page photographs of them appearing regularly in *Mayfair*. Everyone else paid through the nose, a 'Man of the Twentieth Century' contributing anything from fifty to five hundred guineas for the privilege of being so designated. So successful was this money-making formula that a member of *Mayfair*'s staff named Nathan broke away and started his own magazine under the title *Men of the Day*. However, the formula did not achieve the peak of its perfection until the post-war years when Gregory founded and edited the *Whitehall Gazette*.

*　　*　　*

Mayfair was Maundy Gregory's finishing school, he being fully versed in the gentle art of con-manship by the time he had completed his education at the Brothers Keen-Hargreaves' hands. For the brothers were social buccaneers of no mean ability. Their methods may seem crude by today's standards, but they were effective, as witness the way the brothers exploited their father's supposed connection with King Victor Emmanuel III, who was always referred to in *Mayfair* as 'Il Re Galantuomo'. Specifically, they used this alleged connection to worm their way into the good graces of 'Il Re Galantuomo's' cousins, King Alfonso of Spain, and the exiled King Manuel of Portugal. When the Portuguese monarch married in September, 1913 the entire issue of *Mayfair* was given over to the wedding in Sigmaringen, and the bibulous Harry Keen-Hargreaves was dispatched to Germany with a water colour portrait of the king as a wedding present.

As for King Alfonso XIII of Spain, the brothers used a wealthy American sportsman named Walter Winans (he was a member of the American Olympic rifle team in 1912) in their approach to His Majesty. Specifically, they persuaded Winans to present a string of polo ponies to the king, the brothers, of course, being on hand for the presentation, as was Maundy Gregory. Among these wolves in silk toppers, spats, and tails, King Alfonso, judging from the group photograph which appeared in *Mayfair*, contrived to look almost sheep-like, no mean feat on the part of this swarthy monarch with the waxed moustaches. The brothers pulled their most audacious coup in June, 1911, five years after their father's death, when 'Baron' Jack Keen-Hargreaves led a group of survivors of Garibaldi's 'British Legion' to Rome for the jubilee celebration of Garibaldi's famous march through Sicily. The phoney baron was received in private audience by King Victor Emmanuel and was 'warmly thanked' by His Majesty, according to *Mayfair*. Seldom can a monarch have been conned so successfully.

None of this was lost upon Maundy Gregory, who in time became the friend of European royalty, notably those crowned heads who were deposed after the First World War. In the 'confidential' memorandum which he drew up for the benefit of clients, Gregory claimed that he had:

'Assisted H.I.H. the Grand Duke Nicholas of Russia with regular quarterly emoluments paid entirely confidentially.

'Materially assisted the Grand Duchess after the death of her husband, the Grand Duke Nicholas.'

Perhaps the most astonishing claim of all made by Gregory was that he held the power of attorney of Prince Danilo of Montenegro, who in turn had made him Grand Cordon of the Montenegrin Order of Danilo for assistance given. Granted that Montenegrin royalty were considerably impoverished after the Serbs had over-run their country, that Prince Danilo and Princess Militza should entrust their affairs to a con-man like Gregory seems incredible. Such, however, was the case.

His longest and most successful friendship was with King George II of Greece, whom Gregory knew during his first London exile when His Majesty put up at Brown's Hotel. While not exactly impecunious, the ex-King of the Hellenes could not afford to run a car in those days but relied upon taxis. He could, however, afford to make Gregory a present of such bibelots as cuff-links and a gold cigarette case. More important, he allowed the latter to exploit this royal friendship for his own nefarious ends.

*　　*　　*

It was as a sideline to his duties as editor of *Mayfair* that Maundy Gregory got into the credit-rating business running his own detective agency. Starting in April, 1912, *Mayfair*, under the heading 'At the Hotels', began to list each week the distinguished guests who had checked in at the Ritz, Claridge's, the Savoy, the Cecil, and the Hyde Park hotels, later expanding the feature to include such establishments on the French Riviera as the Hôtel de Paris at Monte Carlo and the Metropole at Cannes. Thanks to this feature, Gregory soon found himself on first-name terms not only with hotel managers, but with the *maîtres d'hôtel* of London's better restaurants, men like roly-poly Arturo Giordano, then manager of the Savoy restaurant, and later proprietor of Kettner's in Romilly Street, a favourite Edwardian rendezvous.

London's better restaurants in those pre-war days were run

almost exclusively by Italians, who composed a benign mafia to give employment to relatives arriving from Reggio di Calabria and Catania. Everyone was related to everyone else. Giordano of the Savoy was a cousin of Ferrari at the Berkeley Hotel who, in turn, was related to Francesco Mazzina, the owner of the Royal Trocadero in New Oxford Street. (Most probably it was through his connection with this 'jobs for the boys' mafia that Maundy Gregory met his future business partner Peter Mazzina.) Once introduced to this closed circuit, Gregory found that he had a ready-made intelligence network at hand, with scores of informants ranging from waiters to hotel managing directors to act as extensions of his eyes and ears. Thanks to these, he was able to amass a great deal of information concerning the credit ratings of wealthy and titled people.

It was a two-way flow, with Gregory in turn collating this information for the benefit of hotel and restaurant managements, and in some cases of jewellers, all of whom paid a small retaining fee for his services. As time went on his advice was sought concerning continentals arriving by the boat trains from Dover, and he built up an extensive memory bank of those who had propensities to pass bad cheques, or who otherwise were undesirable. This was the information Gregory was able to place at the disposal of MI-5, the branch of Britain's secret services which deals with internal security, following the outbreak of the First World War.

The bottom dropped out of *Mayfair*'s world in August, 1914, when the German guns began to pound Liège. Until then the magazine, faithfully reflecting the Edwardian society for which it catered, had found it too tiresome to comment on the alarums of war, observing in its issue of July 25, 1914, 'If we have not all taken as deep an interest in the political situation as our morning papers would have us believe we should, it is obviously because we have been better employed.' 'Now for the country and the moors,' the editorial concluded. 'France and the continent will call a number of us, while others will journey North in search of sport . . .' Soon France was to call *Mayfair*'s readers in a way that neither they nor the magazine's editorial staff could ever have envisaged. In its issue of August 1 *Mayfair* reported that the gravity of the political situation had forced the King to cancel his visit to Goodwood, adding that 'it will take particularly big "bags" and real shooting weather to bring us all back to normal spirits'.

A week later, with seven German armies poised to overrun Belgium the magazine could find nothing more momentous to report than the cancellation of Cowes Week, fulminating in an editorial, 'No regatta at Cowes! the announcement seems hardly credible! ... People who do not come to London for the season go to Cowes for the regatta. Royalties from the Continent, Indian chiefs, American magnates, Mayfair hostesses ...' The same issue had good things to say about Kaiser Wilhelm, the peace maker ('It must be recognized that another of the most powerful influences working for peace has been the German Emperor'); but by the following week the Kaiser had been labelled 'The Assassin', and cartooned with gouts of blood issuing from his eyes and mouth. The descent into the maelstrom was completed by an article entitled 'The German Spy Peril in England' which appeared on September 19, and which, though unsigned, bore the hallmarks of Maundy Gregory's style ('German spies have been arrested wholesale ... We know that one was discovered with a supply of bacilli of typhoid germs, enough to incapacitate a whole Army Corps. In Paris German waiters have poisoned the food of the customers they are attending ...'). Mercifully, *Mayfair* itself was killed off three months later.[1]

*   *   *

In the 'confidential' memorandum which he gave clients Gregory boasted that during the 1914–18 war he was engaged in counter-espionage work 'in which he employed some 1,000 agents'. This is a typical Gregorian exaggeration. Very possibly Gregory had in mind the extensive network of hotel and restaurant employees who had acted as informants when he ran his credit-rating agency; but even if one counts every doorman, bus boy, commissionaire or waiter who had ever given Gregory a tip, their number could hardly have approached a thousand. As for the MI-5 section of the Secret Service, at the height of the war it employed no more than 850 personnel, and this total included informants whom it used on a casual basis.

However, Gregory had much in common with Captain Vernon

[1] The Brothers Keen-Hargreaves tried to revive it after the war, but without success. The magazine appeared sporadically—that is, whenever the brothers could find a 'live one' to foot the bill—until 1923 when the limited company went into liquidation with £4 cash as its total assets and £2,000 in debts. 'Baron' Jack's bankruptcy petition followed.

Kell, founder and head of MI-5, who was a fearful snob. A veteran of the Boxer rebellion, tall, stoop-shouldered, Kell had the blinkered outlook of the serving officer and was inclined to equate loyalty with attendance at a good public school. As a consequence MI-5 was staffed largely by City gents and the sons of admirals. A parallel dictum that secretaries must be well-bred and have good legs resulted in stocking seams being straight, but in weird spelling and typing mistakes.

More important from Maundy's point of view was the fact that Kell was a deeply religious man. The story is told that during the early days of the war Asquith, as Prime Minister, summoned Kell to a Cabinet meeting on a Sunday morning to report on the internal security situation. To the consternation of all, Kell declined to attend at the appointed time, explaining that he had duties to perform as usher at his parish church in Weybridge. The fact that Gregory was the son of a clergyman would have weighed heavily with Kell, but Gregory had something even more important to recommend him. In the early days of the war Kell was desperately short of just the sort of information Gregory had been supplying to hoteliers concerning the antecedents, habits, credit ratings, and social desirability of guests, particularly of those arriving from abroad.

When MI-5, or the 'Special Intelligence Bureau', as it was first called, was set up in 1909 it had had to start from scratch building up its dossiers on such information as Kell was able to scrounge from the Special Branch at Scotland Yard.[1] Ex-Superintendent Arthur Askew hints that Gregory, on MI-5 orders, continued to operate his credit-rating agency even after *Mayfair* closed down. Askew says that Gregory's agency was used 'for the sort of minor enquiries it was not necessary or maybe not desirable to pass through strictly official channels'. 'Maundy Gregory handled his detective agency with superb organizational skill,' he adds. 'Soon he had an intelligence network that brought him much secret information not only from other parts of Britain but from various parts of the continent.'

[1] As late as 1940, when Kell retired, MI-5's records contained a high percentage of tittle-tattle, according to the authors of *Philby: The Spy Who Betrayed a Generation*. They cite the detailed reports of the MI-5 agents who disguised themselves as witches and warlocks in order to penetrate the coven presided over by Aleister Crowley.

Curiously, in later life whenever Gregory referred to this cloak-and-dagger period, it was to emphasize the theatrical, rather than the organizational aspect. Thus one of his assignments was to get himself hired as a valet at a stately home in Scotland in order to ferret out certain information for MI-5, according to Gregory. The anecdote has overtones of John Buchan and *The Thirty-Nine Steps*, also of Gregory's first appearance on the stage as a butler in *The Brixton Burglary*, and therefore must be accepted with reserve.

The same is true of Gregory's story of the Great Impersonation: Gregory claimed that on one occasion early in the war he had impersonated Winston Churchill, then First Lord of the Admiralty and thought to be in danger of assassination by a German agent. Superficially the two men resembled one another, being the same height (5′ 8″), and having the same domed foreheads, and the same tendency to toe in when they walked. But the story of Gregory masquerading as Churchill at a public banquet, and rising to take the toast on behalf of His Majesty's government, has altogether too much the ring of a tall tale. It should be noted that true detective stories were Gregory's favourite reading.

On July 10, 1917, Gregory was called up under the Derby scheme of deferred enlistment, and posted first to the Household Battalion (Reserve), then as a private to the Irish Guards at Caterham. It was not at all uncommon for a counter-espionage agent to be inducted into the armed services as a 'cover' for his extracurricular activities. It has even been known for such an agent to hold commissions in two separate branches of the armed services.[1] The advantage of such an arrangement from Gregory's viewpoint was that if he were stopped on the street as a draft dodger or deserter he could always produce papers signifying that he was a member of H.M. Forces on 'special duty'. But it must have been obvious to even the most obtuse that Gregory was hardly the material that Kitchener had in mind for front-line duty. At forty, Gregory, who had never knowingly partaken in any form of physical exercise, fell ludicrously below the physical standards demanded of a private in the Irish Guards, being short, paunchy, and bespectacled. In February, 1919, without ever having fired a

[1] See Charles Barry's account of such a situation when he served with Army intelligence in Russia during the First World War in *Unsought Adventure* published in 1939.

[88]

rifle in anger, Gregory was transferred to Class Z, Army Reserve.

Maundy Gregory's wartime activities would be shrouded in even greater obscurity had I not been so fortunate as to find one witness at least who had contact with him during this period. She is Miss Phyllis Barnes, now living in Tankerton, Kent. During the 1914–18 war Miss Barnes was secretary to a Captain H. J. Craig, who was with the procurement division of the War Office, but whose offices in Trafalgar House, 11 Waterloo Place, simply had 'Craig & Company, merchants' lettered on the door. (Other wartime agencies housed in Trafalgar House included the American Volunteer Motor Ambulance Corps.) Captain Craig dealt with armament manufacturers, and a frequent visitor to his office was Mr H. W. Holland, inventor of the Holland breech mechanism which was used with the Nordenfeld 75-mm artillery field piece. I give Miss Barnes's story in her own words:

'One of Captain Craig's associates [who] had a room in the office . . . was an Australian engineer, a D.Sc., and an inventor of a hand grenade that was supposed to be better than the Mills bomb. He spoke German well and said he had lived in Germany. There was correspondence with the Ministry of Munitions, and eventually a demonstration of the bomb was arranged to take place at Hendon. In 1917 Captain Craig told me that the inventor was suspected (he did not say by whom) of spying for Germany. He said a very important member of the Secret Service was going to investigate and I was to carry out his instructions.

'It was Maundy Gregory who came to the office as the Secret Service agent. He asked me to keep a list of all incoming and outgoing telephone calls from this man's room . . . and names of visitors. He said he could not give me his address as it was strictly private and never given to anyone, but he would call for the lists from time to time. He gave me a telephone number which could be used in an emergency. There was a trustworthy person who would take a message. I cannot remember the number after all these years but it was the Gerrard exchange . . . Maundy Gregory was very well dressed but wore too much jewellery. His hair was brown, he was not bald then, and he did not wear glasses, but used a monocle. He was always courteous although he had a pompous and grand manner. There was an air of mystery about him.'

Miss Barnes does not remember what happened to the Australian inventor, but her contact with Gregory had a post-war sequel when

in 1919 she was summoned to Gregory's office in Parliament
Street. 'His manner was as impressive as usual,' she remembers.
'He said he was going to publish an important periodical and he
wanted to engage a confidential secretary and receptionist who was
capable of receiving well-known and famous people, including
royalty. This last I thought was rather amusing.' Miss Barnes
politely turned the offer down.

VII

Mystery Man of Whitehall

Just as the cancellation of Cowes Week in August, 1914 had sig-
nalled the end of the fashionable world chronicled by *Mayfair* so
the revival of the royal regatta at Henley in 1920 ushered in a new
era. That year the 'bright young things' were in evidence for the
first time among the mums in the flowered organdies and the big
picture hats, and from countless punts tied up along the Thames
came the gramophone wail of the latest jazz importations from the
New World.

Still not all of the old order was lost. Among the representatives
of a more staid generation to be seen at Henley that year were
Maundy Gregory and his guests, Frederick Rosse and his wife
Edith, who strolled beneath the gaily striped awnings of the Phyllis
Court terrace. They had been seen together often that summer
either boating on the river in one of the new-fangled 'electric'
canoes, or at Maidenhead enjoying a strawberry tea at Skindle's
overlooking the Thames; and already tongues had begun to wag
about 'The Inseparable Trio', as they were dubbed. The truth was
that Gregory and the Rosses, with whom he had remained fast
friends ever since the *Dorothy* fiasco, were sharing a house in St
John's Wood, Gregory occupying the top floor while the married
couple had the run of the lower. The arrangement was not to last
for long, 'The Inseparable Trio' becoming a twosome when Rosse
suddenly decamped. Thereafter Gregory and Edith Rosse, who remained living together blamelessly in the St John's Wood house,
gave it out that they were brother and sister.

But this was in the future. At the Henley regatta attention
focused less on the middle-aged actress with dyed red hair and her
complaisant husband than upon the third member of this ill-assorted
triangle. For Maundy Gregory was something of a mystery. Judging by his life style, Gregory was a man of wealth, but the source of
that wealth was far from visible. Also his advent on the social
scene had been unheralded: no one could recall having seen him

before the war at Henley. At Henley a government minister, who had overheard Gregory at the next table bandying about the names of Cabinet colleagues, demanded, 'Who the devil is that fellow?' and got four different answers from his companions. One said that Gregory held an important post at the Foreign Office; another claimed that he was associated with Lord Northcliffe in some publishing enterprise; while a third, coming closer to the truth, described Gregory as a political fixer. It needs to be added that the fourth positively identified Gregory as 'C', the head of the British Secret Intelligence Service. To get himself talked about in these terms meant that Gregory had come up very fast, indeed.

*   *   *

Gregory gave Lord Murray of Elibank, Liberal Chief Whip in the pre-war Asquith government, full credit for introducing him to the honours business. It was Murray who recognized the need for an honours brokerage system, according to Gregory, and it was Murray who tipped him, Gregory, for the job. If Gregory is to be believed, he learnt the business from a master. As Liberal Chief Whip in 1910 'Alick' Murray, as he was known to his friends, had had to raise funds to fight two general elections in quick succession against such entrenched interests as the liquor lobby and the Tariff Reform League. To get the necessary he had not hesitated to hypothecate honours in advance of the poll results, thus 'anticipating the favours of the Crown', as one critic expressed it. Again, in 1911, anticipating that the House of Lords was about to throw out a government reform bill, Alick had a list of from 300 to 400 worthies, all with their cheque-books at the ready, whom he intended to recommend for peerages should it be found necessary to pack the Upper Chamber.

The following year he resigned as Chief Whip and exited hurriedly from the House of Commons after it had been discovered that he secretly had invested £9,000 of Liberal party funds in American Marconi shares. When a Select Committee of the House of Commons was appointed to investigate the Marconi scandal, Alick Murray, whose family motto was *Virtute Fideque* ('By Courage and Faithfulness'), fled to Bogota in Columbia, South America, fourteen days by mule from the nearest telegraph office, where the derisive cry of 'Bog-Oh-Ta-Aah!' raised by hecklers at

Liberal meetings could not reach him. It speaks much for the shortness of the public memory and the amnesiac effect of war that by December, 1918, when Maundy Gregory first met him, Murray had acquired the status of an elder statesman whose advice was sought by politicians, not the least among them being Lloyd George.

For in December, 1918, in the wake of the so-called 'Coupon' election, Lloyd George was in a mess of his own making. The fox had been out-foxed. Supposedly the moment of greatest triumph for Lloyd George and his Coalition government, the 'Coupon' election, in reality, heralded his worst defeat. Of the 484 Coalitionists elected to Parliament only 136 were of the Welsh premier's own Coalition Liberal persuasion, the balance being Conservatives. Thus, having broken with the official Liberal party, Lloyd George found himself without a political machine of his own, a virtual prisoner of the Conservatives, who could dump him at any time that suited their convenience.

None more than Alick Murray realized the danger to which Lloyd George had exposed himself. If he was to survive politically the Welsh Wizard must found his own party to fight the next general election. To do this would require an enormous campaign fund—at least £4 million, according to Murray's calculations. The only way such a colossal sum could be raised was the time-honoured one of bartering honours for political fund contributions. The Chief himself had been of no help. No sooner had the election dust settled than Lloyd George had left for the Versailles peace conference table, leaving his advisers—notably Murray and Captain Freddy Guest, the Coalition Liberal Chief Whip—to grapple with the problem of raising the £4 million.

The trouble with the honours business in 1918 was that every Tom, Dick, and Harry had got into the act. On the one hand there was the well-intentioned party worker who hawked honours zealously, if with no thought of personal gain; on the other, there was the outright crook who was working a confidence trick, and whose activities were more properly a matter for the fraud squad. Honours were becoming dishonours, as the 4th Marquess of Salisbury warned in a letter to *The Times*. It was this state of affairs that worried Alick Murray. Specifically, he was concerned with putting the sale of honours on a sound business footing. This meant eliminating unnecessary competition and enforcing some sort of retail price maintenance. The way to do this, as Alick Murray saw it, was to establish a brokerage system with one man— a sort of honours czar—in charge. All business would be channelled through this czar, who would act as go-between for buyer and seller, in this case the Whips' Office, and who, in turn, would be paid a commission. Such a czar would have a priceless advantage over his rivals in that he would have a near monopoly on official patronage as far as the honours traffic was concerned.

Obviously none of Lloyd George's close associates could take on the job, for fear that the Chief himself might be directly implicated. This ruled out Coalition Liberals all the way from junior Whips to party agents in the constituencies. No, the honours broker must be a man who was politically neutral, or one who at least had not openly engaged in partisan politics. He must be thick-skinned, and he must be prepared for instant disavowal if anything went wrong. If he were caught *in flagrante delicto* the party chiefs would not hesitate to disown, even to denounce such a broker. Finally, the honours czar must be a gentleman, or at least have the outward appearance of being one. Preferably, he should be engaged in some occupation that was plausible, and that would make his approach to an honours prospect seem a natural one. It is not known whether any of the Coalition Liberal leaders actually put money into the *Whitehall Gazette* to get the publication started, though Maundy Gregory hinted that this was the case.

Gregory answered these qualifications admirably. Not only was he not identified with any political party or faction, but he had never taken an active interest in politics itself until the war years. His clergyman father, his education at Banister Court and at Oxford, these were badges of respectability should anyone question his credentials. As for his occupation, the *Whitehall Gazette* provided the perfect cover for Gregory's wheeling and dealing.

Gregory claimed that it was Alick Murray who introduced him to Captain Guest late in December, 1918, and that the meeting took place at a weekend party at Elibank House, Murray's family seat, on the river Tweed. A brother of Viscount Wimborne and a cousin of Winston Churchill, Freddy Guest had the reputation of being a playboy and a snob. He was certainly a featherweight as far as political ideas were concerned. Thus, early in 1919, with soldiers mutinying, and Clyde shipyard workers forming soviets, all that Guest could come up with as a panacea for the public unrest was to urge the Prime Minister to release larger supplies of beer. 'The masses are hot and thirsty,' Guest wrote in a memo to Lloyd George on the subject, adding, 'I believe a little "dope" would keep them quiet.'[1] As Coalition Liberal Chief Whip, Guest was given the onerous task of raising the Lloyd George campaign fund, and it was in this capacity that he had dealings with Maundy Gregory.

'Freddy's only concern was that he should not get his hands soiled,' Gregory later told friends in a moment of rare candour. 'That is why he consented to the brokerage system so readily. It eliminated the necessity of him dealing directly with touts whom fastidious Freddy described as grubby little men in brown bowler hats. From now on the touts would be my responsibility.'

Sir Colin Coote has described Guest's relationship to Maundy Gregory as that of 'a sportsman [who] employs a retriever . . . to bring the game into the bag.'[2] It might be more accurate to compare Gregory to the head keeper who employs beaters to flush the game into the open where it can be picked off by those behind the butts.

*   *   *

When Maundy Gregory first opened shop in Whitehall he was by no means the only big fish in the honours pool. His chief rival was a well-to-do horse-breeder and property dealer named Henry Shaw, whose organization was 'Doorway Knights', so-called because Shaw's cable address was 'Doorway, Knightsbridge'. It should be remembered that in the early 1920s there was no law on the statute books making honours trafficking an offence; this came later, in 1925. In any event, here was no grubby little man in a brown bowler. Shaw owned three town houses in Belgravia, a stud farm at Newbury, and farmed 2,000 acres in Leicestershire. In 1921 he had bought for £50,000 the magnificent 17th-century Stowe House in Buckinghamshire, which had been put up for sale by the Baroness Kinloss, and which now houses one of Britain's finest public schools. 'No man of straw,' was the *Morning Post*'s verdict which might have been endorsed by Walter Pyman, a wealthy shipowner of Whitby, Yorkshire. In March, 1922, Pyman

[1] LG Papers, F/21/3/24.
[2] The *Daily Telegraph* magazine supplement, February 27, 1970.

[95]

was approached by Shaw on 'a social matter of a very confidential nature', the usual tout's opening gambit. Shaw gave as reference a well-known baronet from Northumberland, who served as Lord Mayor of Newcastle-on-Tyne.[1] As a result of this importuning Pyman agreed to see Shaw at the Reform Club in Pall Mall. The Whitby shipowner described the interview in the following statement which was read in the House of Lords debate of July 14, 1922 (Pyman's name was suppressed):[2]

> Shaw commenced the conversation by telling me . . . that he was running a horse in the Derby. He then went on to say that my name had been mentioned to him as a suitable person for a baronetcy, and if I agreed he could have it done in an hour. I presume he meant put on the list. He said the Government could not last very long, and that when Lloyd George went to the country he wanted funds to contest certain seats, etc. He did not mention the amount because I very quickly told him what I thought about it. I told him that if it was a question of finding £2,000 or £3,000 to turn this Government out and dipping Mr Lloyd George into the Thames I would subscribe with pleasure but as far as paying anything for a Baronetcy I would not give three half-pence.

Pyman lost his temper before finding out Shaw's asking price for the baronetcy. But Ernest Doxford, J.P., a shipbuilder of Sunderland, whom Shaw approached with an identical offer, was told that a baronetcy would cost £40,000. The operations of 'Doorway Knights' were exposed by the Duke of Northumberland, who wrote to the *Morning Post*: 'There can surely be no doubt in any reasonable mind that Mr Shaw . . . was acting . . . on the authority of somebody connected with the Government. If it were true that he had received no authority of any kind, it would mean that Mr Shaw was trying to obtain money under false pretences, and that the baronet he quoted as reference was his accomplice in this design.' The *Morning Post* itself sent a reporter to interview Shaw at his Knightsbridge flat, whose walls were graced by photographs of the pedigree pigs Shaw bred in Leicestershire. ('No recent re-

---

[1] I have suppressed the baronet's name in the absence of more conclusive evidence that would link him directly with 'Doorway Knights'.

[2] Hansard, Lords, 5th Series, v. 1, col. 507.

[96]

cruits to the honours list [they] had reached the pig peerage some generations before,' the reporter wrote.) Shaw refused to comment on the Pyman and Doxford cases, but in the following bit of dialogue hinted that he was not without influence:

Reporter: Might I ask who is your particular friend in the Cabinet?
Shaw: Oh, I know quite a lot of them.
Reporter: On which side, the Unionists or the Liberals?
Shaw: On both sides.
Reporter: Which side do you favour yourself?
Shaw: Neither. I am a Coalitionist, that's all.
Reporter: I suppose these transactions are with the Whips.
Shaw: You seem to know more about it than I do.

Lloyd George issued a blanket disclaimer to the press: 'I do not know Mr Shaw. I have never heard of him before. I never authorized anyone on my behalf to instruct Mr Shaw, nor anyone else, to act in the way he is alleged to have done.' Half a century later President Nixon's denials of White House complicity in the Watergate break-in and subsequent cover-up were to have the same counterfeit ring.

Once Maundy Gregory began to operate as honours broker, organizations such as 'Doorway Knights' did not stand a chance. For Gregory was 'Mr Honours', as far as the Coalition Liberal Whip's Office was concerned; he alone had the inside track in the honours sweepstakes. Gregory himself was magnanimous as far as his vaniquished rivals were concerned. To the best of the touts he offered better terms to come and work for him. It was thus that he acquired J. Douglas Moffatt, described in an earlier chapter.

Still it was by no means all clear sailing for Gregory. Walter Pyman, the Whitby shipowner, was not alone in his desire to see Lloyd George dipped into the Thames, as Gregory discovered. Other industrialists upon whom Gregory now called had not forgotten Lloyd George's 'soak-the-rich' policies as Chancellor of the Exchequer in Asquith's pre-war government, and they still did not trust him. To counteract this image of Lloyd George as a leveller Gregory proceeded to paint him as a crusader against Bolshevism. In fact, Gregory became a master at invoking the Red menace, whether in the columns of the *Whitehall Gazette*, or in private discussions with clients. On one occasion, in order to impress upon a client the necessity of supporting Lloyd George financially, Gregory strode across the room to the window, which he flung open on to a jobless demonstration in progress down Parliament Street. 'That's the way the Russian Revolution started,' he cried with a dramatic flourish. 'Only Lloyd George can save us from a similar fate.' By August, 1921, the number of unemployed had risen to two million, half of them being ex-servicemen, while another seven million workers had had their wages cut. War veterans paraded down Whitehall with banners proclaiming:

THE LAND FIT FOR HEROES

Over 3,000
Ex-Service Civil Servants
have been sacked
by the Government
and
over 26,000
Non-Servicemen
are retained

Describing one such demonstration in the *Whitehall Gazette* Gregory applauded the 'sportsmanlike spirit' of the mounted police in 'laying about them with their ashen staves and riding about more like polo-players'. From press accounts the mounted police charge was more like the Odessa steps sequence of *The Battleship Potemkin* than a polo match.

*   *   *

As suggested earlier, Gregory had one priceless asset which no other competitor possessed, and that was the *Whitehall Gazette*, which provided a plausible cover for his activities. This journal, whose first issue appeared in August, 1919, was Gregory's masterpiece as far as make-believe is concerned. It put him in the van Meegeren class, for like the art forgeries emanating from the latter the *Whitehall Gazette and St James's Review*, to give it its full title, fooled even the experts. In this case, Gregory's object was to make

[98]

the *Whitehall Gazette* look as much like an official government publication as was humanly possible, from its title (so easily confused with the *London Gazette*), its lay-out and typography, down to the thick, expensive-looking paper it was printed on ('Featherweight Antique Wove, Double Royal 90'), which Gregory had manufactured especially for him.

Not content with making the *Whitehall Gazette* look like a government white paper, Gregory also managed to suggest that it enjoyed royal patronage. On the inside cover of every issue it carried an appeal for King George's Fund for Sailors, whose president was the Duke of York (later King George VI). Colour portraits of members of the Royal Family also appeared from time to time, the Prince of Wales, in the uniform of a colonel of the 12th Lancers, being the favourite subject. Other 'public service' type advertisements which suggested official patronage related to Treasury Bonds, the sale of surplus government stores, and the Officers' Association, this latter being an appeal over the signature of Earl Haig.

The *Whitehall Gazette* was priced at half-a-crown a copy, but one would have searched in vain for it on the newsstands, the reason being that its circulation was almost entirely complimentary. 'We printed a thousand copies of each issue,' A. R. K. Barnard, of the printing firm of Barnard & Westwood, whose father handled the *Whitehall Gazette* account, told me. 'Nearly all of these were mailed free to foreign embassies and legations, Members of Parliament, and to various clubs.' 'It was a very select mailing list,' Barnard added. Finding a complimentary copy in the magazine rack, bishops at the Athenaeum, retired generals at the United Service Club, and politicians at the Carlton, would conclude that their club subscribed to the *Whitehall Gazette*. Thus it gained the reputation of being a reputable journal. Foreign embassies likewise were fooled into believing that the editorials which appeared in the *Whitehall Gazette* often reflected government opinion, and a number of them—notably the Spanish, Italian, and Swedish embassies —bought special supplements of the *Gazette*, hoping no doubt that the propaganda contained therein might reach the eyes of those in power. These special supplements provided Gregory with a lucrative sideline.

From its inception the *Whitehall Gazette* was an organ of extreme right-wing opinion, its aim as stated by Gregory being to conduct 'a consistent and insidious campaign on behalf of monarchy and against the growth of Bolshevism and Communism and their ramifications'. The 'ramifications' of course were the British Labour party and the British trade union movement. The *Whitehall Gazette* tried hard to mirror the prejudices of the upper classes, or what Gregory took to be their prejudices, including anti-Semitism. Thus Bolshevism was presented as 'a conspiracy of the unsuccessful Jews throughout the world' in the *Whitehall Gazette*, which in its issue of October, 1919 drew a homely parallel: 'One can well imagine what would happen in London if twenty or thirty thousand Russian Jews of the East End suddenly, by a *coup d'état*, grasped political power . . .' This image of East London Jewry on the move was dear to the editor, for in the issue of June, 1920 he reported that, 'A confused rabble is pouring into Whitehall from the East End, led by Russian Jew tailors . . . armed to the teeth with any weapon that comes handy.' And not only Jewish tailors but foreign agitators well supplied with *gelt*. These arrived from Soviet Russia with 'pockets full of looted diamonds', which they sold in Hatton Garden, spending part of the proceeds in English pubs. They 'grow extremely angry when asked about their white hands and the sources of their income', the reader was assured. 'They grow even more angry when asked what they were doing during the Great War.'[1]

Very few of the articles that appeared in the *Whitehall Gazette* during its twelve years' existence were signed, their authors taking refuge behind such *noms de plume* as 'Gellius', 'Aurelius', 'Sophist', 'Carfax', and 'Vigilate', this latter being the Gregory family motto. The rubrics under which the various articles appeared give some idea of the magazine's contents: 'The Court of St James', 'The Embassies and Foreign Affairs', 'The Empire', 'British Enterprise', 'The Services', and 'The Clubs'. Just as was the case with *Mayfair* Maundy Gregory seldom allowed his own personality to obtrude. Aside from the lurid 'Inside Reports' from the Soviet Union, in which the imminent collapse of the Bolshevik regime was reported

[1] Stylistically the anti-Jewish diatribes, notably those signed 'Gellius', bear all the earmarks of having been written by Sir Basil Thomson, one-time Assistant Commissioner of Metropolitan Police, who was a friend of Gregory's and who wrote for the *Whitehall Gazette*. Thus Thomson, in his *Queer People*, writes that 'it is inevitable in a country like Russia, when the dregs of the population had boiled to the top, a preponderance of Jews would be found among the scum'.

year after year, the magazine was unbelievably dull, which of course was Gregory's intention.

The jam filling of the *Whitehall Gazette* for which all else served merely as puff pastry was a feature entitled 'Officials I Have Met', which did for this publication what 'Men of the Twentieth Century' had done for *Mayfair*. Under the rubric 'Officials I Have Met', Maundy Gregory was able to corral such Establishment figures as the Archbishop of Canterbury, the Dean of Westminster, the Astronomer Royal, the Comptroller to the Duke of York, the Marshal of the Diplomatic Corps, and the chairman of the British Broadcasting Company, not to mention the Commissioner of Metropolitan Police. These notables, whose inclusion was for the purpose of lending the magazine respectability, were the only ones to be given a free ride. All the other 'Officials I Have Met' paid. I have analysed 140 of these profiles, and the largest group of them (over a third) are businessmen and industrialists, many of whom had made good in the 1914–18 war. Another third are Members of Parliament, senior civil servants, and civic dignitaries. The balance are 'exotics', among whom I include Indian princes like the Maharajah of Patiala who, although he left his 350 wives at home when he travelled to London, still required an entire floor of the Savoy for his needs. The bovine faces of the maharajahs stare repeatedly from the pages of the *Whitehall Gazette*. They were Gregory's best paying customers.

One of those whom Gregory tried to sell a puff piece in the *Whitehall Gazette* was Captain (later Sir) Colin Coote, D.S.O., who was later to become managing editor of the *Daily Telegraph*, but who in 1919 had been elected as a Coalition Liberal Member of Parliament for the Isle of Ely. Apparently unaware of the recently demobbed captain's struggle to make ends meet ('I was poor, and trying to supplement my Parliament salary, the £400 a year, by freelance journalism,' Coote writes), Gregory proposed that Coote, as a promising new MP, should have his portrait done *à la* Spy for inclusion in the *Whitehall Gazette* for the trivial cost of 50 guineas. Thereupon Coote neatly turned the table on him. 'I retorted that I did not possess such a sum, but that if he would pay *me* 50 guineas I would write him an article,' Coote recalls.[1] 'To my astonishment, he burst out laughing, produced a cheque-book and

[1] Colin Coote. 'Scandals of the Century—£12,000 a Knight', the *Daily Telegraph*, February 27, 1970.

wrote out a cheque for the amount with a fountain-pen fitted with a gold nib which seemed to me to be at least an inch broad.' The article, 'Caporetto and After', in which Coote recounted his war-time experiences on the Italian front, appeared in the very first issue of the *Gazette*, after which Coote contributed other articles from time to time.

'Gregory was no fool,' Sir Colin adds. 'He never by a word or a look hinted to me where the money came from. That was psychologically quite acute, because he knew that I had a connection with the Whips' Office, but perceived it would be fatal to try to recruit me as a tout or even as a *confidant*.'[1]

Not all those lured to Gregory's office on similar pretexts were let off as lightly as Coote. Those profiled in the *Whitehall Gazette* paid anything from £50 to £500 for the privilege depending upon whether the subject was a promising but impecunious politician or the Maharajah of Burdwan (the latter's portrait appeared three times). These amounts, of course, were peanuts to Gregory, who was playing for much higher stakes. In reality the profiles were a useful means of sounding out prospects whether they would be willing to pay £25,000 to become a baronet, or maybe just £10,000 to become a plain knight bachelor. When an industrial or a civic magnate approached him unsolicited with a view to purchasing an honour, Gregory, while assuring the magnate that the matter could be arranged, would suggest a profile in the *Gazette* as a preliminary, 'to get your name and face before the people who really matter'. The proof of Gregory's success is the number of people who, profiled originally as plain 'Mister', make a second appearance in the *Whitehall Gazette* as 'Sir So-and-So'.

*   *   *

Lloyd George, of course, was always careful never to let the left hand know what the right hand was doing, leading some writers to suppose that he was largely innocent of some of the more sordid deals made in his name. Immediately following the war Lloyd George was too preoccupied with negotiating 'peace with honour' to give his attention to the mere bestowal of honours, his apologists claim. Acting as his own foreign secretary (he had virtually abolished the Cabinet), Lloyd George was not even in England

[1] *Ibid.*

during much of the time that honours were being sold to the highest bidder, they argue.

Lloyd George in a statement to the *Daily Mail* in December, 1927 gave his own version of how the Honours Lists were drawn up under the peculiar conditions of the Coalition government. That government, it will be recalled, consisted of two wings, Coalition Liberal and Coalition Conservative, working in tandem under the joint leadership of Lloyd George and Bonar Law. The actual lists were drawn up by the two Chief Whips, Captain Freddy Guest for the Coalition Liberals, and Leslie Wilson for the Coalition Conservatives. (Each wing of the Coalition retained whatever amounts its Whips had collected from honours aspirants, but what Lloyd George does not mention is that Guest poached widely on Wilson's territory in order to swell the coffers of the Lloyd George Fund.) 'They [the Honours Lists] were then submitted to the joint leaders of the Coalition, myself and Mr Bonar Law, and afterwards Mr Austen Chamberlain, who succeeded him,' Lloyd George declared. 'We sat together at a joint meeting to consider and settle those lists. Claims were urged purely on public grounds. For my part, I had no information as to who had or had not subscribed towards the party funds . . .'

This explanation brought a sharp rejoinder from Austen Chamberlain, who took exception to Lloyd George's implication 'that I had canvassed with you the personal merits of nominees'. 'I have responsibility for the Conservative names which you included on my recommendation,' Chamberlain reminded his former chief. 'But I have never considered myself . . . in any way responsible for the selection which you made.'[1]

But if Lloyd George personally was not responsible for the sins committed in his name, who then was to blame? The real villains of the piece, according to the Lloyd George apologists, were Captain Freddy Guest, the Coalition Liberal Chief Whip, and his assistant Sir William Sutherland, noted for his foul mouth, uncouth manners, and outsize cigars. Guest it was who wrote to his

[1] LG Papers, G/4/3/4. This archive includes three drafts of Lloyd George's reply to Chamberlain, the actual letter that was sent on December 14, 1927 being considerably toned down. In one of the drafts Lloyd George writes: 'I recollect two cases presented by Leslie Wilson in your day about which I had grave misgivings . . . Subsequently I was informed . . . that substantial cheques had passed in respect of both cases to the managers of your party fund.'

chief early in May, 1919, urging him 'to rely to a certain extent on my discretion' in the matter of honours recommendations, and this at a time when Lloyd George was preoccupied with the Versailles peace negotiations and had no choice but to accept Guest's word.[1] Again, in June, 1922 Guest took advantage of Lloyd George's absence at the Genoa conference to slip through the notorious Birthday Honours List which helped to bring down the government. Such, at any rate, is the apologia put forward for Lloyd George. The Welsh wizard himself in later life played up to this received version of the truth, going so far as to maintain that he was actually frightened of Freddy Guest, the playboy politician. ('I feel certain that Freddie is watching carefully my action with regard to that Fund,' Lloyd George wrote to his old crony Lord Reading concerning the huge war chest raised in his name largely through the sale of honours. 'As long as I keep control of it in my hands, he cannot move . . .')[2]

Documents in the Lloyd George archive at the Beaverbrook Memorial Library tell an entirely different story. They show that far from urging Lloyd George to a course of action to which he was opposed, Freddy Guest tried to act as a restraining influence on him. Thus in a memo dated February 16, 1919, Guest warned that, taking account of the restless mood of the country, Lloyd George would incur 'a grave risk' if he published the belated 1919 New Year's Honours List as it then stood, because 'the bulk of the recommendations are for (a) the Press, (b) the Trade, and (c) Capitalists'. 'I do not suggest that there is a single improper recommendation, on merits, if these had been ordinary times,' Guest added, 'but I point out that the whole burden will be upon you.'[3] The Chief Whip then urged that the list be held over until summer when 'we may have passed this industrial crisis and the bad weather, which emphasises the shortage of coal'. As a sop to the masses, Guest suggested that Harry Lauder, the Scottish comedian and darling of the music halls, be added to those who were to receive knighthoods. Even Sir William Sutherland, who was notorious for hawking baronetcies around the clubs, had the wind up. In a separate memorandum appended to Guest's views, 'Bronco Bill'

[1] LG Papers, F/21/3/24.
[2] Malcolm Thomson. *David Lloyd George*. London: Hutchinson & Co., 1948.
[3] LG Papers, F/93/2/13.

Sutherland, as he was called, warned that 'the appearance of any Honours List at the moment with a lot of wealthy men in it will act as a red rag to the Labour extremists . . .'[1]

If additional proof were needed of Lloyd George's complicity in the honours racket it will be found in The Case of the Suspicious Sheffield Manufacturer. This case is of special interest in that it involves a woman tout, a Mrs Parish, who was a Coalition Liberal party worker and who had been active in the Women's Land Army during the war. Late in November, 1918 Mrs Parish, who said she came from Downing Street, approached G. S. Marple, the Sheffield manufacturer in question, and offered him a knighthood for £8,000, explaining that the Coalitionists were 'very hard up for funds' with which to contest the general election then pending. Marple, who was a Conservative supporter, succeeded in knocking the price down to £5,000. He then made out a cheque for that amount to Captain F. E. Guest, crossed it, and post-dated it January 7, 1919, which meant that he could stop payment on the cheque if his name did not appear in the New Year's Honours List. The post-dated cheque was accepted without a demur.

To check on Mrs Parish's bona fides Marple then wrote to his friend Lord Curzon, a Cabinet minister who belonged to the Conservative wing of the Coalition. It had been Curzon's onerous task, as leader in the House of Lords, to defend the government against charges of honours jobbery, as he now reminded Lloyd George, in a 'confidential' letter heavy with sarcasm. 'You will remember,' he wrote, 'the emphatic assurances that I have given on no fewer than 3 occasions in the House of Lords on your behalf and on behalf of the Government that there neither was, nor had been, nor would be any traffic in honours by your government.'[2] The tetchy Lord then set out the facts in the Marple case, commenting, 'I need hardly say that if a case of this sort—which I am sure will make you as indignant as it has myself—got into the papers it would do the Coalition Party immeasurable harm.' The cheque for £5,000 must, of course, be returned at once 'with a statement that Mrs Parish was unauthorized to enter into the negotiations or to receive the money, and that such transactions are emphatically repudiated by the Government'.

But Lord Curzon was unwilling to let the matter rest there.

[1] *Ibid.*
[2] LG Papers, F/11/9/25.

'This case,' he concluded, 'makes me afraid that similar transactions may be going on elsewhere; and I venture to suggest that a word from you to Captain Guest (who may quite probably be ignorant of the whole affair) would be most opportune.' Although there is nothing in the Lloyd George papers to indicate what action was taken, the money almost certainly was refunded.

VIII
The Robinson Scandal

There was nothing new about the sale of honours, of course. It dated back at least as far as Marcus Didius Julianus, who bought the title of Roman Emperor in A.D. 193. In Britain it was recognized as a time-honoured method of raising party funds, sanctioned among others by William Pitt the Younger who laid down the dictum: 'Any man who is master of £10,000 has a right to a Peerage.' The auction of honours which took place under Lloyd George's stewardship differed from the others that had preceded it in that it was conducted on a vaster scale. 'He [Lloyd George] ran the system too hard,' A. J. P. Taylor writes. 'Not only did he sell more honours with less excuse. Lacking a party, he sold them for his own account.'[1]

Also there was a recklessness, a blatancy about the trafficking in honours under Lloyd George which previously had been absent from such transactions. 'Lloyd George,' writes Sir Colin Coote, 'did not mind how the money was raised provided he was not told. Freddy Guest . . . was completely cynical about it. His side of the Coalition had to have the sinews of war, and this was the only way to get them quickly.'[2] This cynicism filtered down, of course, to Guest's lieutenant, the man he had set up in the brokerage business, Maundy Gregory. Gregory was in the happy position of reaping all the benefits of the honours harvest, without incurring any of the risks.

'It was computed that there were some 340,000 wealthy war profiteers in England in 1919,' Lord Kinross writes.[3] While this estimate may appear excessive there were certainly enough *nouveaux riches* with a deep craving for the kind of respectability

[1] A. J. P. Taylor. *Politics in Wartime*. London: Hamish Hamilton, 1964.

[2] Colin R. Coote. *Editorial*. London: Eyre & Spottiswoode, 1965.

[3] Patrick Balfour (Baron Kinross). *Society Racket: A Critical Survey of Modern Social Life*. London: John Long, Ltd., 1933.

that a title confers to keep Maundy Gregory busy. 'Thus gentle-men received titles whom no decent man would allow in his home,' Lt-Col Henry Page Croft complained in the House of Commons debate of May 28, 1919. 'Several of them would have been blackballed by any respectable London social club,' he added.

Having no political allegiances himself, Maundy Gregory, although nominally employed in the Coalition Liberal interest, felt no inhibitions about crossing party boundaries and poaching on Tory preserves. In fact, he was encouraged to do so by Guest, who, of course, bore the brunt of the recriminations which followed. Complained Sir George Younger, the Coalition Conservative Chief Whip: 'These damned rascals come to me demanding to be made knights and when I refuse go straight to Lloyd George's Whip's Office and get what they want from him.' Younger's cries became shrill when in the 1921 New Year's Honours List a baronetcy was bestowed upon Frederick Mills, Tory supporter and chairman of the Ebbw Vale Steel and Iron Company, for whom Younger had been trying to find a seat in the Commons. 'There must be a stop to Freddie poaching our men,' Younger protested in a memo to Bonar Law. 'I haven't a doubt that if I had got Mills a seat, & got him into the House he would have proved a generous annual subscriber, & it was for us & not for Freddie to give him something more later on.'[1] As it was, Mills's subscription presumably went straight into the coffers of the Lloyd George Fund.

In this same Honours List pride of place went to a convicted food hoarder, Rowland Hodge, who was made a baronet 'for public services, particularly in connection with shipbuilding'.[2] As a Conservative supporter, Hodge, a Newcastle shipbuilder, had first made overtures to the Conservative party to obtain his baronetcy, but his 'offers were so brutally frank that I made up my mind to have nothing to do with him', Sir George Younger recorded.[3]

[1] BL Papers, 100/1/2.

[2] Convicted in April, 1918 under the Defence of the Realm Act and fined £600 plus costs, Hodge was found to be hoarding at his home in Gosforth, 1,148 lbs. flour; 333⅓ lbs. sugar; 148 lbs. 6 oz. bacon and ham; 29 lbs. sago; 19½ lbs. split peas; 32 lbs. lentils; 31 lbs. rice; 25 tins sardines; 10 jars ox tongue; 19 tins salmon; 85 lbs. jam and marmalade; 61 tins preserved fruits, among other items.

[3] Among others whom Hodge approached was Winston Churchill. In a letter dated December 9, 1918 and intended for Lloyd George's eyes,

Maundy Gregory was not so squeamish. Gregory's friendship with the food hoarder dated back to 1912 when he had profiled Hodge in *Mayfair* as 'Man of the Day No. 106'. In the prose poem which had accompanied the full-page colour portrait of Hodge, Gregory had referred to him in rather ambiguous terms as 'one of those all-around, good men, of whom no country can have too many'. Gregory also claimed that the shipbuilder managed to be 'a keen politician without arousing any animosity'. This, of course, was long before Hodge's conviction under the Defence of the Realm Act, which aroused so much animosity against him in the north that he was forced to sell his Gosforth house and move to Kent.

King George V, of course, had approved Hodge's baronetcy without knowing that the man was a law-breaker. When he found out he was furious. By a rather weird coincidence Hodge's shipyard, where barges were being built for the Admiralty, had been one of five Tyneside shipyards which the King had visited in June, 1917, at which time His Majesty had met Hodge himself. As Lord Stamfordham wrote to Lloyd George's secretary, 'The King . . . said he perfectly recollected the man as the only individual of a personally unattractive (to say the least of it) character whom he met on that tour.' Lord Stamfordham added that 'the King has expressed to me his feelings of annoyance and indeed disgust that this man should have received any honour, let alone a Baronetcy'.[1]

Nor was the King alone in his disgust. On March 1 in the House of Commons Lt-Col Henry Page Croft questioned Lloyd George about Hodge, without mentioning the latter by name. Was the Prime Minister aware that 'a recent recipient of a high honour' had been convicted for food hoarding, and if so did he propose to take any action? Lloyd George answered to the first part of the question in the affirmative, with the rider that although Hodge accepted technical responsibility for the hoarding, it was done without his knowledge. 'As regards the second part of the

---

Churchill's secretary, Sir Edward Marsh, wrote: 'Mr Churchill thinks he ought to let you know that he was approached on Saturday . . . with a suggestion that he should procure a baronetcy for a certain Rowland Hodge, a Newcastle shipowner, and receive £5,000 on delivery of the goods. Naturally the intermediary received short shrift.' LG Papers, F/8/2/44.

[1] LG Papers, F/29/4/34.

question,' the Prime Minister pursued, 'I do not propose to take any action, as the recipient rendered conspicuous public services to the country during the war.' It also developed that since his hoarding days Hodge had suddenly become religious and had actually been chosen to represent the diocese of Rochester, Kent on the Central Board of Finance of the Church of England. In response to further questions from Croft the premier whipped out a letter from the Bishop of Rochester congratulating Hodge on his 'well-deserved' honour. (One wonders whether His Lordship the Bishop was aware when he sent his congratulations that Sir Rowland Hodge, Bart, was a law-breaker.)

The Hodge case called into question the use of the citation 'public services' to conceal the real nature of the honour bestowed, which in too many cases was a cash transaction. It was not until October, 1917, as a result of a heated debate in the House of Lords, that the Lloyd George government felt compelled to give any reason at all why an honour was conferred, but too often it sheltered behind the omnibus term 'public services'. In the case of Rowland Hodge, for example, the *Morning Post* questioned whether the delivery on time of barges he built for the Admiralty was 'a service sufficient to extinguish conviction for food-hoarding of a particularly gross and flagrant kind'.

Viewed in this light other peerages take on a new aspect. Sir William Vestey, head of the Union Cold Storage Company, Ltd, was made a baron in the 1922 King's Birthday Honours because he had 'rendered immense service' during the war by providing 'gratuitously' cold storage accommodation for war purposes at Le Havre, Boulogne, and Dunkirk, according to his citation. Yet under prodding in the House of Commons, the Secretary of State for War admitted that these cold storage facilities had been paid for. Furthermore, it developed that Sir William himself was a wartime tax-dodger. In 1915, in order to avoid paying income and excess profits taxes he had moved his £20 million meat-packing concern to Buenos Aires, thereby throwing some five thousand Britons out of work.

In the Vestey case, as in the Hodge case, vital information was withheld from the King, in asking him to approve the honour. The same was true in the case of Sir John Stewart, a whisky distiller of Dundee, who was made a baronet in June, 1920, for unspecified 'public services'. One wonders what the King's reaction would have been had he been told that Stewart paid Maundy Gregory £50,000 for his baronetcy. Afterwards Sir John's financial position had become so precarious that the £50,000 had had to be refunded out of the Lloyd George Fund. When he died in 1924 of a self-inflicted gunshot wound in the head Stewart's debts amounted to more than half a million pounds. At a creditors' meeting held not long after his death the following dialogue took place, according to the *Daily Telegraph*:

Mr Gavin Ralston (solicitor representing one of the largest creditors): I don't believe for a moment that £50,000 was all Stewart paid for that baronetcy. I know what baronetcies have fetched in the past. More likely it was £150,000.
Chairman: I am not sure that I agree with my friend as to the prices of baronetcies—£50,000 may have been sufficient at the time . . .
Ralston: I want to know the name of the man with whom he dealt.
Chairman: That may be difficult to obtain. I think you may take it as certain that every brass farthing Sir John Stewart could have got back was obtained.
Ralston: In any event he was a Lloyd George whisky baronet. He was a bootlegging pal of Mr Lloyd George. Is there no means by which the trustee could force those who handle the Lloyd George political fund into the courts by some method equivalent to what we call 'discovery'?

The *Daily Telegraph* concludes its account of the hearing with the comment: 'It was stated last night by one of Mr Lloyd George's secretaries that the ex-Premier had no knowledge of such a transaction.'

*   *   *

That the government should publish its reasons why a particular person had been recommended to the Crown for an honour was not the only concession which his critics had wrung from Lloyd George. After a full-dress debate in the House of Lords on October 31, 1917, Lord Curzon, as Leader of the House, entered into a specific undertaking on the part of the government: 'That the Prime Minister, before recommending any person for an honour or dignity, shall satisfy himself that no payment or expectation of payment to any party or political fund is directly or indirectly associated with the grant or promise of such honour or dignity.' As the Marquess of Salisbury had pointed out in an earlier debate, 'A man is not allowed to give a money consideration in order to get an ecclesiastical living. That is called simony, and it is a criminal offence. A man is not allowed to give money in order to get a seat in the other House of Parliament. That is called bribery. Why should he be allowed to give money in order to get a seat in your Lordships' House?'[1]

On the face of it, Lord Curzon's undertaking would appear to have been binding. In reality, it was one that was honoured only in the breach, as Lloyd George, who entertained nothing but contempt for their Lordships, had no intention of satisfying himself whether or not money had changed hands in connection with the honours recommendations of his Chief Whip. The Rowland Hodge case and the hostility it had aroused should have served as a warning to Lloyd George of the danger that lay ahead, but he chose to ignore it, and in doing so brought down the Coalition.

*   *   *

The straw that broke Lloyd George's back was the barony conferred on Sir Joseph Robinson in the 1922 Birthday Honours List. The Robinson scandal lacked the glamour of the Profumo affair that precipitated the Macmillan government out of office in 1963—there were no call girls, no midnight swimming parties at Cliveden, no British defence minister sharing a mistress with the Russian naval attaché—but its effect was no less deadly.

Its central figure was no Christine Keeler, but Sir Joseph Robinson, a hard-bitten, sour-visaged pioneer of the South African gold fields. Many times a millionaire, Sir Joseph was so stingy that he never entered the saloon bar of the Queen's Hotel in Johannesburg without first making sure that there was no one inside to whom he would have to stand drinks. The man had 'a tombstone on his soul', in the words of one of his critics. Sir Joseph may have been short of the milk of human kindness, but he was long on boasting. Thus he claimed that he was the first to discover

[1] Hansard. Lords, vol. 26, cols. 172–212.

the great Kimberley diamond field, the first to export diamonds to England, the first to sink a mining shaft on the Rand.

Curiously, Robinson never made a killing in diamonds, though he was one of the first diggers to reach the Vaal river after the discovery of diamondiferous rock there. In fact, he was badly in debt and his bank about to foreclose when in July, 1886, word came of the gold strikes in Witwatersrand. Robinson, with money borrowed from Alfred Beit, set out for the Rand in a buck-wagon. In later years Robinson used to boast how he panned gold in his sun helmet on the Widow Oosthuizen's farm which he bought for a song, though it seems unlikely that the tight-fisted Robinson would have ruined a perfectly good sun helmet in this fashion. By taking options on the neighbouring farms he was able to parley a £26,000 initial investment into a fortune estimated at £18 million.

In 1908 'the Buccaneer', as Robinson was known to his associates, developed a hankering for respectability, and as his first step towards acquiring the same, bought a baronetcy from the Campbell-Bannerman government that was then in power. Next he bought Dudley House in London's Park Lane, stocked it with masterpeices by Rembrandt, Romney, and Franz Hals, and settled down to live the life of an English gentleman. In November, 1911 the quest for respectability led Robinson, aged 71, straight to Maundy Gregory's office in Albemarle Street to see about getting his portrait in *Mayfair*. Gregory, of course, was only too happy to oblige—for a price. And so Robinson, in a frock coat, appeared in four colours in *Mayfair*'s issue of December 14, 1911 as No. 78 of its portrait series 'Men of the Day'. The prose poem which accompanied it spoke of Robinson's 'diplomacy and tact' in dealing with the labour problem in the goldfields. 'He was instrumental in having the Chinese sent back to China,' the profile continued, 'and the prophecy he then made that the requisite labour could be found in South Africa has turned out to be correct.' In reality, Robinson had an almost pathological hatred of the coloureds who took the place of the Chinese coolie labour he had had deported, a hatred dating back to his childhood when his home was attacked by Kaffirs. As the coloureds became organized he transferred his hatred to the trade unions. *Mayfair* concluded its profile by describing Robinson as 'one of those whom Britons have to thank for the successful growth of the Colonies'.

When Maundy Gregory set up in the honours business his

filing-cabinet mind, of course, remembered Robinson, whom he called upon at his Park Lane mansion. This time it was no tuppence coloured portrait which Gregory dangled before the gold-and-diamond merchant, but a barony. By this time Robinson was 82 years old and deaf, but all the more reason why he should consider crowning his career. A barony, Gregory pointed out, would give Robinson a seat in the House of Lords, which was not only a fitting climax for a man who had pioneered the Rand, but a rebuke to his enemies who had criticized Robinson for his pro-Boer stand during the South African war. Sir Joseph eagerly swallowed the bait, but not without knocking Gregory's original asking price of £50,000 down to £30,000.

Robinson's barony 'for National and Imperial services' was duly gazetted in the Birthday Honours List, which described him as 'chairman of the Robinson South African Banking Company'. Reference was made earlier to the fact that in asking the King's approval of certain honours vital information had been withheld from His Majesty. But here is a case of the facts being deliberately falsified by the Chief Whip's Office, for the bank of which Robinson was supposed to be chairman had been liquidated seventeen years earlier.[1] Lloyd George's reckless contempt of public opinion appears to have been infectious, for his subordinates likewise concealed the fact that Robinson had been convicted of fraud in connection with his Randfontein Estates Company, and fined £500,000 by the South African Supreme Court. Moreover his appeal against this conviction had been dismissed by the Judicial Committee of the Privy Council as recently as November, 1921.

The sort of fraud in which Robinson was engaged was described by Lord Harris in the House of Lords' debate of June 22, 1922. As chairman of the Randfontein Estates Company, it became Robinson's duty in 1906 'to acquire for the company the freehold of certain mining properties', Lord Harris explained. 'His method of performing this duty was to purchase the freehold for himself and then to resell it to the company at an enormously higher price.'

---

[1] In April, 1921 Charles McCurdy, one-time Food Controller, replaced Freddy Guest as Coalition Liberal Chief Whip, Guest being made Secretary of State for Air. Of McCurdy Sir Colin Coote writes: 'He had . . . rather inherited than exploited the dubious methods of raising the money which later became the Lloyd George Fund.'

As an example of Robinson's manipulations, he sold land and options he had originally purchased for £60,000 to his shareholders for £275,000.

* * *

The scandal of the Robinson peerage broke over Parliament like a storm, setting up eddies in the lobbies of both Houses. Their Lordships were particularly incensed, for their number included Privy Councillors who had dismissed Robinson's appeal against conviction only seven months earlier, and the facts of the case were still fresh in their minds. What Britain was faced with was a 'public scandal of the first magnitude', cried Lord Selborne, who went on to link the scandal with the 'immense sums of money [which] continue to flow into the coffers of the political party in power at the moment'. Nor was the Robinson peerage the only one to come in for criticism. In the ensuing parliamentary debate four out of the five men whom Lloyd George had recommended for baronies in the 1922 King's Birthday Honours were suspected, some of them unjustly, of having obtained their peerages by corrupt means.[1] Mention has already been made of Robinson, and of Sir William Vestey, who moved his meat packing business to Buenos Aires allegedly to avoid taxes; the other two peerages that came under fire were those of Sir Samuel James Waring, former head of the department store Waring and Gillow, and Sir Archibald Williamson, whose oil firm was accused of trading with the enemy. Waring, who was accused in the House of Commons of wartime profiteering, created a sensation when he stood up in the Distinguished Strangers' Gallery of that chamber, and shouted, 'That is a lie!' Needless to say the press had a field day with these disclosures.

Having raked the peerages with the buckshot of criticism the press turned its attention to other names on the Birthday Honours List. Among those recommended for baronetcies was Sir John Drughorn, a shipowner, who had been convicted in 1915 for trading with the enemy, it was pointed out. True, the judge in fining Sir John had given him a good character, but he was considered in many quarters to be unsuitable for an honour. Possibly even

---

[1] The fifth baron's chief claim to fame appears to have been that he was a manufacturer of custard powders.

less suitable for an honour was Hildebrand Aubrey Harmsworth, younger brother of press lords Northcliffe and Rothermere, who was awarded a baronetcy 'for public services'. Commenting on this baronetcy, his nephew Cecil King writes: 'Hildebrand had never done a stroke of work in his life. So when the baronetcy was announced the family inundated him with sarcastic telegrams on the lines of, "At last a grateful nation has given you your due reward".'

* * *

Meanwhile, the Robinson farce (for that is what it had degenerated into) had not quite played itself out. Having been made a baron for 'National and Imperial services', the old man must now be persuaded to disgorge his barony. With this end in view on June 23 Robinson was visited in his suite at the Savoy Hotel where he was waiting to assume his title. Almost stone deaf, the South African pioneer thought he was being pressed for more money, reached for his cheque-book, groaning, 'How much more?' When the nature of the visit was explained to him he grudgingly consented to write a letter to the Prime Minister declining the peerage. On June 29 the Prime Minister's reply was delivered to Robinson at the Savoy by A. J. Sylvester, Lloyd George's principal secretary. It said that the King had agreed to Robinson's request to decline the proposed honour, and pointed out that had Robinson not adopted this course, 'the House of Lords would . . . have petitioned His Majesty not to issue the Patent, without which no Peerage can be created'. This visibly upset the octogenarian, who having had second thoughts about the peerage, was preparing to fight the matter out in the House of Lords. 'This is a breach of faith, and I shall be covered with ridicule,' he cried, according to Sylvester's account. 'I cannot now live in South Africa and it will be said that I could not face the charges against me in the House of Lords . . . I particularly did not desire that the King should be approached.'[1]

That same afternoon Robinson's letter declining the barony was read aloud in the House of Lords by Lord Birkenhead, the Lord Chancellor, who actually dictated the letter, according to some accounts. Addressed to the Prime Minister, it read in part: ' I am

[1] LG Papers, F/252.

now an old man to whom honours and dignities are no longer matters of much concern. I should be sorry if any honour conferred upon me were the occasion for such ill-feeling as was manifested in the House of Lords yesterday, and while deeply appreciating the honour which has been suggested, I would wish if I may, without discourtesy to yourself and without impropriety, to beg His Most Gracious Majesty's permission to decline the proposal.' It says much about this whole sorry episode that, in the end, Robinson was the only one of the principals involved to emerge from it with even a shred of dignity.

King George V was so infuriated over the Robinson peerage, which he described as 'little less than an insult to the Crown', that he took the unusual step of writing to Lloyd George personally to express his disgust. In the letter His Majesty called attention to 'the excessive number of honours conferred; the personality of some of the recipients; and the questionable circumstances under which the honours in certain instances have been granted' as causes of 'growing public dissatisfaction'. Referring to the Robinson case again, the King ended by appealing 'most strongly' that the Crown and government be protected from 'similar painful if not humiliating incidents . . .' Lloyd George's reply to the King was one of studied insolence. He blamed the outcry over Robinson on the fact that the South African digger had always taken an 'independent' line in politics—i.e. that he was pro-Boer. 'This has caused him to make very powerful enemies in Africa and also on the Stock Exchange in London . . .'[1]

As stated earlier, the Robinson peerage and the other 'tainted' honours in the 1922 List as much as any one factor were responsible for Lloyd George's fall from power, which came some four months later. He was never again to be entrusted with public office. As Lord Beaverbrook remarked, 'Without a doubt the sale of honours for the benefit of Lloyd George's personal Political Fund had damaged his prestige and injured his standing in Parliament and in the constituencies.'[2] Robert Blake expresses it another way. Commenting on the brilliance Lloyd George brought to public life, Blake writes: 'There was an obverse side to that brilliant sparkle: the sale of honours and the prostitution of the

[1] LG Papers, F/29/4/104.
[2] Lord Beaverbrook. *The Decline and Fall of Lloyd George.* London: Collins, 1963.

highest judicial office. The world of Maundy Gregory was never far away.'[1]

What of Gregory—how had the Robinson scandal affected his fortunes? At the first sign of the storm Gregory made for cover, and he remained there until the storm had blown over, when he emerged unscathed. Not once while the scandal was being aired in Parliament and in the press had Gregory's name been mentioned, though there were dark hints in both places that a brokerage system was in operation. (The current tariff for honours was given during a House of Lords debate.) The silence concerning Maundy Gregory was a tribute not only to his skill in keeping out of the public eye, but to the fear he inspired in certain quarters. That fear, in turn, had bred contempt on his part. The story is told that after the furore had died down Gregory was called into Chief Whip Charles McCurdy's office and informed that Robinson was demanding a refund of the £30,000 he had paid for his barony—did Gregory know what had become of the money? 'Of course I know what has become of it,' Gregory snapped. 'I have spent it.'

[1] Robert Blake. 'Baldwin and the Right.' *The Baldwin Age.* (John Raymond, editor.) London: Eyre & Spottiswoode, 1960.

PART THREE

'. . . if I admired him for nothing else, I certainly
admired his gift of silence about his particular
line of business.'
GERALD HAMILTON

'I make it a rule never to open my mouth on such subjects,' said Taper, 'a nod or a wink will speak volumes.'
DISRAELI

'I never thought him more despicable than the clients he
obtained. He generally managed to deliver the goods for
which they ought not to have asked.'
SIR COLIN COOTE

'Could any man *ever* have been quite such a rogue as
most people think Maundy Gregory was?'
PROFESSOR ROY DOUGLAS
in a letter to the author dated October 26, 1972

IX

The Cheerful Giver

Waiters at the Ambassador Club in Conduit Street had a standing
order that promptly at 12.45 each day they were to put two magnums of *Moët et Chandon* in a bucket of ice and wheel it to a table
near the centre of the dining-room to await the arrival of Maundy
Gregory. The 'High Table', Gregory called it—the venue where
he and his guests were on display daily. He was entitled to call it
anything that took his fancy, for from April, 1927 Gregory owned
the Ambassador Club. In many ways it was his most audacious
undertaking.

What was the Ambassador Club like under Gregory's aegis?
No two people I have talked to who knew the club are agreed as
to the exact purpose the club served in the Gregorian scheme of
things. One charter member explained it thus: 'You've heard of
feasting with panthers, the phrase Oscar Wilde coined to describe
the deliberate courting of danger? That is what the Ambassador
Club was like. As host Gregory was a very playful panther indeed.
The guests at the High Table were like goats tethered to stakes.'

Not all those who accepted Gregory's hospitality did business
with him. There was a fair sprinkling of sheep among the goats.
Gregory's luncheon guests in the late 1920s might include the Earl
of Birkenhead, one-time Lord Chancellor; Major-General John
Hanbury-Williams, Marshal of the Diplomatic Corps; and the
first secretary of one of the foreign embassies. At a nearby table
Austen Chamberlain, the British Foreign Secretary, might be
spotted lunching with Sir Warden Chilcott, who hunted wild boar
on his Corsican estate with the huntsmen dressed in pink and
carrying pikes.

'The Ambassador Club became a favourite lunchtime rendezvous for Members of Parliament,' says John Baker White, one-
time Tory MP for Canterbury, who ate there often. 'Its charm
lay in its distance from Westminster. MPs felt that they were far

enough away from the sound of the division bells for them to relax; and for those who liked to keep in touch, Gregory had a direct telephone line to the House of Commons installed.'

This was the Ambassador Club by daytime. At night its character changed completely. From the outset Gregory had been torn between trying to please the 'bright young things' of the 1920s— 'the rather hectic modern type', as he called them in a *Whitehall Gazette* article—and catering to the Establishment. It was the heyday of the night club, an importation from the continent, and Gregory would have liked to cash in on the craze. But the night club brought with it 'an undesirable promiscuity', as he pointed out in the same article. By making the Ambassador Club an all-male preserve in the daytime, and throwing it open at night to what he called the 'leisured seekers of the lighter life', Gregory had hit upon a compromise solution that worked.

The London night club craze of the 1920s was born of a desire to wallow in the mud shared by the aristocratic and the bohemian alike. The Crown Prince of Sweden and Prince Nicholas of Rumania were regular customers at Kate Meyrick's '43' club, as were Jacob Epstein and Augustus John. Lancashire millionaire Jimmy White would arrive at the '43' with six chorus girls on each arm and proceed to run up a champagne bill for £400. Threading in and out among the guests was 'Brilliant' Chang, who peddled only the highest grade heroin. The Ambassador Club achieved a *louche* reputation of a different kind. 'No one knew what went on under its glass roof, though everyone suspected that it was suitably squalid,' John Baker White explained. Some said that its managing director Peter Mazzina was, in reality, a fence for stolen goods; others, that the de luxe flats above the club were used for the showing of blue films.

Louche or not, the Ambassador Club received the accolade of social approval when the Prince of Wales, who was a dab hand at panther-feasting, took to dropping in. Out of deference His Royal Highness was never referred to by name. He was simply 'Number One'. ('Number One will be arriving at midnight with a party of six,' Gregory would inform Mazzina, adding, 'The Marchioness of Dufferin and Ava will have to give up her table, as Number One doesn't like to be too near the orchestra.')

*   *   *

Maundy Gregory acquired the Ambassador when its previous owner Ritzie went broke and had to sell it in a hurry. Ritzie had opened the Ambassador Club early in 1926 with the aim to make it a rival to Ciro's and the Kit Kat Club, but the General Strike of May, 1926, had intervened to put paid to his hopes. 'Many hostesses who would normally have given their "little season" parties are reserving them until industrial tranquillity is restored,' wrote the gossip columnist of one of the London dailies. But Ritzie could not wait. Within the year the little restaurateur was dead (of a broken heart, some said) and his club had come on to the market to be snapped up by Gregory with the aid of a £20,000 mortgage from Barclays Bank.

The story is told that Gregory bought the Ambassador as a present for Peter Mazzina, a 23-year-old waiter at the Carlton Hotel, who looked after Gregory attentively whenever the latter dined there. The *Sunday Dispatch* of September 12, 1954, describes the episode thus: 'One day Maundy Gregory, enjoying his brandy and cigar with a companion, nodded at the hovering figure of the waiter and mused, "You know, Peter deserves something better than this." And in that moment was born the idea of the Ambassador Club . . .' This bit of apocrypha, like much else that has been written about Maundy Gregory, belongs to the realm of folklore. The truth was that the Ambassador Club was a bargain Gregory felt he could not ignore. Besides, it answered Gregory's need for self-display.

Mazzina's extreme youth caused some raised eyebrows, and even Maundy Gregory alluded to it playfully in the *Gazette* article already quoted, writing, 'Mazzina, known to so many as Peter, will pass many moons before he needs the assistance of Dr Voronoff or any of his cult.' (Serge Voronoff's experiments in transplanting monkey glands to human beings were then a favourite subject with headline writers and music hall comedians.) Despite his youth, Mazzina earned the £3,000 a year he was paid as managing director, for he fronted for Gregory, holding half of the share capital in the limited company that was formed. The bank's nominee, a stockbroker named Arthur Bissett, held the other half. Thus Gregory's name appeared on no document identifying him as proprietor of the Ambassador Club, or even as a company director. Did he take this precaution, one wonders, because he had burned his fingers on Combine Attractions Ltd? To Maundy Gregory was reserved the exquisite pleasure of being able to inform a guest at the conclusion of a superb meal, 'By the way, I happen to own this club.'

The staircase as one entered the Ambassador Club (now headquarters of the Royal Society of Painters in Water Colour) was lined with the portraits on vellum of dignitaries who attended George IV's Coronation, the collection having belonged originally to the Duke of York. The dining-room itself with its classic Greek columns and a gallery running around three sides was surprisingly small, but the mirror walls gave a *trompe l'oeil* effect of a much larger salon, while the Rose du Barry colour scheme was echoed by tinted light filtering through its glass roof to give an overall impression of cheerfulness.

Under the Gregory–Mazzina management there was a distinct falling off in the standards of service set by Ritzie in the early days of the club. Gregory put the attendants in velvet knee-breeches, but club members complained that they were surly. Club members were given their change in crisp new banknotes and newly minted silver for which Gregory sent to the Bank of England by special messenger each morning, but they were kept waiting an unconscionably long time before the bill for dinner was presented. As for the food itself, it was on the whole excellent, such delicacies as frogs' legs, Rouen duck and Avignon asparagus being flown from the continent daily by Imperial Airways. The wine was a different story.

'The reason why Gregory had two magnums of champagne put on ice for him every day, and why he drank nothing else at the Ambassador Club, was that he knew that champagne could not be re-corked,' Mrs Mabel Pirie-Gordon told me. 'All the other wines served at the Ambassador were subject to being re-corked. In fact, Gregory once told me in a burst of confidence that he bought French corks by the gross so that the members could not tell that their wine had been tampered with.' 'Gregory,' she added, 'used to swirl a stick of toast around in his glass of champagne to remove all the bubbles. The bubbles gave him a headache, he complained.'

Mention was made earlier of the Ambassador Club as fulfilling a particular need felt by Gregory. The need partly was for a place where Gregory could entertain prospective clients in style, and in turn be seen by them hob-nobbing with celebrities on terms of intimacy. But the main purpose which the club served was quite simply that of a listening post. It enabled Gregory to pick up information from politicians and diplomatists whom he saw in relaxed surroundings, and to pass on information that he wanted to plant with them. The club thus took on a sinister aspect. It was as though all the strands that made up the tapestry of Gregory's life—the bogus, the criminal, the make-believe—were interwoven in the 'Social Alpine Club', as Richard Aldington called it, at 26 Conduit Street.

*   *   *

The use of the word 'criminal' in the foregoing paragraph is apposite. Since August, 1925, when the Honours (Prevention of Abuses) Act received the Royal Assent, the sale of honours had been a criminal offence. This law was passed by Parliament on the recommendation of the Royal Commission on Honours which Lloyd George had set up as one of his last acts in office. The Welsh premier had made sure that the Commission's findings would be toothless by restricting the scope of its enquiry to 'future' policy, thus leaving 'unexplored one of the gravest abuses concerning the nominations for honours', in the words of Arthur Henderson, the Labour member of the commission, who signed a minority report.

The Commission had heard the testimony of all living Prime Ministers except Lord Rosebery, who was too ill to attend, as well as that of party Whips, past and present. But not a single honours tout had been called upon to testify, nor had their clients been subpoenaed. In other words the Commission had gone about 'its somewhat unsavoury duties with nose held firmly between finger and thumb', as the *Morning Post* pointed out.[1]

Just as the Robinson scandal had if anything given Maundy Gregory's business a boost by advertising the fact that honours could be bought, so the new law on balance made swindles easier. For the new law made no distinction between buyer and seller in

[1] The Commission did recommend that an honours scrutiny committee composed of three Privy Councillors should be set up to vet honours nominees, which is the procedure now followed. In pruning from honours lists persons deemed to be 'unsuitable' the scrutiny committee works in complete secrecy. No minutes of its meetings are kept, nor is it answerable to the House of Commons.

the matter of honours trafficking. Hitherto only fear of ridicule had ensured the silence of the client who had been defrauded. Now the fear of finding himself standing in the dock alongside the honours tout made him clam up even more readily. The great honours auction ended with Lloyd George's fall from power, but Gregory continued to do business. The chief difference was that whereas 'guaranteed delivery' had been his slogan in the past, now he flogged the occasional 'non-existent' knighthood or baronetcy, safe in the knowledge that the victim of his swindle would not squeal.

Gregory had taken the advent of Britain's first Labour government in his stride. Swallowing his pride, Gregory, in the issue of the *Whitehall Gazette* for January, 1924, hailed the Labour government as 'The New Dispensation', writing, 'Mr Ramsay MacDonald and his Cabinet have in no way indicated—in fact the opposite—that they stand in any shape or form for anything except the sound conduct of pressing affairs . . .' A cartoon showed MacDonald being invested with the chain of office by Britannia while a figure labelled 'Prejudice' was being carted away feet first. In the same issue an article signed 'Lex' praised the Labour leaders for their courage ('They have certain definite aims, and they have pursued them openly, without deviation, with sincerity and persistence . . .'). To appreciate the irony of this *volte face* it should be borne in mind that for five years the *Whitehall Gazette* month in and month out had been damning the Labour party and its leaders as agents of the devil, if not of the Third International.

While trimming his sails to the Labour wind Gregory was careful to keep on excellent terms with the Tories. Among the Conservative and Unionist MPs whom he persuaded to write articles for the *Whitehall Gazette* were Major Sir George Hennessy, O.B.E., Tory party vice-chairman; J. C. Gould, a Lloyds Insurance broker; and Sir Martin Conway (later Lord Conway of Allington) who represented the universities in the Commons. Other Tory MPs with whom Gregory was on intimate terms were Sir Percy Newson, Sir Nairne Stewart Sandeman, Sir Fredrick Wise, and Edward Marjoribanks.

Gregory's honeymoon with Labour came to an abrupt halt with the General Strike of May, 1926. Gregory held that the General Strike was a Soviet conspiracy ('It was now or never—Russia could wait no longer') hatched by 'Hebrew–Russian brains'. The writer who signed himself 'Lex', and who earlier had praised the Labour leaders for their courage, now held that they should be tried for high treason. Another contributor saw in the strike's failure a glorious opportunity 'to cleanse British Enterprise of the blight that can do nothing but kill it'. As the *Whitehall Gazette* appeared at the end of each month, the April issue, which was labelled 'Emergency Issue', consisted of nineteen galley-sheets bound together and badly proof-read. Gregory hastily switched to a non-union printer in time for the May issue.

*   *   *

On the whole the 1920s were a happy time for Gregory. During most of the decade he shared with Edith Rosse a house in St John's Wood not far from Lord's cricket ground, then a fashionable area. Abbey Lodge, as the house was called, stood well back from Abbey Road, and was approached by a curved driveway with entrance gates at each end.[1] Gregory had the top floor to himself; Mrs Rosse had the ground floor, and her bedroom had French doors opening on to the garden at the back of the house. Each had a housekeeper, each had a baby grand piano (as an early jazz devotee Gregory also bought himself a set of trap-drums with which he accompanied Paul Whiteman and his orchestra on the gramophone). There were even unisex versions of the same clothes. 'When I bought myself a fur coat I bought Edith one, too,' Gregory told a friend. 'We were like Tweedledum and Tweedledee.' To their housekeepers as well as to their friends Gregory and Mrs Rosse were careful to maintain the fiction that they were brother and sister, though Mrs Rosse complicated matters by referring to Gregory as 'Uncle Jim'. To one person at least Gregory referred to Edith Rosse as his wife. This was Mrs Mabel Pirie-Gordon, whose husband C. H. C. Pirie-Gordon was employed by Gregory to edit *Burke's Landed Gentry*. 'I heard so much about "Mrs Gregory" that, in a neighbourly spirit, I offered to call on her,' Mrs Pirie-Gordon recalled, when I talked to her at Polesacre, her home at Lowfield Heath. 'At the prospect of my visiting his "wife" Gregory

[1] Abbey Lodge has long since been converted into a recording studio by E.M.I. (His Master's Voice). It was here that the Beatles recorded their famous song hits of the 1960s, including their LP album entitled 'Abbey Road'.

became all flustered, and quickly discouraged me from doing so.' Another who was quick to see through the relationship was the late Sir Harry Preston, who owned the Royal Albion in Brighton, where Gregory and Mrs Rosse often stayed—in separate rooms. 'They were the perfect platonic couple,' Preston recalled. 'They were in complete harmony, yet a long way from married bliss.'

What did Edith Rosse see in Gregory? Mention has already been made of the fact that she drank heavily as a result of emotional instability. She appears to have been one of those middle-aged women who dote on homosexuals, possibly because they have been unhappy in their love affairs or marriages. They feel 'safe' in neutered company. From Gregory's viewpoint, Mrs Rosse, when sober, made an admirable hostess for the restricted circle of friends whom he invited to Abbey Lodge. 'Milady'—Gregory's pet name for Mrs Rosse—was high-spirited, amusing—'sharp as a needle' is the cliché he used to describe her when talking to a newspaper reporter later. Gregory took 'Milady' with him everywhere— to Henley, to Ascot, to garden parties at Buckingham Palace. Only when he was the week-end guest of Lord Birkenhead at Charlton, or of Sir Warden Chilcott aboard the latter's yacht the *Dolphin* did Gregory leave Mrs Rosse at home. It would have been difficult, if not impossible, to explain Mrs Rosse in such sophisticated company. There is no doubt that 'Uncle Jim' was generous with Mrs Rosse: after she separated from her husband, he helped her with investments, paid for her holidays abroad.

The cuckoo in this particular nest was Mrs Rosse's niece Ethel Davies, who supposedly was the daughter of Mrs Rosse's brother Frederick Davies, a carpenter living in London. Considerable mystery surrounds this girl, who was to come between Mrs Rosse and Gregory, and in general to play havoc with her aunt's life. According to one version Mr and Mrs Frederick Rosse adopted Ethel in 1914 when the girl was nine years old, though why the girl's father would have parted with her has never been explained. A second version has it that Ethel was Mrs Rosse's daughter born out of wedlock and raised by Frederick Davies until it was convenient for her mother to take the girl under her own roof.

Mrs Rosse, it will be recalled, had enjoyed a stage career under the name of Vivienne Pierpont, touring in such musicals as *The Quaker Girl* and *The Arcadians*. While on the road she would have had little time to look after Ethel properly, and it may well be

J. Maundy Gregory in his prime, when he was undisputed kingpin
of the honours racket.

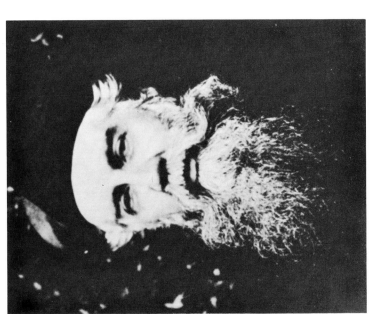

Left The Reverend Francis Gregory, vicar of St Michael's, Southampton, where he created a furore by introducing Anglo-Catholic ritual. Today Maundy's father is regarded by parishioners as having been a saintly man.

Right J. Maundy Gregory shown as a budding theatrical impresario, aged 27. The pose suggests a dream-like trance, as he may slot for the main chance. (*Photo British Museum*)

WALDORF THEATRE
ALDWYCH, STRAND

Proprietors   WALDORF PRODUCTIONS, LTD.

By kind permission of the
Messrs. MAUNDY-GREGORY,

A SPECIAL BENEFIT MATINEE

OF

DOROTHY

By STEPHENSON and CELLIER,

WILL BE GIVEN ON

TUESDAY AFTERNOON, JANUARY 26th, at 2.30.

IN AID OF

The Lord Mayor's Mansion House Fund

FOR THE SUFFERERS IN THE RECENT

Italian Earthquake

Under the Distinguished Patronage of

THE LORD MAYOR AND SHERIFFS

(Who have kindly promised to attend in State) and of

HIS EXCELLENCY THE RUSSIAN AMBAS-
SADOR, COUNT BENCKENDORFF
HIS EXCELLENCY THE AMERICAN AMBAS-
SADOR, THE HON. WHITELAW REID
H.S.H. PRINCE ALEXANDER OF TECK

PRINCESS LOWENSTEIN WERTHEIM
HIS GRACE THE DUKE OF ARGYLL
THE DUCHESS OF NORFOLK
THE DUKE AND DUCHESS OF DEVONSHIRE
THE DUKE AND DUCHESS OF SOMERSET

[For further Patrons see page 4]

WALDORF THEATRE
MATINEE PERFORMANCE, JAN 26, 1909
DOROTHY

IN AID OF THE SUFFERERS FROM THE EARTHQUAKE
AT MESSINA & REGGIO

Programme for the benefit performance of *Dorothy* held in aid of the Messina earthquake sufferers. This experience opened Gregory's eyes to the possibility of roping in wealthy and titled patrons in the name of charity.

Above David Lloyd George campaigning in Wales during the so-called 'Coupon' election of December, 1918 which saw the triumph of the 'hard-faced men who look as if they had done well out of the war', in Stanley Baldwin's phrase. (Photo *Radio Times Hulton Picture Library*)

Below Captain Freddy Guest, Coalition Liberal Chief Whip in the Lloyd George government, who set Maundy Gregory up in the honours business, using Gregory as a retriever to bring the game to the bag. (Photo *Radio Times Hulton Picture Library*)

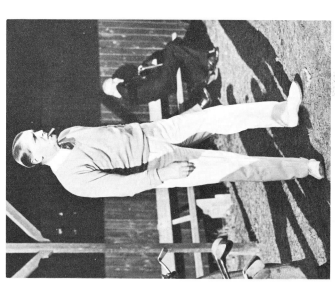

Left The Earl of Birkenhead, formerly F. E. Smith, and one-time Lord Chancellor of England. His friendship with Maundy Gregory, whom he dubbed 'the Cheerful Giver', was highly indiscreet. (Photo *Radio Times Hulton Picture Library*)

Right Lieutenant-Commander Edward W. Billyard-Leake, D.S.O., to whom Maundy Gregory tried to sell a knighthood for £10,000. Billyard-Leake, who was godfather to Lord Louis Mountbatten's daughter, was to act as Gregory's nemesis.

Left Edith Rosse and Maundy Gregory shown in an informal mood at the bungalow on Thames Ditton island where they entertained friends at boating parties.

Right Edith Rosse's will, written in pencil on the back of a Carlton Hotel lunch menu, leaving everything she possessed to Maundy Gregory, whose signature appears in the upper left-hand corner.

Above Edith Rosse's grave, surmounted by a cross in the foreground, showing how close she was buried to the water's edge at Bisham-on-Thames.

Below The exhumation of Mrs Rosse's remains in the churchyard cemetery at Bisham. Dr Roche Lynch, the Home Office analyst, has his back to the camera as he unwraps apparatus. Chief Inspector Arthur Askew is the gentleman in the bowler with the pipe.

Left The Christmas card which 'Sir Arthur' sent out in 1938 to his friends. Gregory was inordinately proud of his handwriting.

Right Madame Anne Yvinec, who successfully hid Maundy Gregory from the Germans for nearly four months at the Hotel Belle-Vue in Brittany.

that she left Ethel with the child's uncle. However, Mrs Rosse quit the stage around 1914 when she was forty-one years old, and henceforth she had time to devote to Ethel's upbringing. The adoption, of course, could be a convenient means of disguising the girl's irregular birth. Whether or not the second version is correct it was believed by Mr and Mrs MacKinlay, who were perhaps Mrs Rosse's closest friends (Sterling MacKinlay was her voice teacher). Miss Leila MacKinlay, their daughter, tells me, 'My parents were convinced that Ethel Davies was Mrs Rosse's illegitimate daughter. It explained why Ethel had such power over Mrs Rosse and could make her feel so miserable. It explained why the girl was so uncontrollable—her fits of temper may have dated from the discovery that Mrs Rosse was her real mother and not her aunt.'

It would also account for Ethel's hatred of Maundy Gregory as the outsider coming between the girl and her mother, and thus deflecting some of the mother's affection from herself. There is no way of checking on Ethel's adoption as adoptions were not registered in England until 1926. In the absence of compelling evidence to the contrary Ethel Davies will be referred to here as Mrs Rosse's niece; but the relationship between the two was no ordinary one such as one might expect to find between aunt and niece. Ethel did her best to make life at Abbey Lodge unpleasant for its occupants.

*   *   *

Maundy Gregory made an excellent host at Abbey Lodge, according to Miss Leila MacKinlay. Whenever he spotted guests arriving, he whipped out the cocktail shaker, and he would be pouring Martinis or Manhattans by the time his friends had shed their coats. (Gregory was probably the first person in Abbey Road to own one of those monstrosities known as a 'Hollywood Cocktail Cabinet'.) On Guy Fawkes' Night Gregory would build a big bonfire in the back-yard, and would invite all the neighbours' children in for an elaborate fireworks display. Afterwards, he would entertain them with his ventriloquist act, dating back to the 'Signor Gregorio' of his Southampton schooldays, or he would accompany himself on the trap-drums singing, 'Ain't She Sweet' or 'My Cutey's Due at Two-to-Two Today'.

It was the age of the flapper, Sigmund Freud, Oxford 'bags', and the Eton crop. To advertise the latest importation from America, a dancing instructor toured Regent Street Charlestoning on top of a taxicab. Preaching against the new dance vogue, the Vicar of St Aidan's, Bristol, cried: 'It's neurotic! It's rotten! It stinks! Phew, open the windows!' But the Charleston quickly won social acceptance when the Prince of Wales was seen doing it expertly at the Kit Kat Club.

Sterling MacKinlay and his wife Dagny were the most welcome of the guests at Abbey Lodge. 'With Gregory and Mrs Rosse my parents made up a foursome for New Year's Eve parties at the Savoy, and for regatta week at Henley,' Leila MacKinlay, who is a novelist, told me. 'My mother also went on holidays abroad with Mrs Rosse, with Gregory paying all the expenses. One year it was Monte Carlo, the next year they went to Florence, where they stayed for nearly a month.' Keeping up with Gregory's style of living in the end proved embarrassing for the MacKinlays. 'My parents couldn't afford it,' Miss MacKinlay explained. 'Taking holidays abroad meant that my mother had to buy clothes which she would not have bought in the ordinary way. Recently I came across an ancient snapshot of my father done up for Henley in white flannels and blazer, which, as a voice teacher, he would have no need of.' What did Gregory get from such a friendship? I asked Miss MacKinlay. 'I think Gregory found my parents useful and reasonably decorative and not at all connected with all these people he was trying to impress. He could relax in their company.'

It was through the MacKinlays that Maundy Gregory met Lionel Logue, the man who cured King George VI of stammering. (The Duke of York, as he then was, had a grave speech defect; he could not for example, articulate the words 'King' and 'Queen', but referred to his parents in public as 'Their Majesties'.) His Royal Highness had been treated by no fewer than nine specialists when in October, 1926, as a last desperate resort, he went to see Logue, an Australian-born speech therapist who had opened up offices in Harley Street. After examining him, Logue assured the Duke, 'I can cure you, but it will require a tremendous effort on your part.' Gradually, by means of breathing exercises, but above all, by building up the Duke's confidence in himself, Logue helped him to overcome his handicap.[1]

[1] On Coronation Day in May, 1937, Logue's was the stage whisper that was heard around the world. Sitting beside the newly crowned King when he broadcast to Britain and the Commonwealth, and thinking the

Owing to Logue's connections with Buckingham Palace, his friendship was an important acquisition for Gregory in his climb upwards on the social ladder. Hardly a week passed but that Logue and his wife Myrtle were entertained at bridge at Abbey Lodge. They were also frequent guests of Gregory at his bungalow 'Vanity Fair' on Thames Ditton Island, where Gregory kept an electric canoe and a motor launch tied up. 'Vanity Fair' was little more than a boathouse, in reality, its amenities being of the crudest (the island was without main drains until 1939), but it had a tiny, enchanting garden running down to the Thames on the Middlesex side where Henry VIII's gilt barges had once glided on their way up to Cardinal Wolsey's palace at Hampton Court. Gregory's friendship with Logue did not pass unnoticed, but created a feeling of grave disquiet in certain quarters.

* * *

Mention was made earlier of the fact that the Ambassador Club acquired a certain chic precisely because it had a *louche* reputation. All that was smartest in London society flocked to the club for such gala occasions as Schiaparelli Night, Napoleon Night, and the Ivory Cross Ball, the latter being under the patronage of Her Grace, the Duchess of Portland. At the height of its popularity the club carried 11,000 members on its books, though many of these were 'honorary' members who paid no subscription.

The Ambassador Club, in fact, did not begin to pay its way. Kate Meyrick, the celebrated queen of the London night clubs, ended her reign with £50,000 worth of rubber cheques, some of them issued by 'visitors whose names are household words—real "pillars of society"', in her own words. Gregory's losses were not nearly so spectacular, but a bundle of worthless cheques reposed in his safe and the club in time accumulated book debts of £2,000 representing meals not paid for by members. When Gregory's accountant Benjamin Pengelly suggested that they go to court to collect on some of these debts, Gregory hastily vetoed the idea. 'As you know, it is against the rules of the Ambassador Club to issue writs against members,' he reminded Pengelly. The truth was that Maundy Gregory dare not become involved in a court action

---

microphone was dead, Logue, just before His Majesty began to speak, whispered, 'Now take it quietly, Sir.'

of any kind, for fear that his own activities would be exposed. The Ambassador Club had never been intended to pay its way. Cheerfully Gregory continued to subsidize it with money earned by other means, recognizing its importance to him as a listening-post.

Of all the Judas goats who were led to the sacrifice at the High Table, none was more important than King George II of Greece. The King of the Hellenes, who made Brown's Hotel his home in London, was a popular social figure, active in Freemason circles, but he was likewise susceptible to flattery which Gregory laid on with a non-Masonic trowel. What did Gregory find to talk about with His Majesty? Sir Colin Coote, who lunched with the pair on several occasions, says that Gregory laced his conversation with amusing gossip, which King George enjoyed. 'Gregory was fond of quoting from the Latin classics, though he usually got the quotation wrong,' Sir Colin recalls. 'He was a great show-off,' he adds, 'but sometimes a chap like that can be amusing.' Gregory by all accounts was a good conversationalist, though no one I have talked to can remember anything memorable that he ever said. Certainly the brilliant and sarcastic Lord Birkenhead, of whom it was said that he would rather keep a live coal in his mouth than to withhold a witty saying, found Gregory sufficiently amusing to honour him with his company repeatedly at the Ambassador Club.

How many of those who enjoyed Gregory's hospitality realized that they were being used by him? King George II of Greece, who was impressed by the articles in the *Whitehall Gazette* advocating a return of the Greek monarchy, was probably a genuine dupe. So too were Major-Generals Jack Seely and Hanbury-Williams, both of whom were babes-in-the-wood as far as Gregory was concerned. Not so Sir Warden Chilcott, who was operating a racket not dissimilar to Gregory's, and who threw business Gregory's way.[1]

[1] Chilcott in 1925–26 used his alleged influence with Lord Birkenhead, then Secretary of State for India, to swindle a group of Indian princes out of £100,000 (see Stephen Roskill's biography of Maurice Hankey, the Cabinet secretary). The fund was 'to enable Chilcott to exercise his personal influence on the affairs of the Princes in London'. A small part of it was siphoned off into the *Whitehall Gazette* where the nabobs were profiled as 'Officials I Have Met'. Birkenhead, when he found out the extent of Chilcott's cupidity, referred to him as 'that sewer rat', according to his son, the present Earl of Birkenhead, who adds, 'Personally I think that this was a slander on sewer rats.'

As for Lord Birkenhead, he walked into Gregory's trap with his eyes open. 'Birkenhead didn't give a damn,' Sir Colin Coote told me. 'If you had asked him to comment on Gregory, Birkenhead would have dismissed him with, "What? That little squirt!"'

*   *   *

The present Earl of Birkenhead is the first to admit that his father accepted expensive gifts from Gregory, who was known to the Birkenhead household as 'the Cheerful Giver'. The Earl of Birkenhead however thinks that the word 'friendship' is too strong to describe the relationship which existed between the two men. 'No one knew anything about Maundy Gregory when he first came to my father's attention,' Lord Birkenhead writes to me. 'It was not then suspected that he was engaged in nefarious purposes.' 'My father was very puzzled by the series of magnificent presents that reached him from Maundy Gregory [who] as you probably know, ran a very good club called the Ambassador. He used to take to it important people with whom he had succeeded in ingratiating himself, such as my father, Austen Chamberlain, etc., and by being seen with them there he produced the impression that he himself was a man of great influence, and used this fact, no doubt, when arranging his deals in the Honours racket.'

'I always thought that my father's acceptance, to a certain extent, of this man's acquaintance was most unwise,' Lord Birkenhead concludes. 'Unwise' is probably too mild a term to apply to F.E. (Birkenhead was known to his cronies as 'F.E.', dating from the days when he was plain F. E. Smith.) By being seen constantly in Gregory's company he left himself open to all sorts of speculation, including the inevitable rumour that he was being blackmailed. F.E.'s biographer William Camp goes so far as to maintain that Birkenhead 'was personally implicated in the honours traffic and caused his colleagues considerable embarrassment by accepting a "cut" from Gregory on more than one occasion . . .'[1]

I have found no evidence to substantiate this charge, but F.E. was certainly a poor judge of men. 'He remained incapable of detecting a bad man,' his son writes in his biography of F.E., citing

[1] When I wrote to William Camp and asked him for his authority in making this statement he cited conversations with Viscount Davidson and Randolph Churchill, both of whom are now dead.

Birkenhead's friendship with Horatio Bottomley, the swindler, who later tried to blackmail him. It is significant that when Birkenhead resigned as Secretary of State for India in October, 1928 two of his friends, Lord Beaverbrook and Viscount Davidson, both leapt to the conclusion that 'either the bailiffs had pushed him out or there was a scandal in the offing'.[1]

Brilliant, erratic, a genius with more than a touch of the swash-buckler in his make-up, Lord Birkenhead had swept the board of all its prizes by the time he had reached his 53rd birthday to become 'the cleverest man in the kingdom', in the words of his friend Lord Beaverbrook. He had been, in turn, president of the Union at Oxford, Vinerian Scholar, Fellow of Merton College, youngest King's Counsel and Bencher of his time, youngest Lord Chancellor of modern times, Solicitor-General, Attorney-General, Rector of Glasgow University, Secretary of State for India. His advocacy at the Bar was considered the most brilliant of his day, his best-known client being Ethel le Neve, the mistress of the murderer Crippen. He was also thought to be the best debater in Parliament. 'Not even Wellington had such a career as this,' as one of Birkenhead's biographers remarks.

As if this were not enough, Birkenhead was endowed with rare good looks. His hat pushed to the back of his head, a red flower in his buttonhole, and a long cigar stuck into his mouth at a jaunty angle, 'F.E.' was the darling of the political cartoonists.

And yet Birkenhead's character was fatally flawed. There was a streak of recklessness in his make-up that amounted almost to a death urge. Mention was made earlier of Birkenhead's lack of judgment when it came to other men, but this applied also to gambling and to other money matters. When another inveterate gambler, the Duke of Marlborough, asked him, 'What shall we play for next?' Birkenhead replied: 'Your bloody palace at Blenheim if you like.' His sin was extravagance, which threatened to land him in Queer Street on more than one occasion. 'I can always make money, but I can't keep it,' he complained to Sir Edward Carson. Even after his bank overdraft had begun to look like the national debt, he continued to maintain a yacht, six motor cars, three chauffeurs, eight horses and their grooms, a town house in London's Grosvenor Gardens, and Charlton, his house in Oxfordshire.

[1] Viscount Davidson's papers. Davidson memorandum dated October 30, 1928, but not catalogued.

When reminded of his debts, Birkenhead's reaction was to rush out and buy another motor car.

Birkenhead's last years were darkened by the sudden death in December, 1928 of Mona Dunn, daughter of the Canadian steel magnate Sir James Dunn, a girl thirty years Birkenhead's junior with whom he nevertheless had fallen hopelessly in love. 'The happy profligate of all she owned' is the way Birkenhead described her in a poem which might almost have served as his own epitaph. After Mona's death Birkenhead drank more heavily, and was less able to hold his liquor (Viscount Davidson in his memoirs speaks of having seen 'F.E.' often 'fuddled, reeling, dragging his dignity and his manhood into the dirt . . .'). It was during these troubled years that Gregory was most often a weekend guest either at Charlton, which was just north of Oxford, or aboard Birkenhead's yacht, the *Mairi*. At Charlton Birkenhead, in a red velvet dinner jacket, played the country squire, presiding over the company in a dining-room which he had had panelled with Jacobean oak to resemble an Oxford common room. Gregory's fellow guests might include Austen Chamberlain and Winston Churchill, then out of office. After one of these Charlton week-ends Gregory strolled into Elkin Mathews, the bookseller's, and announced, 'F.E. wants me to buy his yacht, but I don't want it—I've got four already.' In Gregory's megalomaniac mind a motor launch, an electric canoe, a punt and a dinghy had been metamorphosed into yachts.

At Christmas time 'the Cheerful Giver's' generosity to F.E. and other favoured friends knew no bounds. Gregory employed three secretaries for weeks in advance to do nothing but scour the shops for suitable gifts. 'Gregory used to make a display in his office of the gifts he had bought for his friends,' A. R. K. Barnard, the printer, recollects. 'It looked like the window display of a Bond Street jeweller, with costly pieces of antique silver prominent among the gifts.' (Tom Bramley, Gregory's chauffeur, who delivered the presents in his cab one year, estimated that they were worth several thousand pounds.)[1]

[1] Gregory designed his own Christmas cards, one of which A. R. K. Barnard, who printed them, remembers because it was so unique. 'On the cover', says Barnard, 'there was nothing but Gregory's coat of arms, but inside there was a quotation from Omar Khayyam written in Gregory's beautiful script on the lefthand side, while on the right the hand-

The present Earl of Birkenhead defends his father against the sinister interpretation which has been placed on 'F.E.'s' acceptance of gifts and hospitality from Gregory. 'I should like to make it quite clear,' Lord Birkenhead writes to me, 'that there was nothing whatsoever venal in his acceptance of presents from Maundy Gregory, although doing so showed a naiveté which is amost incredible.' 'It never occurred to him for a second that it might be said that he had thus placed himself in Maundy Gregory's debt,' the son adds. 'I know that this is difficult to believe but it is absolutely true. My father had certain faults but in money matters he was the soul of honesty and honour. I do not think there is now, at this late date, any way in which I can prove this statement to you, and unfortunately my mother, who knew more about all this than I do, is now dead.'

In reply to my question whether Gregory alone, or Gregory acting in conjunction with Chilcott, had ever attempted to extort money from his father by blackmail, the Earl of Birkenhead writes, 'Nothing would surprise me about either of them.' 'Certainly I have no knowledge of such an attempt,' he adds, 'but I should think you are pretty safe in your conclusion that Gregory's income derived quite as much from blackmail as from the flogging of honours . . .'

---

writing had been reversed, as though it were seen in a mirror.' The quotation: 'Though reflection turns the image/Making things to seem awry,/Still it holds a veiled message/For the wise and seeking eye.'

X
'We Are Odd, Very Odd'

The possibility that he might be blackmailing the Earl of Birkenhead resulted in the first determined effort to halt Maundy Gregory
in his tracks. The stop-Gregory attempt came from an unexpected
quarter: Colonel O. A. Harker, who was second in command to
Vernon Kell at MI-5. The story goes that early in 1927 Colonel
Harker was taken to lunch at the Ambassador Club, and was horrified to observe the Earl of Birkenhead dining tête-à-tête with
Maundy Gregory. As Secretary of State for India, Birkenhead was
a member of Baldwin's Cabinet, and hence privy to Cabinet
secrets. Harker was quick to sense the security risk involved. 'I
couldn't believe my eyes when I saw F.E. sitting there with that
villain in the middle of the dining-room,' Harker explained to a
crony afterwards. 'I felt like rushing up to the Honourable Secretary of State with my coat in order to cover his nakedness,' he
added. Instead, the colonel, who had been a commissioner of Indian
Police, launched an investigation of Maundy Gregory.

Strictly speaking, Gregory's activities were no concern of MI-5,
whose business it was to frustrate foreign powers from getting hold
of Britain's defence secrets. Gregory's friendship with Birkenhead,
which involved the risk that the latter might be blackmailed into
divulging Cabinet secrets, was more a matter for the Special
Branch, Scotland Yard, which dealt with internal security. But
Scotland Yard had shown itself to be strangely reluctant to act as
far as Gregory was concerned. Gregory, of course, was a close friend
of Sir Basil Thomson, the one-time Director of Intelligence at
Scotland Yard, who contributed articles regularly to the *Whitehall
Gazette*; and he had succeeded over the years in ingratiating himself with other senior police officials by running their portraits plus
flattering articles about them in the *Gazette*. Gregory went so far
as to present a silver trophy to be competed for annually at the
Metropolitan Police Tournament and Horse Show held at Imber
Court, and he persuaded his good friend Rodman Wanamaker, the

Philadelphia department store magnate, to do likewise. When Brigadier-General Sir William Horwood, the Metropolitan Police Commissioner, entertained the Deputy Prefect of the Paris Police and other senior French police officers at a banquet in April, 1928, it seemed only natural that the Ambassador Club should be chosen as the venue.

Colonel Harker, of course, was aware of Gregory's connections at Scotland Yard. But something else occurred at about this time which decided Harker that the move against Gregory could no longer be postponed, and that was Gregory's capture of the Derby Dinner. Founded shortly after the war by Lt-Colonel Walter Faber, a sportsman and Tory MP, the Derby Dinner was one of the premier social events of the London season, attracting government ministers, peers, and members of the Jockey Club. Winston Churchill was a regular attender at the Derby Dinners; so were three former Prime Ministers, Lords Balfour, Rosebery, and Asquith. To be seen and photographed with such illustrious men, and to have his name bracketed with theirs, was of incalculable value to Gregory, who cheerfully picked up the tabs for these banquets.

The Derby Dinner had originally been held at the Naval and Military Club, then transferred to the Carlton Hotel. In June, 1927, Gregory snatched it from under the nose of the Carlton Hotel by the simple expedient of adding to the governing committee of the Ambassador Club the two men responsible for issuing the invitations, Colonel Faber and Lord Southborough. After Colonel Faber's death in April, 1928, Major General 'Jack' Seely presided, though the non-partisan character of the dinners was carefully retained. By common consent politics were banished for the evening, giving way to an all-consuming interest in the Derby, to be run on the morrow. In the course of the dinner the owners of leading Derby candidates were urged to predict the winner, and to assess their own chances in the field, which they did amid much jollification. There was usually some coy reference to the anonymous host in the company's midst (Gregory wisely had stipulated that silence be maintained concerning his role as 'angel'); thus Seely, in his opening remarks at one of the dinners, observed, 'Despite the strenuousness and economy of the times, our dinner is again able to take place, but over some things we must observe anonymity.' This drew an appreciative murmur from his hearers.

[138]

Obviously Colonel Harker could not take aside each of the 150 guests who were invited to the Derby Dinner each year and explain to him that it was unwise to accept such an invitation. The only thing to do was to expose their host, Maundy Gregory. This would put an end not only to the Derby Dinners, but to the Ambassador Club as well, the MI-5 official reasoned. With this end in view, he decided to launch his own investigation of Gregory and his activities. 'God alone knows what I will find when I start turning over the stones,' he confided to a colleague at MI-5.

*   *   *

Ironically, it was his friendship with Lord Birkenhead that led to Maundy Gregory becoming a collector of first editions. Most of Gregory's friends were distinctly philistine in their outlook. He never felt more at home than when among the backroom boys of industry whose long suit was not book learning but technology. In Lord Birkenhead, who had been selected a Fellow of Merton College, Oxford at the age of 24, Gregory encountered a real love of learning, and just browsing in Birkenhead's magnificent library at Charlton made Gregory keenly aware of deep gaps in his knowledge. Just as 'F.E.'s' interest in yachting had prompted Gregory to look upon his own electric canoe as a yacht, so now, in emulation of Birkenhead, Maundy began to patronize such rare book dealers as Dulau's at 32 Old Bond Street, which was known as the 'Palace Bookshop' because it was patronized by Queen Mary, and Elkin Mathews, which was located opposite the Ambassador Club in Conduit Street.

Predictably, Gregory's tastes ran to the homoerotic in literature, to Wilde, Beardsley, and Pierre Louÿs, but he also collected classics that were mildly titillating. Miss Leila MacKinlay remembers Gregory lending her parents a beautiful edition of Boccaccio's *Decameron*. 'My governess and I pored over it one night when my parents were out,' she recalls. Mrs Maisie Saunders while lunching with Gregory at the Ritz happened to mention that a French friend of hers, Marie-Thérèse Beraudière, was planning to sell a rare edition of Rimbaud's poems in a jewel-studded binding. 'Gregory was so eager to get his hands on the book that he made a special trip to Paris to buy it,' Mrs Saunders tells me.

As part of his passion for secrecy, Gregory insisted upon dealing with only one partner at each of the booksellers he patronized. At Elkin Mathews it was tall, spindly Greville Worthington, scion of the Burton-on-Trent brewers of the same name, who collected dixieland jazz records and vintage cars (he drove a one-cylinder de Dion-Bouton in the Brighton Run). At Dulau's it was Alfred Shipton, who was commissioned to buy various bibelots which Gregory gave away as presents. 'Gregory would call in at Dulau's, and leave his taxi waiting outside for hours while he talked to Shipton,' Percy Muir, a Dulau partner now retired and living in Norfolk, recalls. 'I never liked Gregory myself,' Muir adds. 'He was always impinging upon one's existence.' To test his stricture that only Shipton should have access to his account, Gregory would ask other members of the firm how the account stood. But they were well versed in this eccentricity, and he was never able to catch them out. Whenever the account reached £200 Shipton would inform Gregory, who paid up promptly.

Strangest of all, however, was Gregory's interest in representations of Narcissus, which amounted to almost to a fetish with him. Shipton was commissioned to buy statuettes of the mirror-gazing boy, which he did in bronze, porcelain, and terra-cotta. Gregory eventually amassed more than a hundred of these knick-knacks which cluttered up his Hyde Park Terrace flat. The connection between the cult of Narcissus and homosexuality is so obvious as to require no comment; however, Dr Donald J. West, in his study of homosexuality, might almost have had Maundy Gregory in mind when he writes, 'The typical "narcissistic character" delights in the devotion of others, but gives little warmth in return. The "narcissistic type" of homosexual takes enormous pride in his appearance . . . In personal relationships, however, he tends to be cold and self-centred.'[1]

Gregory's bibliomania was not without its humorous side. Hearing that T. E. Lawrence's *The Seven Pillars of Wisdom* contained passages of a homoerotic nature, Gregory ordered from Dulau's several copies of the book at thirty guineas each prior to its publication in December, 1926 in a limited private edition.[2]

[1] D. J. West. *Homosexuality*. London: Penguin Books, 1960.
[2] The first edition with illustrations by Eric Kennington was limited to 128 copies, one of which fetched £570 at auction a year after the book was published, so much were they in demand.

It was his intention to give the book to friends as a Christmas present. Having placed his order Gregory then awaited the book's appearance with a great show of impatience. One can imagine Gregory's consternation therefore when travelling up to London in the train with Lord Birkenhead after a week-end at Charlton he saw his lordship casually take a copy of *The Seven Pillars of Wisdom* from his briefcase and begin to read it. Gregory could hardly wait to get to his office in Parliament Street in order to get Shipton at Dulau's on the telephone and to give him a dressing down. Patiently Shipton explained that the publication date was still some days off; therefore Lord Birkenhead's copy must have been a review one. Gregory then verified by a telephone call to Birkenhead that this was so, and, looking somewhat sheepish, he called in at Dulau's later in the day to apologize to Shipton.

It seemed inevitable that Gregory's specialized literary tastes should lead him to Frederick Rolfe, alias Baron Corvo, the then little-known author of *Hadrian the Seventh*. Gregory's interest in Rolfe's writings which stemmed from his interest in the homo-erotic, led in turn to what was perhaps the most bizarre friendship of his career, that of A. J. A. Symons, the author of *The Quest for Corvo.* As Sir Shane Leslie expressed it, Gregory occupied the fourth chair at the game of double dummy which Symons played with the ghosts of Baron Corvo and Oscar Wilde, whose bio-graphies he worked on intermittently.

*   *   *

The encounter of Maundy Gregory, the son of an Anglican clergyman, with A. J. A. Symons, whose Russian emigré father is said to have earned his living as a jockey, was straight out of Proust, at once as miraculous and as richly comic in its possibilities as the chance encounter of the Baron de Charlus with the little tailor Jupien. It was a reprise of the miracle of the pollen-bearing bee's visitation to the orchid, the marvellous imagery with which Proust opens the Charlus–Jupien episode of his novel, for surely some supernatural force directed Gregory's footsteps to 17 Bedford Square within whose shagreen walls stippled with silver A.J. dwelt. Gregory explained the purpose of his visit briefly. He was a great admirer of Baron Corvo, he declared, and as such was acquainted with the paper on Corvo which A.J. had read at a meeting of Ye

Sette of Odd Volumes, the dining club to which he belonged.[1] It was to felicitate Symons on his research and to acquire further knowledge about the mysterious Baron Corvo that he had come, armed with a letter of introduction from their mutual friend Shane Leslie.

A.J., who was a good twenty years Gregory's junior, was clearly enchanted with his visitor, of whom he has written that he was 'a plump, rubicund, middle-sized man in the fifties, with an expensive flower in his buttonhole, an air of constant good-living, an affable smile, a glittering watchchain, good clothes and (as I noticed when he sat down) very beautiful boots.' The description could almost be that of Palamède de Charlus if one were to add the imperious beak that stamped the latter as a Guermantes. (Gregory's own nose was more of the pug variety though it became fully as roseate as the baron's with the passage of time.)

It was not so much Gregory's appearance that fascinated Symons, however, as 'a certain watchfulness in his manner, an expression of worldliness far beyond mere literary curiosity, [which] seemed to hint at something more'. Just such a look did Palamède bestow upon Jupien in the courtyard of the Hôtel de Guermantes ('M. de Charlus . . . let his eyelids droop; every now and then he raised them, and at such moments turned on Jupien an attentive gaze'), and with similar effect. Just as Jupien found himself 'quivering in ecstasy before a stoutish man of fifty', so A.J. reacted. 'My reserve vanished before such pertinacious and tactful amiability, like mist before the sun,' he writes. 'I began to like Mr Gregory.'

However, it was the Baron Corvo, and not the Baron de Charlus, who had brought the two together. As Symons produced his treasures for Gregory's inspection—the Corvine manuscripts, the letters on multi-coloured notepaper that Rolfe had written in his beautiful calligraphy—he watched the expression on Gregory's face change to 'that open envy which is the pleasantest form of flattery to the collector'. Finally, with a fine show of diffidence, Gregory asked if A.J. would consider selling one of the less important manuscripts, a fragment or a duplicate perhaps. 'Money was no object,' Gregory added, with characteristic hauteur.

[1] Published as No. 81 of Ye Sette of Odd Volumes, this paper was read on November 23, 1926. Of the 199 copies printed, seventeen had a sheet of Rolfe manuscript pasted in them as frontispiece.

'Actually I had no particular wish to sell anything that morning,' Symons wrote; 'but something in his hint that he was immensely wealthy . . . prompted me to pass him . . . a small poem of Rolfe's composition and in his hand, and say, "You can have that for £20."'[1] Gregory snapped it up like a salmon might snap at a fly. As A.J. escorted his visitor to the door a taxicab drew up from nowhere. 'Goodness,' Symons exclaimed, 'has that cab been waiting for you all this time?' 'Oh yes,' Gregory replied, 'you see, I own it.'

Thus began what in many ways was a literary partnership. For Gregory not only subsidized the research that went into *The Quest for Corvo*, but encouraged A.J. when the latter was inclined to give the book up. In consequence Gregory could claim to be the 'onlie begetter' of this minor masterpiece of literary detection, for without his generous patronage it most probably would never have seen light of day.

* * *

This initial encounter was followed by a series of champagne lunches—'Arabian Nights' feasts', A.J. called them. Not for a moment was Gregory 'taken in' by A.J., whom he recognized as a fellow con-man. On the other hand, he had always secretly admired dilettantes of Symons's stripe, and he had envied them their attainments. Possibly Gregory saw in the tall, foppish Symons with the soft, white hands a mirror image of himself as a young man with his way to make in the world. Whatever the reason, Gregory was clearly out to dazzle his young admirer. That he succeeded in his purpose was all too evident. 'In a dozen ways during lunch I became aware that I was talking to a very rich and influential man,' A.J. wrote admiringly. 'It was not the gold cigarette case he produced (a gift of the King of Greece), nor his superb sleeve links (platinum balls covered with diamonds), nor the beautiful black pearl in his tie which produced this impression of vast wealth, so much as the implication behind everything he said . . .' Gregory listened sympathetically as A.J. explained his efforts to recover the lost manuscripts of the Baron Corvo. 'I gathered that the publication of Corvo's unissued works, the establishment of Corvo in his proper place of repute as an author, were in future to be among

[1] A. J. A. Symons. *The Quest for Corvo*. Penguin Books, 1940.

his major interests, and that I could draw upon him for any reasonable sum to advance these purposes.'[1]

At the second of their rendezvous, which was held at the Ambassador Club, Gregory arrived late, 'breathlessly full of apologies . . . he had been detained at Buckingham Palace on urgent affairs'. Symons noted that Gregory's cuff-links 'were no less resplendent than before, though not orbicular' (A.J. appears to have had a fixation about cuff-links, was shocked to learn that his friend Vyvyan Holland, Oscar Wilde's son, possessed only two pairs), and that the gold cigarette case that Gregory sported on this occasion 'bore an inscription, not from a King, but from the Duke of York'. Maundy Gregory saved his *coup de théâtre* until the cigars and brandy, when 'looking round the magnificent but now empty restaurant, he whispered confidentially, "Of course this place belongs to me."'

Gregory quickly settled into the role of Lord Bountiful, showering his newly found protégé with unusual but valuable gifts. Among the strangest of these was Mussolini's passport issued to Il Duce at Milan in 1921, nine months before his march on Rome. The passport described Mussolini as a journalist and entitled him to travel anywhere in the world except to Russia and Fiume. Gregory refused to tell A.J. how he had obtained it.[2] But Gregory took greatest delight in placing alongside A.J.'s wineglass at lunch one of the supposedly lost manuscripts of Frederick Rolfe, much as another man might slip his mistress a diamond bracelet. The expression of wonderment giving way to rapture on A.J.'s face was ample reward for Gregory's efforts.

Symons told several versions of how Gregory, or rather an agent acting for Gregory, rescued a copy of Corvo's 'lost' masterpiece, *Don Renato: or an Ideal Content*, from the warehouse of an insolvent printer in Birmingham. In the most complete version Gregory's agent knocked up the Birmingham printer on a Sunday morning, and being a Methodist the printer was 'extremely vexed' at the

[1] *Ibid.*

[2] After leaving Gregory's hands the passport had a somewhat checkered history. Symons sold it at auction in March, 1937, to Ian Fleming, the creator of James Bond, who had a special silk-lined morocco case made for it. In May, 1972 the passport was sold by Sotheby's to a private buyer for £1,200, which was exactly four times what the auctioneers thought it would fetch.

intrusion.[1] 'But not even the principles of bankrupt Methodist printers are proof against the allure of gold and silver,' he added lightly. So ultimately Gregory's envoy was directed to a 'rat-infested cellar, wherein by candlelight he sought and recovered a single copy of one of the strangest romances ever penned.' This version contains several errors of fact. In the first place Francis Griffiths, the printer in question, far from being insolvent, was active in the publishing business until 1934 at least. The 'rat-infested cellar' may be doubted, too: the copy of *Don Renato* which Gregory presented to A.J., which was a bound-up proof copy, showed no signs of having been gnawed by rats, but was in mint condition. It bore Gregory's nameplate, and was inscribed, 'To my friend A.J. [A. Symons]. From *his* friend A.J. [Maundy Gregory]. As from one Corvine to another Corvine. (No. 2 of the 1st Edition of only *oo* copies) 13.1.30.'

Maundy 'Money-is-no-object' Gregory not only made gifts of manuscripts to A.J., but continued to buy them from the latter as well, notably the so-called Venice Letters for which he asked A.J. to name his price. Symons was only too glad to oblige, setting their value at £150, which was exactly six times what he had paid for them. 'So far from demurring, my host,' Symons writes, 'questioned (without the slightest irony) if I was asking enough for such remarkable documents . . .'

The letters which Gregory thus acquired were twenty-three in number, and were written by Frederick Rolfe in Venice in the years 1909 and 1910 to Masson Fox, a well-to-do Cornish timber merchant with Quaker connections and paedophiliac tastes (Fox was a patron of the Falmouth Boys' Club football team). Rolfe was proposing to act as Fox's cicerone on a forthcoming visit by the latter to Venice, and the letters form a sort of *catalogue raisonné* of the various gondoliers whom Rolfe proposed to introduce to Fox, namely Zozzi ('simply splendid. He grows on one'), Zildo ('So sweetly modest . . . so bursting with young vigour'), and Piero ('He was scarlet all over, blushing with delight'), not to mention Amadeo, Fausto, and Ermengildo. Far from shocking, the letters would appear comic in the light of present permissiveness were it not for the fact that Rolfe was starving when he wrote them.

Gregory undoubtedly enjoyed himself in the role of patron, but

[1] A.J.'s remarks at a Corvine banquet held at the Ambassador Club on December 12, 1929.

this does not explain why he allowed himself to be conned into backing the Corvine Society which A.J. founded in 1929 with Gregory as anonymous treasurer. 'Symons would talk anyone into anything as long as it involved the prospect of good food and wine,' James Laver, the art historian, who attended both of the Corvine Society's banquets, explained to me. Granted A.J.'s persuasive abilities as the promoter of dining clubs, one is left wondering what Gregory hoped to gain by picking up the tabs for these Lucullan beanfeasts whose guests without exception were A.J.'s friends. Gregory was hopelessly out of his depth in this company of poets, critics, art historians, wine connoisseurs, all reflecting A.J.'s myriad interests. Worse still, he found himself the butt of their ill-natured comments. Sir Francis Meynell, who attended one of the banquets, says that during a conversational lull one guest could be heard informing his neighbour, 'No, no, that is not Gregory—that's the wine waiter.'

Dedicated to honouring Rolfe as 'a Pope in imagination, a Baron in fiction, and a Genius in life', the short-lived Corvine Society bore unmistakable traces of the jejune humour with which Symons enlivened the proceedings of Ye Sette of Odd Volumes. 'We are odd, very odd! You may take it—we are odd!' runs the refrain of the song which the Odd Volumes sang before dinner. The Corvines eschewed singing, but some of them were very strange indeed.

Shane Leslie, in a saffron-coloured kilt, presided at the first Corvine banquet, which was held at the Ambassador Club on June 27, 1929, with seventeen members in attendance. The table was garlanded with white and yellow flowers 'in conformance with the Papal predilections of the author of *Hadrian the Seventh*', and the printed menu gave to the entrées and wines such whimsical names as 'Epigrammes d'Agneau Pio Nono en Aspic', and 'Corvo Gran Spumante'. Maundy Gregory had stipulated that he was not to be named as the footer of the bill, but Shane Leslie paid him indirect tribute by declaring in 'Corvinese', the picturesque speech reminiscent of the Baron, that 'your liparose soups, your lickerish dishes . . . your picric liquors, and even the fumificables have been generously provided.'

At the second Corvine banquet, held on December 12, 1929, anathema was pronounced on Lord Northcliffe, the press baron, in the form of a Papal Bull written in 'Corvinese' and excommunicating him as 'the Enemy of the whole Anglican race'. Attendance

[146]

had doubled, among the newcomers being the waspish Wyndham Lewis, the novelist, and the rotund Professor Tancred Borenius, who looked like Mr Pickwick, but who used scent. As part of the intellectual horseplay a Corvine grace was recited before the banquet to the effect that the Lord feedeth the ravens (*Deus pascit corvos*).

The Corvine banquets helped to stimulate interest in Rolfe leading to the reissue of some of his books that were long out of print; but opinion was sharply divided as to their merits as social occasions. The late Sir Shane Leslie thought that the banquets were worthy of the baron himslf, but Sir Francis Meynell found them a bore. The impression that Gregory left on the latter was that of a 'frightened and dubious-seeming character, though he had not yet achieved his notoriety as fake seller of Papal honours'.

The intriguing question is, who dropped whom first—Gregory or Symons? Most probably Gregory grew tired of being used by Symons; weary, too, of the snide comments which A.J.'s friends made about him, sometimes within his hearing. As a result the intervals between the Arabian Nights' lunches lengthened. The Corvine Society had proved to be an unprofitable excursion into the realm of the intellectuals, which had brought him nothing but ridicule. From now on he would be confirmed in his philistine prejudices. As for Symons, to the end he remained unwavering in his admiration for Gregory, writing: 'His memory remains like that of an incandescent meteor in the sky of high finance, an acquaintance as fantastic and unlikely as the wildest passage in the books of the weird Baron whom we both admired.'

Symons was careful however not to dedicate *The Quest for Corvo* to Gregory, who had financed his research. Neither does he mention in that book the source of Gregory's wealth, nor the fact that Gregory ended up in Wormwood Scrubs, having been convicted of an offence under the Honours Act. Instead, the reader is left with the impression that A.J. dwelt in ignorance of the fate of his friend. ('Since he left England to live abroad eight months ago, my inquiries have remained unanswered, and I have looked in vain for any letter in his sturdy square handwriting,' A.J. writes.) That the contrary was true is borne out by Percy Muir, who was Symons's neighbour when the latter lived in the village of Finchingfield, Essex. Giving A.J. a lift up to London in his motor car one morning shortly after the summons had been issued against Gregory, Muir fell to discussing the case with his passenger. 'Well, regardless of the outcome of the trial I shall be a candidate for Gregory's job now,' Symons announced smugly.

* * *

The Nazi swastika was probably the last thing Colonel Harker expected to find when he started turning over the stones that concealed Maundy Gregory's activities. Yet the colonel quickly discovered that Gregory was involved in White Russian political intrigue that was being financed by the Hitler movement from Berlin. The Ambassador Club itself was being used as headquarters by the Anglo-Ukrainian Council which Gregory founded, and of which he was chairman. Thus the claim put forward by the *Daily Sketch* at a later date that Gregory was at one time 'regarded as the English head of the movement to restore the autonomy of the Ukraine' did not fall short of the truth. Gregory himself was more modest in his claim, asserting in the 'confidential' memorandum which he gave to clients that he was merely 'a principal co-organizer of the great secret anti-Bolshevist movement'. His confederate in this enterprise was His Highness Paul Skoropadsky, the so called Hetman of the Ukraine.

His head shaven, and wearing a Cossack's uniform trimmed with silver cartridge cases, Skoropadsky was a familiar figure at Nazi rallies in the 1920s, where he was regarded as the protégé of Alfred Rosenberg, Hitler's adviser on Eastern affairs. That Gregory did not immediately fall under Skoropadsky's spell is evident from an article in the *Whitehall Gazette* for November, 1921, in which the Hetman was dismissed as a puppet of the German Kaiser during the First World War. 'Had not the Central Powers been defeated in the West, the creation of a vassal Ukraine State would have been one of the most complete . . . victories ever dreamt of by the great German conquerors,' the article states. By June, 1924, however, Gregory had seen the light, and was plumping enthusiastically for the Hetman's cause, reminding British businessmen that in the brief interim Skoropadsky held power in the Ukraine before being chased out by the Red Army, 'one pound sterling was given for forty Ukrainian roubles, and in the grain stores of the Hetman government lay 2,000,000 tons of grain ready for export'.

Thereafter Gregory found himself caught up in the game of 'Bulava, Bulava, who's got the Bulava', which was his private, almost contemptuous term for emigré politics, the Bulava in question being the Hetman's mace. Gregory discovered that none of the White Russian emigrés he talked to was interested except in the most superficial way in overturning the Soviet regime in the Ukraine, but that each was concerned with cutting the throat of some rival faction. Ukrainian nationalists clashed with White Russian generals, and both combined against the followers of the bandit Petlura, who made his headquarters in Paris. There was even a Hapsburg faction, certain Ukrainian emigrés looking to Prince Wilhelm Hapsburg as their leader. As for Gregory himself, his interest was purely financial. By making the *Whitehall Gazette* the official organ of the Hetmanite movement in Britain, Gregory got money from Skoropadsky, who in turn got it from Alfred Rosenberg. (Gregory very carefully steered clear of the homegrown variety of fascists, such as Sir Oswald Mosley and his Black Shirts, who would have queered the pitch for him.)

Gregory's extreme right-wing views led him to support 'Butcher' Mannerheim and his Schutzcorps in Finland ('really a magnificent sight to watch these staunch enemies of Bolshevism march voluntarily'), which in turn earned him the Order of the White Rose of Finland. His views also led to friendship with Werner von Alvensleben, the man who is credited with having put Hitler in touch with the senile President von Hindenburg. (Dr Erich Eyck, the historian of the Weimar Republic, compared von Alvensleben to the squirrel in the Norse saga who hops from tree limb to tree limb 'supplying everyone from the eagle at the top to the dragon underneath with the latest news'.) Gregory made von Alvensleben an honorary member of the Ambassador Club. Then in November, 1930 Maundy Gregory travelled to Berlin to attend a rally of von Alvensleben's 'League for the Protection of Western European Culture', an anti-Communist organization, which Gregory's good friend Brigadier-General Sir William Horwood was to address. 'As I entered the Sports Palace, Berlin, I was at once astonished and overjoyed,' Gregory reported in the *Whitehall Gazette*. 'His Highness the Hetman of all the Ukraine,' he continued in a typical prose passage, 'told me that he wished the enthusiasm of this Meeting could be, in some way, electrically heard by the people of the Ukraine, who are chafing in the toils of Bolshevism.'

Gregory's comings and goings in Berlin were duly reported to Colonel Harker at MI-5, as were his tête-à-têtes over lunch at the Ambassador Club with Vladimir Korostovets, Skoropadsky's hatchet man in the United Kingdom, and author of many of the anonymous articles on the Ukraine which appeared in the *Whitehall Gazette*, and which were reprinted later as a 77-page pamphlet. But MI-5 in those days, of course, was not interested in crackpot movements financed directly or indirectly by Adolf Hitler and his Nazi party. Gregory's continued activity in the honours field, however, gave Colonel Harker an opportunity to act, which he seized. In particular he was able to document a case involving a Midlands industrialist who, having paid money to Gregory for an honour which was not forthcoming, was warned off when he sought a refund in terms which amounted to a veiled threat of blackmail. 'It is by no means complete,' Colonel Harker declared, tapping the dossier he had assembled on Gregory, 'but it should satisfy the Director of Public Prosecutions.' The correct procedure was to consult the Commissioner of Metropolitan Police first, so Colonel Harker made an appointment to see Brigadier-General Sir William Horwood, who then filled that post.

Colonel Harker had enlisted the help of Lt-Colonel John Baker White who, as director of the Economic League, had previously carried out his own private investigation of Gregory at the request of some of the league members. So the MI-5 head asked White to accompany him to see Horwood. White takes up the story from there: 'On the appointed afternoon we went along to New Scotland Yard and rang for Horwood's private lift, which was used by himself and a few senior police officials. The lift appeared to be stuck at the third floor, which was where the commissioner had his office. Finally, the lift came down and out of it stepped Gregory, immaculately dressed as usual and with the smug expression on his face of a canary that has just swallowed a cat. Colonel Harker, who had Gregory's dossier under his arm, looked at me, then his shoulders came up to meet his ears in a comic shrug and he said, "That does it—there's no point in going up." With that he tore the dossier into small pieces which he deposited in a rubbish bin as we went out. That was the end of the matter.'

XI

Baldwin Opens War

Although Colonel Harker was unaware of it, a parallel attempt to get rid of Maundy Gregory as honours broker had been launched at about the same time as his own. This second attempt had the backing of no less a person than the Prime Minister, Stanley Baldwin. Baldwin had taken office in November, 1924 with the avowed purpose of undoing all the evil done by Lloyd George, whom he regarded as 'a real corrupter of public life', as he told Geoffrey Dawson, the editor of *The Times*. If Baldwin regarded the sorcerer as the embodiment of corruption, how much more did he regard the sorcerer's apprentice, Maundy Gregory, with loathing. The Squire of Bewdley's name is not to be found among those who attended the Derby Day dinners.

Yet there is something pharisaical about Baldwin's attitude towards the sale of honours. During the Lloyd George Coalition Sir George Younger, as Conservative party chairman, had doubled the party fund from £600,000 to £1,250,000 largely by means of contributions connected with honours. In a letter to Baldwin dated August 27, 1927, Younger denied that he had engaged in honours trafficking ('I never, so to speak, sold an honour, nor did I ever make any bargains'), but in the next breath he forgot himself and admitted that he had 'superintended the collection of . . . the contributions occasionally made by the medium of the Honours List.'[1] It was this same Younger, it will be recalled, who accused Freddy Guest of 'poaching', when the latter hawked baronetcies to men who were nominally Tory.

A case recently brought to light by the historian A. J. P. Taylor places the ball even more firmly in Baldwin's court. In December, 1928 Lord Beaverbrook approached Baldwin with the suggestion that Andrew Holt, a Canadian banker, should be knighted for his services to commercial aviation.[2] Baldwin promised to give the

[1] Robert Rhodes James. *Memoirs of a Conservative.*
[2] The story is told fully in A. J. P. Taylor's *Beaverbrook*. London: Hamish Hamilton, 1972.

matter his 'personal attention', whereupon Beaverbrook made out a cheque for £10,000 to J. C. C. Davidson, the Conservative party chairman. 'I am sure you know the source of supply,' Beaverbrook wrote to Davidson, adding, 'I only scribble this note in case you might think that I am the good Samaritan myself.' Davidson knew the source all right, as he readily acknowledged, but cautioned that there might be some delay in putting the honour through.

Holt's name did not appear in the 1929 New Year's Honours List, nor in a supplemental list in the weeks that followed. In May came the general election, in which the Conservatives were turned out of office. On June 12, 1929, Davidson returned the cheque to Beaverbrook with a cryptic note, 'I have had no occasion to make use of the money'. What happened? Did Davidson or Baldwin get cold feet, or had they simply been stringing Beaverbrook along in the hopes of securing the backing of the Beaverbrook newspapers for Conservative candidates in the election? The answer probably will never be known. But A. J. P. Taylor has this comment to make about the Holt case: 'Money was paid. A knighthood was promised. Baldwin's claim to clean hands is hardly redeemed by the fact that the promise was not kept.'[1]

This episode may explain why Baldwin, who was admittedly lazy, was slow in moving against Gregory.

*   *   *

When Baldwin did act it was because 'the Royal Prerogative was being prostituted for sordid reasons', in Davidson's words. Unlike Lloyd George, Baldwin was a great respecter of the monarchy, as he was to prove in the Abdication crisis that lay ahead. Baldwin's respect for the Crown was shared by J. C. C. Davidson, who was angered to find, on his only visit to Gregory's office at the Ambassador Club, signed photographs of King George V and of the Duke of York (later King George VI). 'Neither of course had any connection whatever with Gregory,' Davidson hastened to explain. 'He had acquired the photographs . . . and put them on display to impress clients.'[2]

But was this true? There was no more reason to doubt the

[1] *Ibid.*
[2] *Op. cit.*

authenticity of these signed photographs than there was to question the genuineness of the gold cigarette case which the Duke of York presented to Gregory. Both were tokens of royal gratitude for Gregory's services on behalf of King George's Fund for Sailors of which Prince Albert, the Duke of York, was president. Maundy Gregory had served as one of the stewards at the Duke of York's wedding. He had also attended numerous levees and garden parties at Buckingham Palace. Moreover Gregory had such good friends at Court as Lord Southborough, who was on intimate terms with the Royal Family, and at the same time on the governing committee of the Ambassador Club.

These connections emboldened Gregory to play the court cards in the pack more often than was wise, according to Mrs Maisie H. Saunders, who knew Gregory well in the Ambassador Club days. 'The source of Gregory's influence and power was his supposed connection with Buckingham Palace,' Mrs Saunders told me. 'He gave people to understand that he had the ear of King George V, and that he had only to drop a word in that ear and—presto—the lucky person's name would appear in the next Honours List.' 'One of the King's equerries was a great personal friend of Gregory's,' Mrs Saunders added, 'and that is how he got his entrée to Buckingham Palace. I have seen letters from this equerry lying on Gregory's desk, and Gregory himself must have pinched some notepaper for I know of at least one letter that he wrote on Buckingham Palace stationery—to impress one of his clients, to be sure.'

*   *   *

When party chairman J. C. C. Davidson and Stanley Baldwin put their heads together at a meeting at 10 Downing Street the problem they were confronted with was not simply how to get rid of Gregory, but how to do so 'without precipitating a major public disclosure', in the words of Robert Rhodes James. 'A public revelation,' he adds, 'would have provided a *cause célèbre* of dramatic proportions. There was little doubt that some men who had been stupid rather than criminal, and others who had no knowledge of Gregory's activities but had accepted hospitality at his club . . . would have been ruined by their association with him.'

The solution arrived at by the Baldwin–Davidson tandem was brilliant in its simplicity, as Davidson explains in a memorandum left among his papers. 'The thing to do was to break him [Gregory] financially,' Davidson recorded, even though 'this involved making many enemies amongst the people—and some were very well-known indeed—who were his clients, and who expected honours in return for their payments to him'.[1] It was to be a war of attrition. Maundy Gregory was to be blockaded in his Parliament Street building, his chancellery laid under siege, his life-line severed. Referring to Baldwin's approval, Davidson noted, 'I had the right to take whatever steps I thought best to prevent Gregory getting any of his names on to the Honours List.'

Davidson had timed his attack upon Gregory cunningly, for death or retirement had deprived the latter of two of his most powerful protectors. In September, 1928, Brigadier-General Sir William Horwood had retired as Commissioner of Metropolitan Police under a cloud of recriminations, which included charges that police vice squad members had been taking bribes from Soho nightclub owners. Two years later Gregory had sustained another loss with the passing of the Earl of Birkenhead, who died of boredom and brandy in equal proportions. Aside from being the biggest political lion Gregory had ever bagged, 'F.E.' was a man he had genuinely admired and had sought to emulate in many ways. Yet when it came to writing an obituary notice for the *Whitehall Gazette*, Gregory suddenly dried up. All he could find to say about his late friend was that Birkenhead had been 'the greatest Imperialist of our age', and withal 'human to the core'.

To ensure Gregory's downfall Davidson planted a spy in Gregory's camp in the person of Albert (later Sir Albert) Bennett, Conservative MP for Nottingham Central, and assistant party treasurer. One of Bennett's duties was to get a list of the clients whom Gregory intended to put forward for honours so that the Conservative Central Office could veto these names in advance and thus ensure that none of them got on any Honours List. (Bennett's own baronetcy, which he obtained in June, 1929, may not have been unconnected with these chores.) 'Gregory's position,' as Robert Rhodes James points out, 'depended upon his ability to deliver the goods for which his clients had paid him. By ensuring that none of his clients received any award, Davidson devastatingly undermined Gregory's entire scheme of operations.'

In the event, Baldwin did not remain in office long enough for

[1] *Op. cit.*

Davidson's grand design to be realized, though the process of attrition begun against Gregory was to bring the latter down in the end. The Conservatives were defeated in the general election of May, 1929, and a Labour government formed with support from the Liberal party. Two years later came dramatic confirmation that Baldwin had been correct in warning of the danger which Gregory constituted. The incident in question involved Gregory 'leaking' information concerning the formation of a National government under the premiership of Ramsay MacDonald, and it might have caused panic on the Stock Exchange had it not occurred on a week-end when there was no time for the interlocking worlds of politics and finance to react.[1]

The story, vouched for by Sir Kingsley Wood, was that on Friday, August 21, 1931, Gregory's equerry friend who gave him all the gossip from Buckingham Palace lunched at the Ambassador Club, and in conversation with Gregory let drop the King's involvement in the current political crisis that was to lead within days to the formation of a National government. The equerry's lament to Gregory ran something like this: 'Bother, here the King's on his way to Balmoral, and now I have to chase all the way to Scotland tonight to fetch him back, all because of this wretched crisis. Wall Street, it seems, is taking a tough line about loaning Britain money, and the Labour government may not last the week-end.' As his friend talked, Gregory's ears pricked up. Here was a juicy morsel indeed for one who knew how to make use of it. Gregory immediately got on the telephone, and in the next few hours he kept the wires humming with calls to persons he wanted to impress. On one pretext or another he let it drop 'in strictest confidence' that the King would soon be on his way back to London 'to lend a hand in settling the Cabinet crisis'. He even went so far as to suggest to Sir Kingsley Wood that a meeting of Tory bigwigs should be convened immediately, and he offered the use of a room at the Ambassador Club for this purpose. Gregory's motive in relaying what had been told to him so carelessly was, of course, to gain kudos as a political prophet, as well as to demonstrate that his informants were highly placed.

*   *   *

[1] The incident was related by Sir Kingsley Wood, one-time Chancellor of the Exchequer, to John Baker White, to whom I am indebted for the information.

His income from the sale of royal honours cut off, Maundy Gregory turned to the sale of foreign titles and decorations, employing for this purpose Gerald Hamilton, whom he had met through A. J. A. Symons. In his autobiography Hamilton, who served as the model for Mr Norris in Christopher Isherwood's *Mr Norris Changes Trains*, lifts a corner of the curtain on this little-known side of Gregory's activities.[1] Gregory's hottest selling line, according to Hamilton, was the Order of Christ of Portugal, and this 'because the Order could be worn with a bright red ribbon which most people mistook for the French Legion of Honour'. Hamilton was impressed by Gregory's open-handedness, writing: 'Any expenses incurred while travelling were generously reimbursed by Maundy Gregory, whom I remember asking what I would require a day; on hearing me say "Oh, about £10," he answered "Oh, you would probably require more than that—probably not less than £15 a day".' Hamilton found Gregory's political views to his liking. ('He had, not surprisingly, a great hatred of any form of Socialism, a sentiment I readily shared.') In the revolving-door politics of the twenties and thirties, Hamilton had been in and out of almost every political movement and had ended up a diehard Tory.

'Diversify!' became Gregory's war-cry in his battle to survive. Too late he realized the mistake he had made by putting all of his eggs in the honours basket; and now, by a series of shrewd investments, he sought to redress the balance. In doing so, Gregory showed himself to be possessed of an acumen which, if put to proper use, would have made him a success in almost any line of legitimate business. As a first step in the new direction, in August, 1931, he took a lease on the sumptuous Deepdene Hotel near Dorking, Surrey in the name of Peter Mazzina and installed as Maître d'Hôtel his old friend Arturo Giordano, who had just succeeded in bankrupting Kettner's Restaurant. The Deepdene Hotel, which stood in several acres of parkland (its cable address was 'Eden, Dorking') had been built as a country seat by one of the Howards in Cromwell's time, and had been admired by diarist John Evelyn. Deepdene's great days of glory did not begin, however, until 1807 when it was bought by banker Thomas Hope, better known as the owner of the world's largest blue diamond, the ill-fated Hope

[1] Gerald Hamilton. *The Way it was with Me*. London: Leslie Frewin, 1969.

Diamond, which had once belonged to Marie Antoinette.[1] To the existing 17th-century mansion Hope added an orangery, a conservatory, an outdoor amphitheatre, and a sculpture gallery, the better to display his Canova and Thorwaldsen statuary and his Etruscan vases. The result was a gem of neo-classic architecture which, unfortunately, was later marred by the son, Henry Hope, who converted Deepdene into a showy Italian palazzo. It was at Deepdene that Disraeli wrote *Coningsby*, which he dedicated to Henry Hope (in his diary for May, 1834, Disraeli noted that he had 'supped off gold and danced in the sculpture gallery' at Deepdene). Lilian, Duchess of Marlborough lived there with twenty-four servants until 1917, when the house was sold and its contents scattered.

Maundy Gregory contributed to the spoliation of Deepdene by causing to be erected on its roof a huge neon sign which at night could be seen five miles away blinking 'Deepdene Hotel' incessantly. To attract the 'leisured seekers of the lighter life' he chopped up the grounds into a golf course and four hard tennis courts, and inaugurated *thé-dansants* from 4 to 6.30 p.m. Thus in the sculpture gallery with its marble floor and decorated ceiling, where Disraeli once had partnered Lady Blessington, tired businessmen now fox-trotted with their secretaries. For the amenities introduced by Gregory did not disguise the fact that essentially the Deepdene was a place to spend a dirty week-end, with the added attraction that it was located only 25 miles from Piccadilly. Under the Gregory–Mazzina management it soon gained the reputation of being 'the biggest brothel in southeast England', in the words of one of the local inhabitants. Witchcraft was added to venery with the discovery in the grounds of an altar with runic inscriptions, and soon all of Dorking buzzed with rumours of strange, orgiastic rites practised regularly at Deepdene. Peter Mazzina somehow managed to keep the hotel going until 1936,

[1] In view of Deepdene's subsequent history Dutch-born Thomas Hope's efforts to buy a peerage by bribing the then Premier, the Duke of Wellington, are worthy of note. Concerning the same Professor David Watkin, of Peterhouse, Cambridge, writes: 'The Duke of Wellington was no Lloyd George where peerages were concerned and, in attempting to bribe him, Hope revealed the extent to which he had failed to assimilate himself into the customs of English society.' (David Watkin: *Thomas Hope (1769–1831) and the Neo-Classical Idea.* London: John Murray, 1968.)

when he went bankrupt. Soon afterwards it was sold for use as a headquarters to British Railways, Southern Region, which completed the historic mansion's destruction by running central heating pipes through its lovely gesso-work ceilings and erecting office partitions against its exquisite wall panelling.

An even shrewder investment was Gregory's purchase of *Burke's Landed Gentry*, the companion to *Burke's Peerage, Baronetage and Knightage*. Both publications had remained in the Burke family for nearly a century when in 1929, owing to bad management, the family was forced to sell them. Unfortunately, they were split up, the *Peerage* going to Sir Henry Mallaby-Deeley, the original 'Fifty Shilling Tailor', who had made his fortune by buying up Army surplus clothing after the First World War. The *Landed Gentry* was snapped up by Maundy Gregory at a bargain price. 'I don't think that he paid more than £2,000 for it,' L. G. Pine, one-time editor of the *Peerage*, told me. 'My guess is that he tried to buy the Peerage as well, but was outbid by Mallaby-Deeley.'

As editor of the *Landed Gentry* Gregory appointed C. H. C. 'Harry' Pirie-Gordon, D.S.C., F.S.A., a burly six-footer. Pirie-Gordon had shared rooms with novelist Compton Mackenzie at Magdalen College, Oxford, and had gone on to become a brilliant genealogist (he is remembered chiefly for his work on the Orkney jarls and on Pope Innocent I). As editorial assistants Pirie-Gordon chose William Smallshaw, who later became receptionist at the Hyde Park Hotel in Knightsbridge, and Frederick Bamberger, who started life as a page boy at the College of Arms, and who ended up as an executive of the Ford Motor Company at Dagenham. These three were housed in offices above the *Whitehall Gazette* at 38 Parliament Street.

Did Maundy Gregory buy the *Landed Gentry* with a view to using it as an adjunct to his activities as honours broker? Certainly it would have made a powerful weapon for this purpose. To mark the centenary of the publication Gregory planned a complete overhaul of the work, which meant re-writing no fewer than 5,000 entries. This entailed enormous expense, but the work of revision would have given Gregory a plausible excuse for approaching certain *nouveaux-riches* who were eager for promotion from the *Landed Gentry* to the *Peerage*. Having gained access to such persons Gregory—or rather his agents, for he himself would be careful not to become directly involved—could then have led the conversation from family pedigrees round to honours.

If this had been Gregory's original intention he later changed his mind, for the *Landed Gentry*, as things worked out, remained free of his influence.

'From the staff's viewpoint Maundy Gregory turned out to be the ideal employer,' L. G. Pine declared. 'He left them strictly alone except at Christmas time, when he gave them worthwhile gifts. He made no attempt to suggest names for the Centenary Edition, possibly because he knew that Pirie-Gordon and his assistants would walk out if he did.'[1]

That Pirie-Gordon was completely ignorant of his employer's activities in the field of honours was confirmed to me by his widow, Mrs Mabel Pirie-Gordon. 'Harry trusted everyone,' she explained. 'He took everyone at face value, and he was genuinely shocked and distressed when he found out about Maundy Gregory, which was not until some time later.'

*   *   *

It was at this time that Gregory blossomed out as a professional fund-raiser. Fund-raising in this sense was by no means new to him. In the 'confidential' memorandum which he gave to prospective clients he noted his achievements in this field:

Financed the entire gilding of the choir stalls in Westminster Abbey—an improvement long desired by the Very Rev Dean and Chapter.

Organized and maintained for Westminster Abbey the gift of all-gold and jewelled Processional Cross, costing over £5,000, from the late Hon Rodman Wanamaker, C.V.O.

Obtained and confidentially handed over an anonymous gift of £20,000 towards saving the roof of St George's Chapel,

[1] The Centenary Edition of the Landed Gentry did not appear until 1937, by which time it had passed out of Gregory's hands and into those of a Chicagoan named Theo John Zimmerman, better known as 'Zimmie', who launched it with typical American flair. The 11-pound, 2,756-page tome's contents had been considerably watered down, more than a third of its entries being landless families who got in on the strength of their pedigrees, or because they had rendered public service. Most of the work on this edition had been done under Gregory's auspices.

Windsor, in the early and crucial stage of this necessary and vital appeal.

The first item refers to the £250,000 appeal which Bishop Herbert Ryle, Dean of Westminster, launched in the early 1920s in an effort to preserve the crumbling fabric of Westminster Abbey. Whether Gregory did in fact raise the money for the gilding of the choir stalls—he certainly would not have done so without first deducting his commission—is open to question. Abbey officials understandably are reticent about discussing the matter. One thing is certain: if Maundy Gregory did have anything to do with refurbishing the choir stalls he skimped on the job, for they were covered with water gilt most of which had worn off by 1966, when the stalls were gilded with gold leaf and burnished.

Gregory's great friend at Westminster Abbey was Sir Edward Knapp-Fisher, then Chapter Clerk, who was responsible for Maundy Gregory being made one of the stewards at the Duke of York's wedding. Sir Edward was twice profiled in the *Whitehall Gazette* as an 'Official I Have Known'. It was probably at Knapp-Fisher's instigation that Gregory talked Rodman Wanamaker, the Philadelphia department store magnate, into donating the processional cross to the Abbey.[1]

Maundy Gregory's relationship with Wanamaker was that of a public relations expert to a client. He conned the American millionaire into believing that he, Gregory, held the key that would unlock the doors to English society. Not that Wanamaker was in need of such a locksmith. His wealth and his reputation as an art patron alone were enough to gain him entrée into the best drawing-rooms. As for the Royal Family it thought so highly of Wanamaker that when the Prince of Wales visited the United States in November, 1919, he decorated Wanamaker with the Royal Victorian Order. Just as Wanamaker had a passion for uniforms and decorations so he liked to surround himself with factotums who bore titles such as 'Chief of Staff'. Gregory, one suspects, belonged to this category. Gregory used to boast that it was

[1] 'The Cross of Westminster', as it is called, originally was studded with sapphires. When Rodman Wanamaker's nephew visited London in 1965 he was persuaded to enrich the gift. Accordingly, the cross was sent to America for alterations, and returned with 72 top-class diamonds inserted.

on his advice that Wanamaker had presented the solid silver altar and reredos to the Sandringham parish church where George V and his family worshipped, but this magnificent gift was made prior to the First World War and before Gregory had gained eminence as a political wire-puller. Whether Wanamaker was the anonymous donor of the £20,000 towards saving the roof of St George's Chapel, Windsor, is not known.

Gregory with his love of mystification makes his early fund-raising activities sound very hush-hush in the 'confidential' memorandum just quoted. But apparently they loomed large enough in certain eyes to recommend Gregory in June, 1931, for the job of Deputy Director of the £100,000 centenary appeal launched by the Most Venerable Order of the Hospital of St John of Jerusalem, whose Grand Prior was a member of the royal family, the Duke of Connaught. In order for Gregory to be brought in as fund-raiser he first had to be made a Commander of the Order of St John, which meant that all sorts of red tape had to be slashed. As Miss Helena Nicholls, curator of the Order, explained to me, 'It would have been unusual for Maundy Gregory to have been made a member of the Order, let alone Commander, without working his passage. Usually a person is not accepted to membership until he has earned it through service with the St John's Ambulance Corps, for example. In Gregory's case all of this was waived.'

One reason why the Earl of Scarborough, Sub-Prior of the Order, and Colonel (later Sir) James Sleeman, C.M.G., C.B.E., M.V.O., the honorary director of the appeal, were so eager to waive the rules is that Gregory had offered free of charge the use of his offices at 38 Parliament Street as the appeal headquarters. What if any Gregory's commission would have been on monies he collected in response to the appeal Miss Nicholls did not know ('There would be no record of that sort of thing'), but she thought it likely that Gregory was paid off simply by being made Commander of the Order. Among the first to respond to the appeal were King George V, the Prince of Wales, and the Duke and Duchess of York.

Meanwhile, Maundy Gregory, who had begun to use the initials 'C. St J.' after his name, travelled in very exalted company indeed. On June 22, 1931, he was a guest at a banquet given by the Duke of Connaught at St James's Palace, Gregory being seated, according to the table plans, at Table 'A' along with Major M. H. Tomlin, Chief Constable of the Metropolitan Police, Colonel G. A. Moor, Assistant Chief Commissioner of the St John's Ambulance Corps, and Sir Gerald Wollaston, the genealogist. The following day he attended an investiture at Buckingham Palace where officials of St John's were received by King George V as the Sovereign Head of the Order.[1]

Despite its avowedly non-sectarian character, the Order of St John is strongly imprinted with Protestantism, owing partly to the fact that reigning British monarchs have always served as Sovereign Heads of the Order since 1888 when it was granted a Royal charter. As if to redress this Protestant imbalance Maundy Gregory now underwent a conversion which was as sudden and dramatic as that of St Paul.

[1] The appeal, whose object was to build an extension to the Order's headquarters at St John's Gate, Clerkenwell, was a failure, only £20,000 having been realized by the end of 1931. It was not until 1956 that the new building was started by which time the original plan to memorialize donors of £100 or more by inscribing their names on tablets in the entrance hall had either been forgotten or abandoned.

XII

His Beatitude and
a Blackmailer

The cynical remark attributed to Henry of Navarre on embracing the Catholic faith, 'Paris is worth a Mass', might well have been taken by Maundy Gregory as a motto. For there is little doubt that, whatever the Catholic Church came to mean to him later—and indications are that it became a great source of comfort to him towards the end of his life—in the beginning he looked upon it as a means of supplementing his income. As one who knew him expressed it to me, 'Maundy would have embraced Islam, and declared Mohamet to be the one true prophet, if he thought that there was a possibility of peddling ribbons or titles to pilgrims to Mecca.'

There are fashions in religious conversions just as there are fashions in hats, and in the 1930s the Jesuits, whose Farm Street headquarters were in the heart of London's Mayfair, were all the rage. The 9th Duke of Marlborough started the vogue by undergoing a Farm Street conversion. Then in July, 1930, after dining with the Marlboroughs at Blenheim Palace ('The Duchess very battered with fine diamonds. The Duke wearing the Garter . . .') novelist Evelyn Waugh sought out Father Martin D'Arcy, S.J. for instruction in the mysteries of Holy Mother Church. Much later Father D'Arcy charged himself with the salvation of Dame Edith Sitwell who 'swathed in black like a sixteenth-century infanta', according to Waugh, was received into the Roman Church at Farm Street. 'Edith recanted her errors in fine ringing tones,' Waugh recorded. 'Afterwards she entertained her guests to lobster Newburg at the Sesame Club.'

However, as early as 1931, when Maundy Gregory saw the light, the movement to Farm Street was well under way, with society matrons sandwiching an hour of spiritual guidance between appointments with the dressmaker and the coiffeur. 'I am rapidly emptying my confessional,' Father Cyril Martindale, S.J., wrote in disgust, 'by telling the ladies to stop dissecting themselves . . . and to tell me whether they seriously try to do unselfish things for anyone else.'[1] Maundy Gregory chose as his preceptor a jolly Jesuit named Father Francis Colchester, who had spent most of his 72 years as a teacher trying to mould into muscular Christians the boys entrusted to his care at Mount St Mary's College, Sheffield. The story goes that the rector of Mount St Mary's, on seeing the good priest sprint down the garden path with his charges, exclaimed, 'My stars, that Holy man will bust [sic] himself yet.'[2] Father Colchester was especially devoted to St Theresa of Lisieux, 'The Little Flower', and so completely did he identify himself with her that he took pains to discover on what day of the week the most notable events of her life occurred so that he could time his meditations accordingly.

Maundy Gregory's instruction was not so much speeded up as it was cut short by the untimely death of Father Colchester from heart failure on January 17, 1932, just five days before Gregory was received into the Church. The resulting gaps in Gregory's knowledge of his religion were to become more noticeable with the years, causing his friend, Marcel D'Roubaix, to comment sourly, 'What kind of a Catholic does Maundy think he is? He doesn't know the first thing about his religion.' His grasp of fundamentals may have been shaky, but Gregory's rise to eminence in Papal circles, accomplished in less than eight months, was little short of meteoric, as the following time-table indicates:[3]

> *January 22, 1932*—Gregory is received into the Catholic faith
> at the Paris convent of the 'Soeurs de la Retraite du Sacré
> Coeur', 34 Rue St Guillaume, in the respectable 7th arron-
> dissement. (The order was a 7th century one with a special
> devotion to Saint Odile.) The simple ceremony was held in
> the presence of His Beatitude Monsignor Luigi Barlassina
> II, Latin Patriarch of Jerusalem.
> *March 1, 1932*—Gregory is made Knight Commander of the

[1] Philip Caraman. *C. C. Martindale, A Biography*. London: Longmans.
[2] For this anecdote I am indebted to *Letters and Notices*, vol. XLVII, the province's internal newsletter.
[3] I am indebted to the Most Reverend Monsignor Kamal Bathish, Chancellor of the Latin Patriarchate of Jerusalem, for supplying me with the relevant dates.

Equestrian Order of the Holy Sepulchre by Monsignor
Barlassina, in his capacity as Grand Master of the Order.

April (?), 1932—Gregory is made Knight Commander of the
Most Noble Order of Pius IX, which ranks as third of the
Pontifical Orders of Knighthood.

September 9, 1932—Gregory is promoted to Grand Cross of
the Holy Sepulchre Order, and becomes His Beatitude's
'special representative' in England, while his offices at 38
Parliament Street are designated as the Chancellery of the
Order.

The rank of Knight Grand Cross of the Holy Sepulchre Order
was usually reserved for 'ecclesiastical or secular princes, Ministers, and ambassadors', according to the Order's statutes. In pro-
moting Gregory to this exalted station rules and regulations were
waived, including the requirement that he pay a visit to the Holy
Land.

The common factor at each stage in Gregory's progress up the
Papal ladder, it will be noted, was His Beatitude Monsignor Barlassina, who also doubled as titular Bishop of Capernaum (his
episcopal coat of arms, taking some liberties with geography,
shows Mounts Zion and Carmel arising like twin breasts from the
Sea of Galilee on the north shore of which Capernaum is located).

A Piedmontese from Turin enjoying rude good health, Barlassina was so busy raising money for various grandiose schemes that
he had a portable typewriter installed in the episcopal limousine,
and he tapped away while being driven by his chauffeur Giovanni.
It is unclear where and how Maundy Gregory met the wily
patriarch, whose features were notable for a square beard and
liquid brown eyes. But one thing is clear: these two were made for
each other. Above all, they saw eye-to-eye on the desirability of
building up the coffers of the Holy Sepulchre Order. The fact
that Maundy Gregory hopped over to Paris to be received into the
Catholic Church at the hands of this prelate would suggest that
they had done business together, long before Gregory fell down
blinded by the light on his particular road to Damascus.

By reason of seniority the Earl of Denbigh, aged 73, was the
nominal head of the Holy Sepulchre Order in England and Wales,
but a lieutenancy was not established until 1954, which left the
field wide open for Maundy Gregory to operate. As one of only

eight Knights Grand Cross in the British Isles, 'His Excellency J. Maundy Gregory', as he was now entitled to style himself, found himself on an equal footing with both the Earl of Denbigh and Cardinal Bourne, the Archbishop of Westminster, and two grades above such ecclesiastics as the Bishops of Brentwood, Middlesborough, and Galloway, and such martial figures as General Sir Edward Bulfin, Major-General Lord Treowen, and Major-General Sir William Western.

The origins of the Holy Sepulchre Order are clouded in obscurity. Some historians claim that the Order originated with the guard which St James the Apostle posted around the Holy Places immediately after the Crucifixion. Others trace its origin to the community that settled in Jerusalem during the reign of the Emperor Constantine, when St Helen ordered the pagan temples which covered the sites of Calvary and the Holy Sepulchre to be removed. What is known for certain is that when Godfrey of Bouillon captured Jerusalem from the Saracens in 1099 he recognized the successors of this devoted band of Christians as the guardians of the Holy Places. Among other quaint privileges which knighthood in this Order conferred at one time were the power to create notaries public, to legitimize bastards, to change a name given in baptism. (Should he chance to meet a prisoner being led to the gallows, a Knight of the Holy Sepulchre could, if the spirit moved him, pardon that prisoner.) In view of these unique privileges, and the fact that Holy Sepulchre Knights took precedence over all others except those of the Golden Fleece, knighthoods had been in demand down the ages, so much so that in 1868 the Holy See fixed the tariff for Knight, Knight Commander, and Knight Grand Cross at 1,000, 2000, and 3,000 *francs d'or* respectively.[1]

*   *   *

That Maundy Gregory did a brisk business in selling Papal honours has now been established beyond any doubt, thanks to the attempts to blackmail the Patriarch of Jerusalem made by Gregory's accountant, Benjamin Pengelly.

Pengelly was altogether a pitiable creature. For one thing, he had a police record, which may explain why he is not listed as a

[1] *Le S.M. Ordre du St. Sepulchre: Extrait des Statuts.* Paris, 1868.

member of either of the two bodies covering his profession—the Institute of Chartered Accountants of England and Wales, and the Association of Certified and Corporate Accountants. In 1913 he had been involved in a shoot-out in Buenos Aires during which one man was killed and Pengelly himself was wounded, leaving him partially paralysed from the waist down. Tried for manslaughter, he was convicted, serving one year in prison.

A social outcast of this sort was made to order for Maundy Gregory, who sensed that Pengelly would have difficulty in getting work, not only because of his prison record, but because of his physical disability. Pengelly's loyalty to Gregory his benefactor would therefore be absolute. So the crippled bookkeeper had gone to work for Gregory in 1921, at first keeping the accounts of the *Whitehall Gazette*, later taking on the Ambassador Club as well. In time Pengelly had become privy to all of Gregory's secrets; indeed, he had aided and abetted Gregory in the honours racket by rustling up candidates on his own account. Later when Gregory got into financial difficulties the two had fallen out, and Pengelly had palmed some of Gregory's cancelled cheques with the end in view of blackmailing their recipients. It was on the strength of two of these cheques totalling £1,000 that Pengelly tried to shake down His Beatitude the Patriarch of Jerusalem, only to land in the dock of the Central Criminal Courts charged with extortion. The first of these cheques signed by Gregory was dated January 24, 1932, or two days after Gregory had been received into the Church.

As the Pengelly blackmail case throws light on Gregory's methods, it is worthwhile examining more closely. On December 20, 1933, Pengelly, in his opening gambit, wrote to the Patriarch about the cheques in his possession, claiming that certain un-named newspapers wished to publish them—did the Patriarch have any objection? His Beatitude evidently thought that Gregory was behind the scheme, for he replied through his secretary with a threat of counter-blackmail. 'We think it would not be wise to publish these cheques, since it might force us also to publish letters signed by prominent persons referring to money paid to Mr Maundy Gregory for the Order', was the way the letter was phrased. (Were these 'prominent persons' complaining, one wonders, that Gregory had pocketed their money without delivering the Order?) At this point Pengelly opened the flood-gates. The tale he poured out to the Patriarch in a letter dated January 9, 1934, was no less harrowing in that its begging intent was obvious. Gregory, he wrote, had absconded owing him several hundred pounds. 'In consequence my home is sold up, my family are in great poverty and distress, we are suffering hunger, cold, and degradation...My two-year-old son is constantly crying for food...' (Gregory cannot be held responsible for all of Pengelly's misfortunes, but the fact remains that when a detective inspector called at Pengelly's house in Fulham with an arrest warrant he found that the bailiffs were already in possession, and he did hear the baby crying.) Blackmail was the only trump card left for someone of Pengelly's mentality, and he now tried his hand at it in clumsy fashion. He proposed to write his memoirs, he informed the Patriarch, and would 'give the inside story of his [Gregory's] dealings with honours and titles, British and foreign', liberally illustrated by photographs of the cheques in Pengelly's possession. 'If you are prepared to assist me financially in this respect,' the accountant concluded, 'I will withhold publication of the matter so far as the Order is concerned and stop reproduction of the cheques.' It was at this point that the Patriarch decided to go to the law.

His Beatitude did not travel to London for Pengelly's trial at the Old Bailey, which opened on March 1, 1934, but he sent his secretary the Reverend Alexander John Kirby, who testified that the Patriarch was 'very upset' when he received Pengelly's letter as 'he did not wish to stir up any mud with regard to certain people'. Father Kirby claimed that the two cheques totalling £1,000 were 'personal gifts to the Patriarch for the use of his mission', and not in payment for knighthoods, as had been suggested. Gregory, he said, was merely the transmitting agent. Under cross-examination the cleric admitted however that he had been Gregory's guest at the Ambassador Club. Further cross-examination wrung the admission from him that Gregory was rather more than a collection agent.

Mr P. Gordon Bamber (defending): Was Maundy Gregory appointed as his [the Patriarch's] representative in this country?
Fr Kirby: I don't think so. I don't know definitely.
The Recorder (interrupting): It rather looks as if he were?
Fr Kirby: Yes.

[168]

The jury, without leaving the box, found Pengelly guilty of demanding money with menaces, and the judge sentenced him to six months imprisonment, despite his physical condition. There had been one horrifying moment in the courtroom when Pengelly, in testifying, had let drop the name of a 'distinguished man'. The judge had quickly intervened to express the hope that no newspaper would publish it. As the judge declared in sentencing Pengelly, 'Once it is imagined in this country that people can hold a pistol at the heads of public men and say, "If you don't pay money we will publish something about you", then the social order would be at an end.'

Maundy Gregory's activities as Papal honours salesman, as revealed at the Pengelly trial, did much to harm the Holy Sepulchre Order, for when the English Lieutenancy of the Order was established in 1954, only eight members applied to join, and three of these were priests.[1] Since then more than one hundred Knights and Dames have been created in the Lieutenancy.

* * *

Before leaving the subject of Maundy Gregory's conversion mention should be made of a curious incident which involved Gregory posing as 'confidential agent of the Vatican', and hoodwinking Hollywood film-writer and director John Villiers Farrow, husband of Maureen O'Sullivan, father of actress Mia Farrow, and winner of a best screenplay Oscar in 1956 for 'Around the World in 80 Days'. In April, 1932, Farrow, however, was just a struggling screen-writer employed by Cecil B. DeMille and had still to win his spurs. Moreover, the 28-year-old, Sydney-born scenarist had just divorced his first wife, and was staying at White's Club in London. Being Catholic Farrow was anxious to have his first marriage declared a nullity by the Church authorities in Rome so that he could make a second marriage within the Church. A friend at the Danish Embassy said that he knew just

[1] Apparently after the Gregory scandal some members in disgust ceased to wear the medals of the Order. One such was John H. Dixey, solicitor, Catholic convert, and an old boy of Harrow. I am indebted for this information to Dr James Walsh, one-time proprietor of the *Catholic Times*, who has served as Chamberlain to four Popes, and who is Grand Cross of the Holy Sepulchre Order, as well as being its first Lieutenant for England and Wales.

the man for the job, and promptly introduced Farrow to Maundy Gregory, who invited him to lunch.

What followed is best described in the affidavit Farrow filed in March, 1934, in the High Court action which grew out of his dealings with Gregory. The young screen-writer went along to 38 Parliament Street where he found Gregory 'very agreeable and his offices . . . most sumptuous'. 'He had a chapel there and also a place called the "Chancellery",' Farrow deposed. 'He showed me many documents purporting to have come from the Vatican, giving him the title of "Chancellor of the Order of the Holy Sepulchre in the British Empire".' Gregory then opened a closet and showed Farrow the gorgeous white robe with black facings which was his uniform, and his insignia as Knight Grand Cross of the Order—the Silver Star, the red, five-fold Cross of Godfrey of Bouillon which he wore suspended from a wide ribbon in the form of a sash. They then went to lunch at the Ambassador Club, where Gregory introduced Farrow to Major-General Seely and to two Members of Parliament 'with whom he seemed to be on very friendly terms'. 'He also invited me to a big dinner given by him the night before the Derby was run, at which dinner I met many notable people.'

When Farrow broached the matter of obtaining the marriage nullity Gregory, who must have been primed beforehand by their mutual friend at the Danish Embassy, told the screen-writer 'that as confidential agent of the Vatican he was in a position to obtain the said dispensation . . . [but] required payment of the sum of £320 for distribution among Catholic charities, which said John Maundy Gregory represented as customary in cases of that kind, telling me that it would put me in a favourable light with the Church authorities . . .' Accordingly Farrow made out a cheque for that amount in Gregory's favour. Two weeks later Gregory, who knew a good thing when he saw it, put the bite on Farrow again, stating that the dispensation was going through 'but that he would require a further sum of £1,000 for distribution among charities . . . [to] make a better impression with the authorities'. If the £1,000 were forthcoming he could obtain the dispensation in two weeks' time, Gregory claimed.

When Farrow protested that he didn't have that kind of money Gregory countered with the suggestion that he draw a £500 bill of exchange on Farrow to be made payable on September 30, 1932,

with the understanding that if the dispensation had not been obtained by that date he (Gregory) would cancel the bill of exchange.
Meanwhile, Gregory would advance the £500 to Catholic charities
on Farrow's behalf. Farrow agreed to this proposal, whereupon
Gregory began to stall him whenever the screen-writer pressed
him for news of the nullity. On August 20, 1932, Farrow, his
suspicions now fully aroused, stopped payment on the bill of
exchange.[1]

With his youth to excuse him Farrow nevertheless showed himself to be incredibly naïve in supposing that Gregory could obtain a marriage nullity for him. Even a cursory enquiry on his
part would have disclosed that a case such as his had to be prepared
for submission to the Rota, which alone was empowered to grant
such nullities. This would have involved the collection of evidence,
and in all probability Farrow's appearance before a tribunal of
Catholic priests versed in canonical law. Gregory was simply
trading on the screen-writer's gullibility.[2]

*   *   *

Maundy Gregory at the beginning of 1932 appeared to be at the
zenith of his power as prince of con-men and influence peddler
extraordinary. He was on first-name terms with courtiers and,
as Stanley Baldwin had feared, had managed to build a magic
aura around himself as one who enjoyed royal favour. As Deputy
Director of the Order of St John's appeal fund, Gregory had been
bidden to lunch with the Duke of Connaught at St James's Palace,
and had been presented to His Majesty King George V at a
Buckingham Palace investiture. As ex-officio Chancellor of the
Holy Sepulchre Order, Gregory mixed on terms of equality with
such notables as Cardinal Bourne, the Earl of Denbigh, Gwen-
dolyn, Duchess of Norfolk, and Enid, Dowager Countess of
Kinnoull.

[1] The High Court action resulted when Gregory's trustee in bankruptcy sued Farrow to recover the £500 bill of exchange. Alleging 'mis-
representation and fraud', Farrow made a counter-claim for the £320 he
had paid Gregory. Nothing more was heard from the trustee.

[2] Farrow eventually obtained his nullity, and on September 12, 1936,
he married Maureen O'Sullivan at the Old Mission Church in Santa
Barbara, California. They had seven children, of whom Mia Farrow was
the eldest daughter.

To the crestfallen J. C. C. Davidson it must have seemed as though the strategy he had worked out with Baldwin for destroying Gregory—i.e. breaking him financially—had failed. They had succeeded in cutting off Gregory's source of revenue from the sale of honours, but this had only driven him into new fields of endeavour. Far from containing the evil which Maundy Gregory represented, the Baldwin–Davidson strategy had served merely to spread it, like those cancerous cells that are 'seeded' when the surgeon's knife bungles. So, at least, it must have seemed to the two Conservative party leaders.

Seldom have appearances been more deceptive, however. The moment of Gregory's greatest triumph was, in reality, the moment of his greatest weakness, for the war of attrition launched by Baldwin had begun to make serious inroads into Gregory's finances. The Gregorian façade which he had built up so elaborately over the years had begun to crumble. No one would have guessed Gregory's plight from his demeanour—if anything, he appeared more arrogant, more unassailable than ever—but it taxed all of his resources as an actor to maintain this pose.

Looking back, one would find it difficult to single out that moment before the fall when Maundy Gregory appeared to have reached the pinnacle of his success as a public figure. Was it the Feast of Corpus Christi when Gregory, resplendent in his robes as Grand Cross of the Holy Sepulchre Order, went in procession to Westminster Cathedral to attend Mass? Or was it that other occasion, the Buckingham Palace investiture when Gregory received the Badge of the Order of St John with the eight-pointed Maltese Cross emblazoned on it from the hands of His Majesty the King? On balance, neither of these occasions, brilliant though they may have been, were as glittering as the Derby Dinner held at the Ambassador Club on June 2, 1931. This most probably was the high point of Gregory's career.

No sooner had the 162 dinner guests been seated than there was a blinding flash followed by a whoosh of black smoke as Swaine, the Court photographer, photographed the assemblage, thus imprisoning in a single frame for all time Gregory's past. For the men in the photograph, which was duly reproduced in the *Whitehall Gazette*, are from all periods and all layers of Gregory's life, men who had moulded and influenced him, and whom he, in turn, had moulded and influenced. Those seated at the top table were, for the most part, merely window-dressing—they ranged from Conservative politicians then in Opposition like Sir Austen Chamberlain and Winston Churchill, to two Cabinet Ministers, J. R. Clynes and J. H. Thomas, of the Ramsay MacDonald Labour government then in power, and included such peers as the Duke of Marlborough, who was Churchill's cousin, Viscount Craigavon of Stormont, who was Prime Minister of Northern Ireland, and the Marquess of Reading, who had been first Lord Chief Justice of England, then Viceroy of India. Considering that the dinner was held on the eve of the Derby, there was a curious absence of sportsmen, unless Captain Woolf 'Babe' Barnato, heir to the Barnato diamond millions, could qualify as such (Barnato once raced the Blue Train from Cannes to Paris in his $6\frac{1}{2}$-litre Bentley and won). One cannot help but feel that the guests came less to exchange tips on a possible Derby winner than to free-load at Gregory's expense (it is idle to pretend that they did not know that Gregory was their host, as Major-General Seely, as chairman, made several pointed references to him during the evening).

As for Gregory himself, his confused sensation must have been that of Proust's Narrator at the Princess de Guermantes' reception, the coda of Proust's novel, when past and present appeared to swim together in the slipstream of time. By casting his eye round the banquet room Gregory could pick out men whom he had helped along the road to power and social prestige, knights and baronets and even the occasional baron who had bought their honours at Gregory's emporium. Far from bearing him ill-will, they appeared to be satisfied customers, chatting with Gregory amiably as they consumed his food and drink. There were others present who themselves had given Gregory a helping hand when he needed it most. Seated not far from Gregory was that genial playboy Captain Freddy Guest who, as Coalition Liberal Chief Whip in the Lloyd George government, had set Gregory up in the honours brokerage business. Guest had since crossed the floor of the House of Commons to become a Tory MP, after having been thrown to the wolves by his erstwhile hero Lloyd George.

Dotted around the room were other ghosts from Gregory's past. Sir Warden Chilcott, for example, who two years earlier had stood down from Parliament, declaring himself to be 'sickened by the hypocrisy of that hollow game of party politics' (in the eleven years

[173]

he represented the Walton Division of Liverpool in the Commons he made but a single speech). Then there was Brigadier-General Sir William Horwood, who had taken Gregory under his wing during the eight years he was Commissioner of Metropolitan Police at Scotland Yard.

Gregory's non-political interests were also represented among the revenants at the feast. There was that relic of Gregory's brief experiment as patron of the arts, A. J. A. Symons, of the fancy waistcoats and florid cravats, his interest in the Derby inherited no doubt from his jockey father. Symons was flanked by such fellow Corvines as Harry Pirie-Gordon, Vyvyan Holland, and Professor Tancred Borenius, who could never resist an opportunity to dine out. One wonders what the politicos thought of this strange band who kept vigil at the shrine of the Baron Corvo, and what the Corvines, in turn, thought of the politicos. Finally, Gregory's eyes must have strayed to the corner where sat the man who inevitably was cast for the role of Judas, J. C. C. Davidson. In his memoirs Davidson has left a record of how he went about preparing himself for this role, softening up Gregory for the kill while maintaining every appearance of friendliness towards him. 'Some weeks before an Honours List was about to be published,' Davidson noted in a memorandum on the subject, 'I used to lunch at the Ambassadors' [sic] Club. . . . There I had to sit, a marked man of course, at his [Gregory's] table and consume an excellent lunch washed down by half a bottle of champagne followed by at least one sherry glass of green Chartreuse. He would discuss the qualifications of his Honours List candidates and I would depart full of expressions of sympathy and explanation of how difficult these things were, and having made arrangements that the list of men and the honours for which they were suitable should be conveyed to me secretly by hand.'[1] That list, of course, went straight into the waste-paper basket.

As chairman of the Conservative party, Davidson had a public duty to stop the honours racket, which had spread alarmingly. But the spectacle of Davidson years later accepting the hospitality of the man whose destruction he had ordained is one that many will find repellent.

*   *   *

[1] *Op Cit.*

To this same period belongs an anecdote told to me by Mrs Maisie Saunders of Megève. 'A propos of some homicide that was in the headlines, Maundy told me over lunch at the Ritz that he knew how to commit the perfect murder,' Mrs Saunders related. 'He said that recently he had obtained from South America some curare, a poison which was used chiefly by the natives to make poison arrows. Its effect upon the human body if administered in overdose, Maundy told me, was to relax the abdominal muscles to the point where breathing stopped. If the body were then immersed in water all trace of the poison would disappear as curare was soluble.

'Maundy told me that the sample he had obtained was curare in its crude form, a sticky, dark-brown substance that smelled rather like tar. Curare was comparatively unheard of in those days, and its medicinal qualities were unknown, so I listened to what Maundy had to say with curiosity, even though it seemed a rather gruesome topic for lunch. Gregory touched on curare's homicidal possibilities lightly, but not too lightly—you could tell that he was deeply interested in the subject.'

XIII

She Sleeps, Milady Sleeps

Maundy Gregory might still have weathered the storm—he had shown considerable ingenuity in finding new ways and means of supplanting income lost from the sale of honours—had it not been for the death in July, 1930, of Sir George Watson, millionaire owner of the Maypole Dairy, which set in motion a whole chain of disastrous events. Sir George, who was made a baronet in 1912, had been High Sheriff for Berkshire, and among public benefactions had endowed a university chair for the study of American history and institutions (the Prince of Wales had politely declined the honour of having the chair designated by his name).[1] Whether Sir George gave £30,000 to Maundy Gregory out of sheer goodness of heart, or with a view to being made Baron Watson of Sulhamstead (his home in Berkshire) and thus obtaining a seat in the House of Lords, is a matter of conjecture. What is clear is that £30,000 in bonds changed hands as early as 1923; and that Gregory then asked Sir George to write down the particulars about himself, including his contributions to various charities. Sir George complied with this request, giving as reference Viscount Esher, who was closely connected with the Royal Family. (Viscount Esher had supervised both the funeral of Queen Victoria and the Coronation of her son Edward VII.)

Incredible as it may seem, Gregory then was able to string Watson along for the next seven years, always finding excuses why Sir George's name had not appeared in the most recent Honours List. Thus, in a letter dated June 29, 1926, Gregory blamed the General Strike for the delay ('The strike has butted in and caused the entire side-tracking of our collection of names, which was

[1] Sir George's youngest son Peter Watson was a notable patron of the arts, having been one of the founders of the Institute of Contemporary Art, and having financed the magazine *Horizon* which Cyril Connolly edited.

otherwise fully approved'). When the date to redeem the bonds fell due early in 1930, the ever-trusting dairy-owner replaced them by British bonds, French Rentes, and Consols worth £4,000. Seven months later Sir George died of heart failure on the operating table, whereupon the executors of his estate sued Gregory to recover the £30,000.

The executors' contention was that Watson, shortly before his death, had lost patience with Gregory and had instructed him to hand over the bonds to Lloyds Bank; but that Gregory, instead of following instructions, had converted them to his own use. If the case had gone to trial Gregory's defence would have been that the stocks and bonds were an outright gift to him. The trouble was that he could not afford to let the suit be called for trial. The resultant publicity would have destroyed him completely.

On the other hand, if he settled out of court he faced financial ruin. He would be saddled with an enormous debt at a time when the Baldwin–Davidson strategy of attrition was beginning to pay off. Gregory however had no choice. On January 13, 1932, when the Watson case was called, he entered into a settlement with the estate executors whereby he agreed to repay £10,000 at once, and the balance in two £10,000 instalments due on July 13, 1932 and on January 13, 1933. He also agreed to pay court costs amounting to £380. Gregory's financial position on January 13, 1932 after he had paid the first instalment was that he was overdrawn at one bank and had borrowed money from another. Meanwhile, there were printing bills overdue, staff salaries, and Ambassador Club overheads to be met, not to mention the mortgage on his house at Hyde Park Terrace. There was even trouble at the Deepdene Hotel in Dorking, the management having neglected to pay in the monies it had been deducting from the wages of the twenty-eight hotel employees for health and unemployment insurance.

*   *   *

Misfortune such as now dogged Gregory is almost tangible. It is as though the bearer of it gives off an effluvium which attracts vultures and hyenas from afar. Maundy Gregory's relations with his White Russian friends and their Nazi allies is a case in point. In 1931 Gregory had visited Berlin as the guest of Werner von Alvensleben at the famous *Herrenklub*, a right-wing elitist club which

Franz von Papen had helped to found. (Its members included not only Oskar von Hindenburg, son of the Reichs President, and Kurt von Schleicher, one-time Reichs Chancellor, but Paul Reynaud, French Premier at the time of the Nazi invasion.) In his memoirs von Papen makes the *Herrenklub* sound as innocuous as a Boy Scout jamboree ('I often spoke at its meetings, particularly on my favourite topic of Franco-German understanding,' von Papen writes); but the British took a different view. By ordinance dated May 30, 1946, the British Military Government outlawed the *Herrenklub* as a 'criminal organization', and barred its members from standing for public office in post-Hitler Germany.

Warmed no doubt by the schnapps which followed lunch with von Alvensleben and his friends at the *Herrenklub*, Gregory made an unfortunate slip in his conversation, casually letting it drop that he was 'vice-president of the House of Lords' (the remark is so stupid that I can only suppose that it was the effect of too much schnapps, though Gregory may, of course, have been incorrectly translated). Whatever the explanation, the remark was made within earshot of Captain Wilhelm Widenmann, who had served as German naval attaché in London before the First World War, and who knew of course that there was no such office as 'vice-president of the House of Lords'. His suspicions aroused, Captain Widenmann, in turn, wrote to London to his friend Dr Kurt Abshagen, who represented a number of German newspapers in the British capital, and asked him to investigate Maundy Gregory's background. In a letter to me from Bavaria, where he is now living, Dr Abshagen describes a visit to the Ambassador Club. ('In the hall of the club the wall decoration consisted of drawings of guests who had attended luncheons given by Gregory, among the names being a number of prominent politicians.') The journalist was not favourably impressed by what he saw, and as a result of his report to Captain Widenmann Gregory was no longer welcome at the *Herrenklub*. 'Nor do I think that Herr von Alvensleben ever made use of the honorary membership to the Ambassador Club which Gregory had given to him,' Dr Abshagen comments drily.

The repercussions of the affair were not confined within the walls of the *Herrenklub*, but von Alvensleben, who was a born intriguer, made a point of spreading the word to Gregory's White Russian friends that he was a pederast and a phoney who was without any real political influence. This, in turn, led to the Hetman of the Ukraine, Paul Skoropadsky, breaking off relations with Gregory. It will be recalled that Gregory, acting on the Hetman's instructions, had launched the Anglo-Ukrainian Council, whose inaugural meeting was held at the Ambassador Club in December, 1931, with Gregory in the chair. By March, 1932, Skoropadsky, reacting to rumours about Gregory spread by the Nazi grapevine, had ordered the Anglo-Ukrainian Council to be disbanded and had withdrawn his financial support from the *Whitehall Gazette*.

Gregory did not take this lying down. In June, 1932 he began serialization in the *Whitehall Gazette* of a 230-page memorandum on the Ukraine written by Prince Alexandre Wolkonsky, who though Skoropadsky's cousin represented a political viewpoint diametrically opposed to the Hetman's Ukrainian separatism. In a preface to the Wolkonsky articles Gregory wrote that having given a lengthy hearing to the Hetman's views 'we felt that it was only in the public interest that we should give the same facilities for the ventilation of their [the non-separatists'] views.' Then in the November/December, 1932 issue of the *Whitehall Gazette* appeared a letter signed by 'A Student of Russian Politics' questioning the source of the Hetman's finances. After pointing out that the Hetmanite movement had been subsidized by Austria before the First World War, 'Student' writes, 'Are we not entitled to ask whether the present outburst of separatist Ukrainian propaganda is not without particular interest to certain foreign governments, and, if so, why this kind of political venture should continue here?'

The Hetmanites retaliated by founding their own newspaper, *The Investigator*, whose first issue, appearing in November, 1932, announced that it was 'the sole organization in England working with, and with the authority of, the Hetman of the Ukraine Paul Skoropadsky'. Its front men were Sir Michael O'Dwyer, a former lieutenant-governor of the Punjab, and Roderick Macleod, a one-time follower of Lloyd George, who told a Rotary Club luncheon in Wolverhampton that the *Investigator* 'was trying to do for the Ukraine what our fathers and forefathers did for Greece in Byron's day, and for Italy and Garibaldi'. In the background animating these puppets was the Hetman's hatchetman, the ubiquitous Vladimir Korostovets, who signed his articles 'V de K'. The *Investigator* was pro-Hitler and anti-Semitic, seeking to justify Hitler's persecution of the Jews. It was also short-lived, folding after only nine issues, but not before it had attacked Maundy Gregory by name as an enemy to the cause of Ukrainian independence.

* * *

Gregory had run out of bridges to burn by July, 1932, when the second £10,000 instalment to Sir George Watson's executors fell due. He had no option but to turn to his dearest friend Edith Rosse for help, thereby giving 'Milady' the shock of her life. Although she had a shrewd head for business, Mrs Rosse appears to have been completely ignorant as to the true state of Gregory's financial affairs. She was of course under no illusion as to how Gregory made his money—after all, 'Milady' had played hostess to prospective honours clients at the Ambassador Club and elsewhere on a number of occasions. But Gregory, partly from a habit of secrecy, did not encourage her to poke her nose too closely into his concerns.

Gregory, on the other hand, took a keen interest in Mrs Rosse's investments, about which he was kept informed by their joint accountant Benjamin Pengelly. When they had separated back in 1923 composer Frederick Rosse had made his wife a handsome settlement of half of his annual income, and in the intervening years Edith's share had never fallen below £324, and in some years had been £600 and more. This she had added to savings already accumulated in order to make a few forays into the property market with Gregory acting as her adviser. 'After the separation I determined to help Mrs Rosse in every possible way,' Gregory was to write later.[1] 'I advanced her money to buy a bungalow by the river, and I also gave her a guarantee of £5 a week for life.' Gregory admitted that this £260 annuity, which he claimed was drawn up into a deed and signed by himself, was never taken up by Mrs Rosse. As for the 'bungalow by the river', this refers to 'Vanity Fair' on Ditton Island, which Gregory had obtained on a 90-year-lease as far back as July 29, 1910. The records show that two months later Gregory transferred the lease to Mrs Rosse. 'From time to time, with my assistance,' Gregory added, 'she acquired other properties, and was actually managing fourteen at the time of her death.' Mrs Rosse's investments had prospered until in

[1] Gregory by-line story in the *Daily Express*, July 20, 1933.

July, 1932 her estate was worth £18,000, which is roughly the equivalent of £90,000 today.

Morally at least, Gregory felt that he had a first lien on that £18,000 nest-egg. Had he not helped 'Milady' to multiply her savings through his shrewd advice on how to invest them? And had he not paid for her holidays with Mrs MacKinlay at Florence and Monte Carlo? This would explain why he was so stunned when Mrs Rosse refused his request for a loan. She was 'property poor', Mrs Rosse maintained. Most of her money was tied up in property that she could neither sell nor mortgage, not at least without sustaining a loss. Not being privy to Gregory's business secrets, Mrs Rosse was unaware of the seriousness of his predicament. Her feeling was that 'Uncle Jim' could find the money elsewhere, borrowing from his well-to-do friends. Gregory had been in tight squeezes before and had managed to wriggle out of them. Besides, although she was careful not to mention this fact to Gregory, Mrs Rosse had her niece, Ethel Davies, to consider.

Reference has already been made to Ethel's stormy relationship with her aunt, which in its power to wound was what one would expect to find between an over-protective mother and a willful, headstrong daughter. In 1928 Mrs Rosse, in a generous mood, had named Ethel as her beneficiary in a will which made no mention of Maundy Gregory, but the two had quarrelled soon afterwards and Mrs Rosse had torn up the will. Did Gregory persuade Mrs Rosse to tear up the will, as Pengelly later contended? Certainly the quarrel by this date had assumed triangular proportions with Gregory siding with 'Milady' against her niece, in fact, doing everything in his power to drive a wedge between the two. Ethel Davies, for her part, bitterly resented Gregory. Perhaps she saw through his pretences and recognized him as the bogus person he was. More likely she was jealous of Gregory, mistaking him for her aunt's lover, hence as a rival for Mrs Rosse's affections.

Mrs Rosse's quarrel with Ethel was patched up, and in mid-February, 1932 Ethel moved in with her aunt at Hyde Park Terrace, much to Gregory's disgust. The truce did not last for long—apparently Mrs Rosse criticized the company Ethel kept as being 'fast'—and this time, when the niece left, Gregory said that she was not to put her foot inside the door again. If she did so, Gregory hinted, he himself would decamp. Thereafter Mrs Rosse saw Ethel on the sly. Sometimes they met on a bench in Hyde Park.

Sometimes when Mrs Rosse was sure that Gregory would be away for the day she saw her niece at the flat. Once, when Gregory returned home unexpectedly, she hid Ethel in a closet.

The final break came in July, when Mrs Rosse wrote to her brother, 'Ever since I had that girl back I have had daily hell. Another terrible scene this morning, and I feel half dead as if I shall have a bad seizure . . . I have given her £2 this morning and £1 on Friday. I have absolutely finished with her, and she can do as she pleases.' The situation in July, 1932, when Maundy Gregory was pressing 'Milady' for a loan, was that not only was there bad blood between Gregory and Ethel, but that Mrs Rosse had broken off all relations with her niece, and was badly upset by the experience. There is some confusion as to whether Mrs Rosse, under Gregory's prompting, had destroyed a second will naming Ethel Davies as beneficiary. This at any rate was the impression of Frederick Davies, Mrs Rosse's brother.

*　　*　　*

On Friday, August 19, 1932, the sun bowled up red and angry, heralding a heat wave in London. As the day wore on the mercury climbed steadily until it reached 83 degrees in the shade as recorded at Kensington Palace. The opening of Lambeth Bridge by His Majesty King George was somewhat marred by the number of spectators who keeled over along the embankment, overcome by the heat. At a garden party elsewhere some of C. B. Cochran's 'young ladies' took off their shoes and stockings and posed for a *Daily Mail* photographer with their legs splashing in a swimming-pool.

Maundy Gregory had a luncheon date with King George of Greece at the Carlton Hotel that day, and at 2.30 the two men still lingered over their brandy and cigars in the nearly deserted dining-room when a message was brought to the table that Gregory was to call home immediately as a matter of urgency. Excusing himself, Gregory went into the lobby and called Paddington 2103. Mrs Lottie Eyres, who was Edith Rosse's housekeeper, answered the telephone and informed Gregory that her mistress had been taken suddenly and violently ill, and that she was asking for Gregory. A doctor had been called—not Dr Blair, Mrs Rosse's regular physician, who was away on holiday, but a Dr Plummer, who had been recommended. Mrs Eyres feared that it might be a heat stroke, she told Gregory.

Mrs Rosse had been complaining of the heat all morning, and at noon, claiming that she had no appetite, had nibbled at a cheese and tomato sandwich washed down with half a bottle of champagne. After lunch she couldn't seem to breathe, Mrs Rosse said, and she had gone to the French windows overlooking the garden in search of more air when suddenly 'it was as though something burst in my head', as she later described it. 'Come quickly, Eyres—I am so ill,' she had called out, after which she had collapsed on the bed. Mrs Eyres and Mrs Kate Wells, who was Gregory's housekeeper, undressed the sick woman and put her to bed, and Mrs Rosse had asked that Gregory be sent for, saying, 'I feel so ill I don't know if he will arrive in time.'

Gregory arrived at 10 Hyde Park Terrace a few minutes before the doctor, and thus was able to open the door to the latter, greeting him with, 'I'm so glad you've come, doctor. My sister is very ill.' Inasmuch as Dr E. Curnow Plummer's competence has been questioned it is only fair to point out that he had never before attended Mrs Rosse and consequently knew nothing about her medical history—the fact, for example, that she was an alcoholic and suffered from high blood pressure. Nevertheless, in the course of treating Mrs Rosse, Dr Plummer was to change his diagnosis of her illness at least four times, and none of his hypotheses was to prove correct. In the first instance, the doctor said that Mrs Rosse appeared to be suffering from 'heat collapse', as distinguished from 'heat stroke', and he prescribed ice packs and aspirin. Later he substituted high blood pressure and indigestion for 'heat collapse', and still later he came down heavily in favour of uraemic poisoning as the cause of Mrs Rosse's complaint.

Ice packs and aspirin sound like a rather trivial remedy to give to a woman who feared that she might not last the twenty minutes or so it took for Maundy Gregory to get from the Carlton Hotel to Hyde Park Terrace. For Mrs Rosse was convinced that she was dying. The conviction was so strong that when Maundy Gregory did finally arrive she insisted upon drawing up her last will and testament there and then. Gregory gave his version of what followed in the by-line article quoted earlier. 'Mrs Rosse said to me, "Jim, get pen and paper—there is something I want you to write." I put my hand in my pocket and pulled out the Carlton Hotel luncheon menu card . . . I found there was no writing on the back, and so I wrote on that . . . I had no pen, and so I had to write in pencil. She dictated the will without the slightest hesitation.' Gregory added, 'I tried to persuade her that there was no necessity to take the precaution of making her will, but she insisted on going on with it.'[1]

The will read as follows: 'Everything I have, if anything happens to me, to be left to Mr J. Maundy Gregory to be disposed of as he thinks best and in accordance with what I should desire.' The will was witnessed by Mrs Eyres and by Dr Plummer. It was the latter who suggested that Mrs Rosse should sign it twice, inasmuch as her first signature had obscured one of the words.

* * *

Thereafter Mrs Rosse's mysterious illness followed a switchback course. At one moment she appeared to be making slow but steady improvement; the next, she complained of severe pains in her head, and had attacks of vomiting and diarrhoea. When Dr Blair returned from holiday on August 23 he took over from Dr Plummer, but a week later Gregory telephoned Dr Blair that he, too, could cease attendance inasmuch as Mrs Rosse was making such splendid progress. Gregory's report was completely at variance with that of Hilda Mary Howard, Mrs Rosse's former housekeeper, who when she telephoned her on Monday, August 29, found her former mistress confused in her speech. Mrs Rosse told Mrs Howard that she had had a stroke, and that although she was feeling better she was unable to remember anything. Apparently the sick woman mistook Mrs Howard for Mrs MacKinlay, for she kept referring to the housekeeper as 'Dagny', which was Mrs MacKinlay's Christian name. When Mrs Howard pointed out the mistake, Mrs Rosse replied, 'Oh, you mustn't take any notice of what I call you.'

Still Maundy Gregory judged that Mrs Rosse was well enough on Thursday, September 1, to go for a drive in the taxicab with the faithful Tom Bramley at the wheel. They went as far as Jack Straw's Castle, Hampstead Heath, where Charles Dickens used to enjoy a chop and a glass of wine, before turning back. 'She felt so much better that she even talked of going away soon to Brighton,

[1] *Daily Express*, July 20, 1933.

where she had a flat,' Gregory claimed, adding, 'I humoured her, although I knew she was not really well enough for that.' When Mrs Rosse returned from the outing she took to her bed again, complaining that she was having trouble with her eyes. 'She said that she could hardly see,' Mrs Eyres testified.

The arrangement at 10 Hyde Park Terrace was that during the week Gregory dined downstairs with Mrs Rosse—on those nights that he was home, that is—but on Saturday night Mrs Rosse dined with Gregory in his upstairs flat, the object of this exercise being to give Mrs Eyres her Saturday night off. The two friends used to joke about dining Chez Gregoire on Saturday night, and on one occasion Mrs Rosse put a fur coat over her best evening dress to climb the stairs to Gregory's flat, and she pretended all evening that they were at Ciro's, and that Gregory was alternately the head waiter and her gallant. Neither was in a playful mood on Saturday, September 3, when Mrs Rosse got up to have dinner with 'Uncle Jim' for the last time. Gregory himself took no part in preparing the dinner, which consisted of liver and bacon and stewed plums (a rather indigestible meal for a sick person, one would have thought), but he did fetch a bottle of champagne from the wine cellar, 'because I thought it would be good for her,' as he later explained.

'We both went to bed early,' Gregory declared. 'Mrs Rosse's bedroom was on the ground floor—it was formerly a billiards-room, and had been built out on to the garden. She had a bell by her bedside which rang in my bedroom, so that she could summon me in an emergency. Soon after I went to bed the bell rang, and I went down to find Mrs Rosse had been taken violently ill. She had fallen out of bed and almost collapsed trying to telephone a friend.' This was about 11.30 p.m. Gregory knocked on Mrs. Eyres' door, telling her, 'Come quickly, Mrs Rosse is very ill again.' He then telephoned Dr Plummer, who had been superseded by Dr Blair ten days earlier. (Gregory later claimed that Mrs Rosse was dissatisfied with Dr Blair.) Dr Plummer made another of his fatuous diagnoses, concluding that Mrs Rosse had been 'overdoing things'. She was suffering from nothing more than acute indigestion, in the opinion of Dr Plummer, who prescribed for her accordingly. But Mrs Rosse was too ill the following day to even talk to Hilda Mary Howard who called to see her. Mrs Howard remained to help with the nursing.

Another week was to elapse before Dr Plummer called in a consultant, during which time Mrs Rosse was mostly in a state of coma. By this time Dr Plummer had come around to the view that Mrs Rosse was suffering from uraemic poisoning caused by Bright's disease, a diagnosis in which the consultant Dr Parsons Smith concurred. When Dr Plummer arrived at Hyde Park Tertace on the night of September 13-14, in response to Gregory's urgent summons, he found that Mrs Rosse was paralysed on her right side. She died without regaining consciousness at 12.45 a.m., and Dr Plummer then opened a vein at Gregory's request (the latter said that this had been Mrs Rosse's wish.) 'Cerebral haemorrhage and chronic Bright's disease' were the causes of death given by Dr Plummer in signing the death certificate. As it happened he was wrong on both counts.

The events of Wednesday, September 14, the day of Mrs Rosse's death, were so extraordinary as to merit a full description in a later chapter. In short, Gregory lost his head entirely. For example, he neglected to notify Mrs Rosse's relatives of her death. Ethel Davies did not discover that her aunt had died until the day of the funeral, when she telephoned to Hyde Park Terrace quite by chance to enquire about Mrs Rosse's health. One can picture therefore the niece's shock and sense of outrage upon learning that her aunt was to be buried that afternoon. Ethel did not attend the funeral, but later she rang up Gregory to find out the cause of Mrs Rosse's death, and also where she was buried. Here Gregory made his second mistake. He gave her the name of the cemetery at Bisham-on-the-Thames all right, but he refused to disclose the cause of Mrs Rosse's death, claiming that this was 'a professional secret'. In adopting this high-handed attitude Gregory was merely storing up trouble for himself, for now Ethel began to suspect that her aunt's death had not been a natural one. Ethel's suspicions came to full flower when she learned that she had been completely cut out of Mrs Rosse's will in favour of Gregory. Gregory did, however, have enough presence of mind to pen the following note to Frederick Rosse:

Dear Fred—Poor Edith passed away peacefully early this morning at ten to one. She had a heat stroke nearly a month ago and a relapse last Saturday week.

We did everything we could for her—three specialists,

[186]

and two nurses. She did not suffer at all towards the end.

Yours, *J.M.G.*

I have just found your address and a packet to be sent to you.

* * *

Maundy Gregory lost no time in proving Mrs Rosse's will, taking out letters of administration on October 8, exactly three weeks after 'Milady's' funeral. In the by-line newspaper article already quoted Gregory tacitly admitted that his speed had been dictated by fear that the will would be contested. 'Mrs Rosse had always thought that after her death my life would be made difficult,' he wrote. 'She said as much when she made her will. I therefore thought it advisable to have her will proved as speedily as possible. I did not wish to give anybody an opportunity of holding up the legal formalities.' Another reason for Gregory's haste was, of course, that his creditors were pressing him.

As sole beneficiary Gregory soon cleaned out the £4,975 Mrs Rosse had saved with the Abbey Building Society, withdrawing £3,500 on October 11, £1,000 on November 17, £425 on November 29, leaving a balance of £50 in the account. At the same time he set about liquidating Mrs Rosse's property holdings. Gerald Macmillan estimates that by the end of November the £18,000 which Gregory inherited from Mrs Rosse had been spent, cites as evidence the fact that the undertaker's bill for £82 which he owed to Harrods was never paid. This means that Gregory ran through the entire inheritance in six weeks, mostly in paying off creditors. It means also that Gregory was broke by January 15, 1933 when the third and final £10,000 instalment under the Watson settlement fell due. If this assumption is correct, it would explain Gregory's recklessness in approaching Lt-Cmdr Billyard-Leake with the offer of a knighthood.

In ordinary circumstances Maundy Gregory would not have gone near Billyard-Leake with such an offer. For the retired naval commander was no jumped-up millionaire from the Midlands eager to buy an honour for the 'missus'. To begin with, Billyard-Leake was by no means a wealthy man, such wealth as he had being tied up in property in Australia and in Ayrshire, Scotland. Again, as already indicated, he was a highly sophisticated individual, not likely to fall for invitations to dine with exiled royalty or any other of Gregory's ploys. Lastly, he was fully aware that his war-time services had been amply rewarded when he was made a member of the Distinguished Service Order. Any other honours that were due to him would come as a result of a recommendation from the Ministry of Defence, and not from some squalid back-alley deal.

In the honours prosecution which now loomed ahead of Gregory it is not necessary to postulate any frame-up or conspiracy. Billyard-Leake was not pushed into Gregory's arms, but was deliberately sought out by the latter. Nor is it necessary to conjure up the sinister figure of 'Blinker' Hall as the master-mind of a plot to ruin Gregory. Gregory was his own ruin. Ten thousand pounds was the amount he attempted to extract from Billyard-Leake as his asking price for a knighthood: it was exactly the amount due to the Watson trustees on January 15.

The first phase of Gregory's trial at the Bow Street police court was covered in an opening chapter. When the curtain fell on this first act the concern of all, it will be recalled, was to ensure Gregory's silence. Under no circumstances should he be allowed to go into the witness-box and tell all, as he had been threatening to do. That Gregory could be persuaded to change his plea from Not Guilty to Guilty was a foregone conclusion. It remained only to see what sort of deal could be worked out, what the *quid pro quo* would be.

XIV

Not with a Bang,
but a Giggle

A comparison of Maundy Gregory with Sacha Stavisky, whose swindles convulsed France in 1934, is instructive because of the contrasts it shows in the handling of political scandals on the two sides of the English Channel. The son of a Russian Jewish dentist who emigrated to Paris, Sacha Stavisky, too, dealt in titles, but of a different sort—his speciality was defrauding investors by means of the bogus companies he set up. Stavisky's empire was built like a pyramid of playing cards, with pawnshops ('Crédits Municipaux', as the French grandly call them) as its flimsy base. Thus the losses of one pawnshop, where fake jewellery was substituted for the diamond rings pledged, were covered by another hockshop, whose losses in turn were covered by the sale of Hungarian bonds. ('Putting capital in circulation', was Stavisky's description of this operation.) It sufficed that one of the playing cards be displaced for the entire structure to tumble down, which was what happened when an insurance company became suspicious of the 200 million francs worth of bonds issued by the Bayonne Crédit Municipal. In the ensuing débâcle, mayors, deputies, and government ministers could be seen scurrying for shelter.

Like Gregory, Stavisky was adept at getting eminent men to front for him. Retired generals, diplomatists, magistrates, senior civil servants with the rosette of the Légion d'Honneur in their button-holes, all served as window-dressing for the fraudulent schemes which Stavisky hatched in his offices in the Place Saint Georges. Shades of the Ambassador Club with its Major-General Seely and its Lord Southborough on the governing board.

The point about Gregory and Stavisky is that neither could have operated without protection from those in power. Stavisky found friends to cover up for him from the Police Judiciaire and the Parquet of Paris on up to and including French Cabinet ministers. Maundy Gregory's friends, as we have seen, were no less highly placed, included a Commissioner of Metropolitan Police at Scotland Yard as well as a one-time Lord Chancellor. Long after death or retirement had claimed his most powerful protectors Gregory continued to enjoy immunity from arrest, so strong was the aura of invincibility which he gave off. Quite simply, those in power were afraid to move against him.

Where the Gregory and Stavisky scandals differed was in the repercussions that they set up. In France *l'affaire Stavisky* brought down the Radical government of Camille Chautemps, precipitated the riots of February, 1934 in which a score were killed and hundreds injured as royalists and right-wing extremists tried to storm the Chamber of Deputies and were stopped by police. In England the political calm was disturbed by nothing more untoward than the Oxford Union voting by 275 to 153 'that this House will in no circumstances fight for its King and country'. ('There is no question but that the woozy-minded Communists, the practical jokers, and the sexual indeterminates of Oxford have scored a great success,' the *Daily Express* commented sourly.)

Stavisky left behind a trail of ruined reputations and wrecked careers. The dismembered body of Judge Albert Prince, who had shielded Stavisky, was found on the railroad tracks near Dijon. Another Paris magistrate took poison, while a director of one of Stavisky's companies cut his throat in the forest of Fontainebleau. In the case of Gregory there was a complete absence of Grand Guignol. A few of Gregory's friends left England hastily on winter cruises, but the majority remained. The death of Daniel Radcliffe, a Cardiff shipowner, may have been hastened by disclosures of honours-dealing at Gregory's trial. At any rate when Gregory's bankruptcy hearing opened Radcliffe's executors lost no time in putting in a claim for £12,789 which the Welsh shipowner had paid out to Gregory—could it have been in expectation of an honour? Again, Radcliffe, whose death certificate gives his age as 73, may simply have died of old age.

The difference in the English and French reactions lay, of course, in the political climates of the two countries. France in the early 1930s was undergoing one of its *crises de foi*, its confidence in parliamentary democracy having been undermined by unstable governments and by the poisons generated by *Action Française* and such anti-Semitic and right-wing leagues as *Jeunesses Patriotes* and *Solidarité Française*, the latter being financed by Coty the perfume king. The absence of any effective libel laws in France meant that public figures like Camille Chautemps and Paul Boncour could be tarred with the Stavisky brush with impunity. In England there was no political crisis. Mosley's black shirts had not yet made their appearance on the streets of London's East End. Strict British libel laws ensured that the names of those whose connection with Maundy Gregory was common knowledge in Whitehall were kept out of the press.

Decidedly the English ordered these things better. Instead of allowing the political scandal to spread until it permeated every phase of public life, which is what happened in France, the English policy was to contain it, or rather, to sweep it under the carpet.

*   *   *

At what time in the interval between February 16 and February 21, when his case was finally disposed of at the Bow Street police court, did Maundy Gregory decide to change his plea from Not Guilty to Guilty? Was it after Gregory had done his Nitti the Enforcer act, in what Gerald Macmillan describes as a 'final and successful attempt at raising money from the traffic in Honours'? Nitti, as students of the prohibition era in Chicago will recall, used to hang his commodious umbrella on the bar of the various Cook County saloons he visited and invite the saloon-keepers to drop their contributions within its folds. These were also the methods employed by Sacha Stavisky, who was more at home with *Jo-la-Terreur* and the pimps who hung around the Porte St Denis than he was with the swells whom he got to front for him in his various *sociétés anonymes*. But to the conventional shakedown technique Gregory added a few refinements of his own.

Among those whom Maundy Gregory visited in the interval between court appearances was Maj-Gen J. E. B. 'Jack' Seely (later first Baron Mottistone). Seely was entirely innocent of any wrong-doing where Gregory was concerned He was 'stupid rather than criminal', in Robert Rhodes James's words, his only fault being that he had supped too often at the Ambassador Club and in doing so had allowed his presence to be exploited by Gregory. 'Jack' Seely had gone one better and had agreed not only to serve on the club's governing committee, but to chair the Derby Dinners by means of which Gregory roped in the illustrious. An old Harrovian (at Harrow he was a contemporary of Stanley Baldwin), Seely had held high administrative office, fought gallantly in two wars, practised at the Bar, and for many years had served as coxswain for the Brooks lifeboat crew in the Isle of Wight. In other words, he was a man for all seasons, which made his friendship valuable to Gregory.

Seely's attitude towards Maundy Gregory in turn had always been slightly patronizing, as is indicated by the nickname 'Friday' which he gave to Gregory. 'If you want anything done, Friday is the man to see—he can produce miracles,' Seely was quoted as saying. Seely used to cite the occasion when Gregory, after a Derby Dinner, had laid on a Daimler to drive him all the way to Portsmouth so that he could enjoy a good night's sleep before addressing a conference there the following morning.

No longer the miracle-maker, it was a subdued Friday who called upon Seely late in February with a hard luck story. The Bow Street hearing, Gregory explained, could not have occurred at a worse time. Not to put too fine a point on it, it had caught him at a moment of acute financial embarrassment, and now he was faced with the inevitable bankruptcy. There was the future to consider as well. 'It's not myself I'm worried about, it's my 85-year-old mother,' Gregory piously declared. 'Her health is so delicate that she may not be able to stand the shock if I'm sent to prison.' (Gregory neglected to mention that his mother was living in an almshouse in Winchester.)

'I'm told that if I plead Guilty and throw myself on the mercy of the court I will be let off leniently,' Gregory pursued, changing his tack. 'But do you know, I'm so disgusted with the attitude of certain erstwhile friends that I've a good mind to let the Not Guilty plea stand and to take my chances in the witness box.' At this point Seely showed his distaste for the turn the interview had taken, according to my informant, but this did not deter Gregory, who hurried on: 'Some of those who now pretend that they never heard of me would look pretty foolish if I were to subpoena them, wouldn't they? It's no good their ducking out of town, for I have their cancelled cheques.' After this remark Seely showed Gregory the door.

Not exactly Nitti the Enforcer, but not far removed from that gangster's technique. Gerald Macmillan confirms that Gregory made a round of calls upon former clients. 'He told them that money was rather short just then,' Macmillan writes, 'and that if a "couple" could be found it would be very useful.' 'Many of his clients,' Macmillan adds, 'apparently thought £2,000 a very reasonable amount to pay to avoid having their names mentioned in court, for it is beyond question that he raised a very considerable sum of money by this means.'[1] Donald McCormick goes one better in writing that 'not one, but certainly five and possibly more people paid up this sum (£2,000) in the hope that their own names and those of their friends would be left unmentioned.'[2]

This was not, in fact, the way it was done. (Gregory would have laughed to scorn any settlement which let his clients off so lightly as £2,000 apiece.) Thanks to the unusually candid memoirs of Viscount Davidson, one-time chairman of the Conservative party, the *modus operandi* is now clear. 'Nobody knew to what extent Maundy Gregory would betray his past in his desperation and financial stringency,' Davidson declared in a tape-recorded conversation quoted by Robert Rhodes James.[3] 'We accordingly organized someone to go to see him, who told him that he couldn't avoid a term of imprisonment, but that if he kept silent we could bring pressure to bear on the authorities to let him live in France after his sentence had been served.' 'When this occurred,' Davidson continued, 'he [Gregory] was met at the prison gates by a friend of mine who drove him in a motor car to Dover, took him to France, ensconced him in previously arranged accommodation, gave him a sum of money and promised him a quarterly pension, on condition that he never disclosed his identity or made any reference to his past.'

Viscount Davidson's reminiscences have led some commentators to suppose that Gregory's remittance came from the Conservative Central Office. Thus Paul Johnson writes that Gregory was 'paid a quarterly pension from Tory funds as the price of silence'.[4] The truth was not quite so simple, according to my researches. Gregory was not paid by the Conservative party. The Conservative Central Office merely acted as 'honest broker', if one may use the term in this context, in bringing together a group of noble lords and

---

[1] *Op. cit.*
[2] *Op. cit.*
[3] Robert Rhodes James. *Memoirs of a Conservative.*
[4] Paul Johnson. *The Offshore Islanders.* London: Weidenfeld and Nicolson, 1972.

knights who had been Maundy Gregory's clients in the past, and who were prepared to underwrite Gregory's future in return for his silence.

The payments to Gregory were made through the liquor lobby at Westminster, which operated under the rather fanciful title of 'National Publicity Agency', and whose job it was to keep Members of Parliament 'sweet' on such questions as State purchase or nationalization of the liquor trade. It was perhaps fitting that Gregory should receive his stipend thus, as men with brewing interests figured prominently among those whom he had helped in their climb upwards into the 'Beerage', as it was sometimes called. The 'National Publicity Agency' had its offices at 3b Dean's Yard, Westminster Abbey, premises now occupied by the Westminster Choir School, all of which caused Maundy Gregory to quip that his remittance, like the quality of mercy, was twice bless'd. One cannot help but feel that the Official Receiver in Bankruptcy, not to mention Gregory's numerous creditors, would have been interested in these ex-gratia payments, had they but known about them.

As to the actual amount of Gregory's pension, Macmillan writes that he was offered £1,000 a year, but held out for £2,000 a year and got it. This sum tax free 'would have been a very reasonable income', Macmillan points out. In purchasing power it would have been the equivalent of £10,000 today, according to my research. Added to this was the fact that Gregory paid no rent on his Paris flat, which was leased for him by his protectors in London. A woman friend of mine who was living in Paris at the same time on an income of much less was able to keep a maid, to give small dinner parties, and otherwise to enjoy life without feeling the pinch.

Viscount Davidson likewise does not reveal that Gregory, although he was quite willing that his lips should be sealed for ever concerning his past, balked at the prospect of banishment to France. Gregory had rather fancied spending his declining years at some watering place like Bognor Regis or Worthing where he could stroll along the promenade with the retired Army colonels or sit on the clifftops gazing seawards, a forgotten lending library book in his lap. But when it was pointed out to him that he would be recognized wherever he went in England, and that he would be cut by these same colonels whose retreat he hoped to share, Gregory with some show of reluctance agreed to take up residence in France.

*   *   *

The Bow Street hearing, when it resumed on Tuesday, February 21, had all the spontaneity of a shotgun wedding. The chief figures showed obvious signs of strain. They were like certain actors who, having over-rehearsed, now appear to sleep-walk through their parts. The Attorney-General, Sir Thomas Inskip, in particular, appeared edgy. 'Inskip looked as though he were afraid that there would be a last-minute slip-up, that someone would say something that wasn't in the script,' recalls John Baker White, who was present in the courtroom. The Attorney-General need not have worried, however, for as soon as the Chief Magistrate was seated Norman Birkett announced that his client on counsel's advice wished to change his plea from Not Guilty to Guilty. 'I do not know whether the Attorney-General wishes to address you on this point,' Birkett added. Coming in on cue, Sir Thomas deferred to his junior, Eustace Fulton, to examine Chief Inspector Askew as to Gregory's character.

Alone of the main actors involved Chief Inspector Askew appeared to have been unaware that a deal was in the making.[1] In response to Fulton's question the detective said that Gregory had never been convicted of any offence before.

Fulton: Have the police had a number of complaints of a similar character to this one?
Askew: Yes.
Fulton: I don't propose to carry it any farther than that.
Chief Magistrate: I don't know exactly what that means.
Fulton: (to Inspector Askew) Have a number of people paid, or been asked to pay, money to Gregory in connection with the receiving of honours?
Askew: Similar transactions.

[1] Commenting on the case nearly forty years later, ex-Superintendent Askew (the grade in which he retired at Scotland Yard) complained to me of being gagged. 'I had uncovered a lot more concerning Maundy Gregory but I was not allowed to make any allusion to this other evidence,' he said.

In rebuttal, Birkett maintained that if these further complaints had been investigated Maundy Gregory would have been able to supply satisfactory explanations. The prosecution's object, he went on, had been achieved inasmuch as Gregory's activities in the honours field were now at an end. Birkett hoped therefore that in 'the difficult circumstances of this case—it was difficult to do justice to Gregory and not to do injustice elsewhere—' the Chief Magistrate would be content with imposing a fine.

In commenting on the evidence, the Chief Magistrate said that the offence was 'doubly mischievous', in that 'anyone who committed an offence under this Act endeavoured to induce some other person to commit a criminal offence'. 'In my opinion the maximum fine of £50 would be wholly inadequate to meet the facts of this case,' Graham-Campbell continued. 'But as this is the first case under the Act I do not propose to impose the maximum penalty allowed by the law to a court of summary jurisdiction.' Thereupon the Chief Magistrate sentenced Gregory to two months imprisonment in the second division, plus a £50 fine and 50 guineas costs.[1]

Judging from the editorial comment the national press seemed as anxious as the Attorney-General to bury the honours case as quickly and as quietly as possible. Typical was the *Daily Telegraph*'s leader headed 'A Salutary Warning', which, after rebuking Gregory for his 'impudence', went on to say: 'There is nothing to show that Gregory really was in touch with any person, official or otherwise, who could exercise the slightest influence in procuring the bestowal of an honour.' The *Daily Sketch* wasn't so sure. Referring to the 'similar transactions' mentioned by Chief Inspector Askew, the *Sketch* declared that 'had these cases been gone into the names of many prominent persons, titled or otherwise, would have been introduced . . . the money involved in the allegations would have amounted to hundreds of thousands of pounds.'

[1] Under the Prison Act of 1898 convicts not sentenced to hard labour were divided into three divisions, the first being composed of 'political prisoners, including those convicted of sedition or seditious libel'. The second division corresponded to Star Class prisoners today—i.e. those considered to be of good character. As Maundy Gregory saw it, second division imprisonment 'is not a blot on your escutcheon; it does not deprive one of any civil rights or title or orders'. (Interview with a *Daily Express* reporter, July 20, 1933.) The whole system of 'divisions' was abolished in 1948.

The following day Candidus, the *Daily Sketch* columnist, joined the fray, pointing out certain 'unsatisfactory features in the trial'. 'It would have been more completely reassuring,' Candidus wrote, 'if it had been proved that Gregory never had any sort of authority, direct or implied, to negotiate, or if he ever had, when so scandalous a connection existed and when it ceased.'

    *   *   *

Sacha Stavisky, of course, was never brought to trial for his swindles. In January, 1934, he was traced by agents of the Sûreté Générale to the ski resort of Chamonix in the Haute Savoie. When the agents broke into the villa where he was hiding they found Sacha dying from gunshot wounds in the head, according to the official version. He was '*suicidé*' according to the Socialist daily *Le Populaire*, which thus enriched the French language with a new verb.

Stavisky's 'suicide' was followed by scenes of wild disorder in the Chamber of Deputies, culminating in the resignation of Camille Chautemps' government. The sentencing of Maundy Gregory was met by deafening silence in the House of Commons. The only reference to *l'affaire Gregory* in the Commons occurred when Frederick Seymour Cocks, Labour Member for the Broxtowe Division of Nottinghamshire, questioned the Home Secretary concerning those 'other complaints of a similar nature' that had been lodged against Gregory. The Home Secretary, Sir John Gilmour, replied that the complaints extended over a period of three years. They had been investigated by police 'but no sufficient evidence had been obtained to justify criminal proceedings'. This brought forth a witty riposte from Cocks. 'Were those complaints from people who paid money and did not receive a title, or were they about people who, having received a title, have not paid?' Thus what might have developed into a political scandal of Watergate proportions ended not with a bang but a giggle.

Maundy Gregory served his sentence at Wormwood Scrubs Prison in London, where he was assigned to light work in the library. He was released at 7 a.m., Wednesday, April 12, 1933, having earned full remission of sentence for good conduct. Viscount Davidson, it will be recalled, claimed that Gregory 'was met at the prison gates by a friend of mine who drove him in a motor car to Dover'. That friend was Captain Richard C. Kelly, Irish Catholic, sportsman, future O.B.E., and self-appointed guardian angel to Maundy Gregory for the remainder of the latter's life. Just how Captain Kelly came to be involved in Gregory's affairs is as mysterious today as it was in 1933. Was Captain Kelly acting in his capacity as secretary of the National Publicity Agency, which represented the interests of the brewing industry at Westminster? Or had he been asked by one of the branches of the British Secret Services to keep an eye on Gregory while the latter was in exile? (As an active member of the Economic Study Clubs, later known as National Propaganda, Captain Kelly had engaged in some 'hush-hush' work in investigating left-wing subversion in industry.) Or was the Captain acting out of the pure goodness of his heart? (That Kelly had enjoyed Gregory's hospitality at the Ambassador Club is attested by the fact that his name appears as a guest at the 1931 Derby Dinner.) The mystery deepened when I wrote to the captain's son, Denis Kelly. 'I am sorry for the puzzlement you feel,' the son replied, 'as the explanation is a perfectly simple and innocent one . . . Unfortunately, this explanation is one that I am not empowered to disclose to you . . .' Whatever the explanation, Captain Kelly was to take Gregory in hand, install him in an apartment near the British Embassy in Paris, and to look after all of his wants, paying him frequent visits both in Paris and in Dieppe.

To return to the morning of April 12, the only glimpse that press photographers caught of Gregory was of his burly back as he climbed into a waiting taxicab with the bowler-hatted Kelly. For the next twenty minutes the ever-faithful Tom Bramley drove like a fiend in a successful bid to shake off pursuing reporters. He then deposited his passengers at a house in Kensington, where Captain Kelly offered Gregory a hearty breakfast of ham and eggs, according to Kelly's widow, whom I talked to at her home in Hove. That night the Captain drove Gregory to Newhaven—not to Dover, as Viscount Davidson supposed—where both men boarded the ferry for Dieppe. Gregory's choice of the poor man's route to France was not dictated by lack of money, but by fear of encountering former acquaintances among the throng of Britons who, encouraged by the promise of fine weather, had started their Easter week-end early.

In Paris Gregory registered at the Hötel Lotti in the Rue de

Castiglione as 'Peter Michael', one of the many changes he was to ring on his given names. It was as well that he went to ground under an alias when he did, for barely a fortnight after his arrival in Paris, Gregory's name was in the headlines again, this time in even bigger and bolder type. Earlier there had been a hint of the coming storm when the *Daily Sketch* appeared on February 23, 1933 with the headlines:

POLICE AND WOMAN'S DEATH SECRET

Composer's Wife Who died in the House of J. Maundy Gregory, Defendant in the Sensational Honours Case

HER £18,000 WILL

The accompanying article contained little that was sensational except that Ethel Davies had been to the police and had made a statement covering sixty foolscap pages concerning the mysterious death of her aunt. Undoubtedly it was the headline linking his name with that mysterious death that had alarmed Gregory. Through his solicitor Gregory, who was then behind bars, had promptly brought suit for libel against the *Daily Sketch* and had obtained an *ex parte* injunction to prevent further publication of the matter. But he could not enjoin Scotland Yard from probing Edith Rosse's death. The delayed storm was now to break with full fury over Gregory's head.

XV

A Watery Grave

The cemetery of Bisham (pop. 997), a Thames-side village near Marlow, lies behind the 12th-century flintstone church of All Saints, and overlooks the river. In fact it is so close to the river that it has been known to flood in winter when the Thames is in spate. Shortly before dusk on Friday, April 28, 1933, this cemetery was invaded by a motley crew which included grave-diggers and stone masons in overalls, bowler-hatted detectives, and uniformed officers of the Berkshire Constabulary, the latter mounting guard at the cemetery gates to keep out curiosity-seekers. Prominent among the officialdom present was Chief Inspector Askew, who earlier in the day had obtained an order from the Home Office authorizing the exhumation of Edith Rosse's remains.

It was Askew who bent down to examine the withered wreath of arum lilies on Mrs Rosse's grave attached to which was a card reading, 'A happy Easter to dearest Marion, situated in so radiant surroundings.—Jim, O.P.N.' ('Jim', of course, had been Edith Rosse's special name for Gregory. The O.P.N. could just conceivably stand for 'Ordo Pio Nono', the Noble Order of Pius IX of which Gregory was still Knight Commander. As for Gregory himself, although he had slipped across to the continent four days before Easter, before leaving he could easily have arranged with a florist to deliver the wreath.) The workmen paid scant attention to this nosegay, now brown and rank with decay. Nor did they appear to be interested in the inscription on the six-foot marble cross which they removed as a preliminary to opening the grave itself. 'In love and remembrance of Edith Marion Rosse (Milady)', it read in part, and beneath this was incised the mournful message from the Apocalypse of St John the Divine VII: 16–17 beginning, 'They shall hunger no more, neither thirst any more; neither shall the sun light on them nor any heat'.[1]

---

[1] Although there is no indication that Edith Rosse had followed him into the Church of Rome, Gregory has used the Roman Catholic translation of the Vulgate.

A canvas screen was then placed around the grave, and for the next hour the predominant sound was that of the grave-diggers' spades as they thudded into the rich Berkshire loam. The grave-diggers could have made short work of it—Mrs Rosse's grave was remarkably shallow, the top of her coffin being barely 18 inches below ground level—had they not been stopped from time to time by Dr Roche Lynch, the Home Office pathologist, who took samples of the soil, and samples of the water that had accumulated in a pool at the river end of the grave. These samples were placed in glass jars, which were sealed and labelled for removal to the Home Office forensic laboratory.

Finally, a big tripod with chains and pulley attached was erected over the open grave. Several attempts to raise the coffin were made before it rose to the surface perfectly balanced. As it did so a *Daily Mail* reporter noted that 'large quantities of water' were running from it. Also present was Percy Hoskins of the *Daily Express* who tells me that the coffin was leaking like a sieve. It was Hoskins who overheard Dr Roche Lynch mutter to his assistant, 'Not a chance—not a bleeding chance.'

*   *   *

For reasons which presently will become apparent, the post-mortem examination of Mrs Rosse's remains was one of the longest and most thorough on record, stretching over a period of three months. The inquest, which opened briefly the day after the exhumation to permit identification of the body, had to be adjourned three times in order to give the forensic experts more time to complete their tests, causing the *Daily Telegraph* to comment on June 23, 'Mrs Rosse's death is providing one of the most mysterious cases that has ever been brought before a coroner's court.'

The delays gave Maundy Gregory a bad case of jitters, but they also gave him time to prepare himself for the ordeal to come. According to those who knew him in Paris at this date Gregory used to inveigle his friends into taking part in a mock trial in which he was the defendant charged with the murder of Edith Rosse. Rearranging the furniture slightly he would pretend that his tiny room at the Lotti was Courtroom Number One at the Old Bailey. He would then persuade a friend to assume the role of the Crown prosecutor while Gregory, himself, played not only the accused, but Judge, defence counsel, and jury, in turn. Shades of 'The Brixton Burglary', in which he had toured the provinces as a stage-struck youth. But this was more than a theatrical performance; it was Maundy Gregory's own Do-It-Yourself Courtroom Survival Kit. Obviously he expected to be extradited to England to stand trial for murder.

*   *   *

On July 19, the morning the inquest finally was resumed, the *Daily Express* scooped its Fleet Street rivals under the front-page headlines:

MAUNDY GREGORY TELLS THE WHOLE STORY

Disclosures to the 'Daily Express' In a Paris Hotel Suite

Life & Death of Mrs Rosse

'My Dear Sweet Friend'

Drama at her Bedside

Will Pencilled on a Menu

Percy Hoskins, the *Express*'s ace crime reporter, had been assigned to play Stanley to Gregory's Livingstone, and had managed to discover the fugitive's whereabouts in the wilds of the first arrondissement in Paris. 'Gregory was astonished when he found I had tracked him down,' Hoskins reported, adding, 'It was a long time before he could bring himself to talk freely.'[1] Gregory, who smoked cigars during the interview, told Hoskins why he had no intention of returning to England for the Rosse inquest. Not only was his presence unnecessary, but he was not in the best of

[1] Hoskins obviously forgot that Gregory had been 'tracked down' earlier by another *Express* reporter, to whom he talked 'with engaging candour about a lifetime devoted to secret intrigue in high diplomacy', whatever that may mean.

health ('My digestion has not been the same since my stay in Wormwood Scrubs'). In the by-line article which Hoskins helped Gregory to write the latter breathed defiance against those who would pry too closely into his affairs. 'It is not I who have anything to fear from the truth being told,' Gregory protested, 'and I shall take strong action if necessary to defend myself against accusations or insinuations that there was anything disgraceful about my association with Mrs Rosse.' Was Gregory's veiled threat of libel action made for the purpose of discouraging other reporters from pursuing him, one wonders? He revealed that he had given to his lawyers 'to use in whatever way they think best' a 14-page statement in writing concerning his friendship with Mrs Rosse and the circumstances of her death. 'I should like my statement to be read in open court,' he added. Gregory concluded with a tribute to Edith Rosse. 'Her friendship,' he declared, 'was the greatest and sweetest thing in my life, and I will allow no one to sully the memory of it.'

Percy Hoskins told me that he obtained Gregory's Paris address from Peter Mazzina, who obviously had cleared the interview with Gregory beforehand. Hoskins also told me that Mazzina had utilized this occasion to try to sell Gregory's memoirs to the *Daily Express*. The proposition was a tempting one—Gregory's memoirs if candidly written would have been the press sensation of the decade—but the *Express* turned it down. 'Quite frankly it smacked too much of blackmail,' Hoskins explained. 'All that Gregory wanted was a letter of agreement from the *Express* to be brandished under the noses of former clients in order to extract money from them.'

*   *   *

Just as the 'Maundy Tells All' scoop of the *Daily Express* dominated the newspaper hoardings on Wednesday, July 19, so did Gregory *in absentia* dominate the proceedings when the Rosse inquest resumed later that morning at the Paddington Coroner's Court. It was like *Hamlet* without the Prince of Denmark; nevertheless Mr Ingleby Oddie, the coroner, who was sitting in this case without a jury, seemed unconcerned with the absence of the principal actor.

At one point Laurence Vine, who represented Ethel Davies and Mrs Rosse's brother, Frederick Davies, asked that the inquest be adjourned in order to compel Gregory's attendance. There were certain questions he desired to put to Gregory on behalf of Mrs Rosse's relatives, Vine contended. If necessary there were 'means of compelling a witness to attend', he added grimly. Chief Inspector Askew in the witness box agreed with Vine that Gregory was a 'very important witness'. He had tried to serve a subpoena on Gregory, but had been forced to leave it with Gregory's solicitor, the detective explained.

In opposing the motion to adjourn the inquest, Walter Frampton, appearing for Gregory, took occasion to remind the coroner of Gregory's libel action against the *Daily Sketch* which was pending in the High Court. Frampton then accused Vine of desiring to conduct a fishing expedition at Gregory's expense in order to elicit information from the latter that might be useful to the defendants of this libel action. It was a masterful stroke, and it brought Vine to his feet protesting, 'This is news to me . . . I have nothing to do with a libel action.' 'It is little short of nonsense,' he went on, 'to suggest that Mr Maundy Gregory, if he is only in Paris, could not be here at 10.30 tomorrow morning . . . This inquiry should be concluded properly, and to do so it is necessary that a very important witness should be here.' But the coroner thought otherwise, and refused the motion to adjourn.

Eleven witnesses in all testified at the inquest, including Sir Bernard Spilsbury, the forensic expert, whose testimony had sent more than one murderer to the gallows, and Dr Roche Lynch, the Home Office's painstaking analyst. One of the first witnesses to be called, Mrs Lottie Eyres, who had been Mrs Rosse's housekeeper since 1931, gave a detailed account of Mrs Rosse's illness from its onset on August 19 until her death nearly a month later, events covered in an earlier chapter. The coroner questioned her about the first series of visits Dr Plummer had paid Mrs Rosse.

Coroner: Was she in bed all this time?—Yes.
—What sort of symptoms did she have?—There was no diarrhoea and no vomiting.
—Did she remain clear in the head?—No, not all the time.
—Was Mrs Rosse a temperate woman?—No, she was not.

The housekeeper then touched on Mrs Rosse's relations with Ethel Davies, disclosing the fact that Mrs Rosse had stopped the latter's allowance of thirty shillings a week before she was taken ill.

Mr Vine: Was Miss Davies told about this illness—No.
—Was any other relative told about it?—No.
Mr Frampton: Was this niece Miss Davies a source of great trouble to Mrs Rosse?—Yes.
—For a considerable period before her death?—Yes.
—Long before August 19 had she refused to see her niece?—Yes.
—Had she also refused to make any allowance to her unless she stayed in a hostel of which she approved?—Quite right.

Mrs Kate Wells, of Drummond Street, Euston, identified herself as Maundy Gregory's housekeeper, said that she knew that Gregory and Mrs Rosse told people they were brother and sister. Mrs Wells then testified that earlier she had been sent to a lumber room upstairs, which was kept locked, and saw some chemicals there. She did not know what they were used for, nor did she take much notice of them.

Coroner: Were they in a box?—In boxes.
—Bottles, tubes and chemicals of various sorts?—Yes.
Mr Vine: Did you notice if any were marked 'Poison'?—No, I did not look that much.

On behalf of his client Mr Frampton objected to this line of questioning, which he described as improper.

Dr E. Curnow Plummer told how he had been called in on August 19 to treat Mrs Rosse, who appeared to have been overcome by the heat, and how he had prescribed for her accordingly. Questioned about Mrs Rosse's will, the doctor said that it was a perfectly genuine one, dictated in his hearing, and signed in his presence. It was he who had suggested that Mrs Rosse sign the will a second time as her first signature had obscured one of the words. At the time her mind was perfectly normal.

Coroner: Did you at any time suspect that anything had been administered to your patient in the way of poison?—No.
—But there was vomiting and diarrhoea?—Yes.

[205]

—Did you not think that they might have been caused by other than food or natural causes?—No.

Mr Vine: The terms of the will you witnessed did not arouse your suspicions in the least?—No, not the least.

—You treated the relatives with rather scant courtesy in this matter, did you not? Did you give them any information?—No, I think not, except to say that I was perfectly satisfied about the cause of death.

—Why not? The relatives were suspicious?—I did not know what their standing was in the matter. I was given to understand that Mrs Rosse wished to have no more meetings with them. It is not usual to discuss a case with strangers.

—Did you know that one of the relatives had been in receipt of an allowance of 30 shilling a week from Mrs Rosse up to within a few days of her death?—I did not know that, but Mr Gregory told me that she had extreme worry and trouble with her niece.

—Did you know the brother was in close touch with Mrs Rosse?—No.

The coroner likewise questioned Dr Plummer concerning the latter's cavalier treatment of Mrs Rosse's relatives.

Coroner: Were you not rather rude to Mr Davies when he called to see you?—I was a busy man. It was after Mrs Rosse's death, and Mr Gregory told me he had had a great deal of trouble with them . . . Under these conditions I think it is a matter of general principle among the medical profession not to impart information without the authority of the representatives of the deceased.

—The only representative was the brother?—I regarded Mr Gregory as the natural representative.

—He was no relation. You knew that?—I knew that.

—Was there any reason why you did not just tell Mr Davies the cause of death so that he would have nothing to worry about?—I listened to what he had to say. I did not immediately show him the door.

—He says you declined to give him information, mentioned something about professional secrecy, and said, 'Here is the door.' Perhaps you got a bit irritable?—Possibly.

Called as a witness, Benjamin Pengelly identified himself as an accountant, said that he had known Maundy Gregory and Mrs

Rosse since 1921, and that he had looked after their financial affairs. Pengelly was questioned about an earlier will of Mrs Rosse.

Coroner: Did you know anything about a will that Mrs Rosse made in 1928?—I saw the will, but I did not know its contents.
—Did you know what it was about and who were to be the beneficiaries?—Yes, Miss Ethel Davies. Mrs Rosse told me that she would remember me on account of my services.
—What about Mr Maundy Gregory?—He was not mentioned.
—What became of that will?—It was eventually destroyed.
—Why?—Mrs Rosse said that Mr Maundy Gregory persuaded her to tear up the will and destroy it on account of the niece giving so much trouble.

On behalf of the relatives, Laurence Vine then took over the questioning, eliciting answers from Pengelly which indicated that the latter was ill-disposed towards Gregory, to put it mildly.

Vine: You said that Maundy Gregory was owing several thousands of pounds on August 19, the day Mrs Rosse was taken ill. Were creditors pressing him very hard?—Yes.
—Just before August 19?—Yes.
—Did he press Mrs Rosse for financial assistance?—Yes he did, according to Mrs Rosse's story to me.
—When?—Before July in 1932.
—After Mrs Rosse's death did you go through her books?—Yes.
—And were they in good order?—Yes.
—Did you find that apparently several pages of one had been cut out of the book?

Before Pengelly could answer Gregory's counsel objected to the question, and it was reframed.

—Where were her books kept?—At Hyde Park Terrace, in a bureau.
—They were all in order?—Yes, with the exception of one sent to me with a lot of pages cut out of it.
—That was what I was asking you about. The pass book was in order?—Yes.

Frampton: You have known both people since 1921?—Yes.
—During that period, I am cutting out 1932, was Mr Maundy Gregory a wealthy man?—Yes.
—Did you know that from time to time he purchased properties for Mrs Rosse?—In Mrs Rosse's name.
—You knew substantially all that she had had really come from Mr Maundy Gregory?—I did not.

The star turn at the inquest was Sir Bernard Spilsbury, pathologist, whose plump, pink face gave him the look of a prosperous farmer as he took the witness stand. For nearly a quarter of a century Sir Bernard had reigned supreme in his chosen field of medicine, ever since his identification of a scar on a minute piece of skin had helped to send Dr Crippen to the gallows. As crime writer Edgar Lustgarten remarks, 'To the man in the street he [Spilsbury] stood for pathology as Hobbs stood for cricket or Dempsey for boxing or Capablanca for chess. His pronouncements were invested with the force of dogma, and it was blasphemy to hint that he might conceivably be wrong.'[1]

Spilsbury had, in fact, appeared as Crown witness at nearly every important murder trial during the past quarter of a century including the celebrated 'Brides in the Bath' case, in which his thoroughness nearly resulted in a fatality. It was Spilsbury's theory—later proved—that George Joseph Smith had murdered his brides in their baths simply by grabbing their legs and tipping his victims backwards until their heads were immersed, thus making it appear that they had drowned while having a heart attack. To test his theory, he tried out the experiment on a nurse who, to the pathologist's horror, came close to dying from shock. Spilsbury's meticulousness had, in fact, come in for criticism in a different context from Coroner Ingleby Oddie, who suggested that his post-mortem examinations frequently were more detailed than the facts in a given case warranted. 'He was not satisfied till he had examined every organ,' Oddie complained; '. . . he would cheerfully sit up into the small hours looking at frozen sections prepared by himself . . .' Spilsbury's findings often were 'not really material, except as a scientific exercise,' he added.[2]

[1] Edgar Lustgarten. *Verdict in Dispute.* London: Allan Wingate, 1949.
[2] Douglas G. Browne and E. V. Tullett. *Bernard Spilsbury: His Life and Cases.* London: George G. Harrap & Co. Ltd., 1951.

Concerning Spilsbury's testimony at the Rosse inquest, Coroner Oddie could have found nothing to quibble about. Sir Bernard's replies were succinct to the point of being cryptic. He did, however, provide one minor sensation when in the witness box he flatly contradicted Dr Plummer's testimony as to the cause of Mrs Rosse's death.

Coroner: Could you say whether there had been any haemorrhage of the brain?—There had not.
—Were there any signs of Bright's disease?—No.
—Is it a fact that the death certificate is quite wrong?—Yes.

But if the death certificate was wrong, neither Sir Bernard Spilsbury nor Dr Roche Lynch, the Home Office analyst who followed in the witness box, could say what was the cause of Mrs Rosse's death, for reasons which became apparent in Dr Lynch's testimony.

Coroner: How deep was the grave in which Mrs Rosse was buried?—The top of the coffin was about 18 inches below the ground level.
—That is very shallow?—Yes, I have never seen one so shallow.

Dr Lynch said that as a result of the churchyard having been flooded by the Thames the body had been immersed in water for some months, and that there had been water in the coffin when it was brought to the surface. Upon analysing the organs he could find no trace of any poison or noxious substance. 'In view of the time that elapsed since death and the condition to which the body had been subjected,' he added, 'it is quite possible that certain poisons could have become decomposed, thus rendering their detection impossible.'

Coroner: Are there poisons which might have produced symptoms or signs similar to those Mrs Rosse suffered from?—Yes.
—Is it a well-known fact that after prolonged exposure certain poisons do decompose?—Yes.
Vine: Did the presence of water render your examination more difficult?—Not more difficult, but there is the possibility that owing to conditions there may have been poisons which had decomposed.

Frampton: You examined for poisons?—Yes.
—You found none?—None.
—Anything else is speculation?—Yes.

After refusing a motion to adjourn the inquest until Maundy
Gregory could be produced as a material witness, the coroner declared that there was only one verdict that could be recorded, and
that was an open verdict. Edith Marion Rosse had died September 14, 1932, of causes unknown. 'I am certain that a more careful
analysis has never been made than that in this case,' the coroner
added. 'The result is a negative one. I do not wish to emphasize
the point which has been mentioned that certain drugs do decompose when exposed, or when they have been buried in soil water-
logged or otherwise. All I will say is that no poison has been found,
and no poison will ever be found in this body. Therefore, no possible charge could arise out of this enquiry.'

*   *   *

Coroner Ingleby Oddie may have thought that by rendering
an open verdict he had disposed of the mystery of Mrs Rosse's
death once and for all. In reality, he had presided at the birth of a
legend, for Mrs Rosse's death has haunted the imaginations of not
a few students of crime. This was true particularly while Maundy
Gregory was alive. He could go nowhere—nowhere at least where
Englishmen congregated—without being pointed out as a 'wife-
poisoner'. Not the least curious part of the legend is how Edith
Rosse was transformed into Gregory's wife in the telling of it.
Novelist Evelyn Waugh, for example, made this mistake.

Waugh used to dine out on the story of how Maundy Gregory
murdered his 'wife' by 'administering strong doses of arsenic', and
of his frantic efforts to remove the traces by burying Edith Rosse
in a watery grave.[1] (That the story should have appealed to Waugh
is not surprising, in view of his liking for the macabre. Indeed he
told it with 'a slight gurgle in his voice', according to his biographer
Mrs Donaldson. Possibly he contemplated using it in a novel.)
According to the novelist, Gregory 'propped his dead wife beside
him in his sports car and drove round the graveyards bordering the

[1] Frances Donaldson tells the story in her *Evelyn Waugh: Portrait of a
Country Neighbour*. London: Weidenfeld and Nicolson, 1967.

Thames until he found one that was known to become submerged in winter. Here he interviewed the vicar [who] . . . agreed to bury Mrs Gregory but asked which undertakers he should consult about the committal. Maundy Gregory then replied that it so happened his wife was with him in the car outside, and suggested the vicar should take over all arrangements.' Waugh need not have embroidered truth in this eldritch fashion—the reality was every bit as bizarre as anything he invented.

I have saved until the last a reconstruction of events on the day of Mrs Rosse's death (she died shortly after midnight, it will be recalled) as warranting more detailed consideration. Mention was made earlier of Gregory keeping a luncheon appointment with the King of Greece ('I felt that no good purpose would be served by postponing it'). It was after lunch that Gregory and his chauffeur Tom Bramley set out on what must surely rate as one of the strangest odysseys on record. In the taxicab which Gregory used as his private motor car they combed the Thames Valley looking for a suitable resting place for Mrs Rosse's remains. Gregory had only the haziest idea as to what constituted a suitable resting place, except for one thing: it must be near the Thames river. ('Milady' had expressed the wish to be buried by the river where she had spent some of her happiest days, Gregory was to insist until his dying day.)

First stop on this weird hegira was Whitchurch (pop. 895), a riverside village on the Oxfordshire–Berkshire border, where Gregory was told by the vicar that the graveyard was reserved for local inhabitants. The taxi then drove east through Reading, following the loop of the river to Henley-on-Thames, scene of gay summer regattas where Gregory had played host to Edith Rosse and their friends. But here the burial regulations were the same: only parishioners could be buried within the precincts of the churchyard. They drove on to Marlow, only to be given the same dusty answer. As the afternoon wore on Gregory's spirits became increasingly depressed until by the time the taxi rolled into Bisham on the Berkshire side of the river and pulled up in front of its 12th-century church of All Saints his mood was one of desperation.

That morning, in making the funeral arrangements with Harrods, Gregory had fixed the date of Mrs Rosse's interment as Saturday, September 17. After selecting a wooden coffin with a lead shell, Gregory instructed the undertaker, Walter Mann, that the coffin should not be sealed, but should be left with the lid resting on it. The usual practice of soldering the coffin was 'too drastic', Gregory explained. Gregory also requested that the grave should be as shallow as possible ('I did not like to think there should be a great weight of earth over poor Mrs Rosse,' he explained later). With the funeral only three days off, the location of a burial plot for Mrs Rosse had become a matter of extreme urgency by the time Gregory knocked on the vicarage door.

This time Gregory was in luck, the Reverend Owen Williams, vicar of All Saints, proving to be unexpectedly sympathetic. Gregory explained to the cleric Mrs Rosse's strange request that she be buried by the river where she had spent so many happy hours. As her friend, Gregory said that he was prepared to subscribe one hundred guineas to any charity that the Reverend Mr Williams cared to mention if Mrs Rosse's wish could be granted. The vicar said that he had no objection, but that the final decision rested with the churchwarden. 'He proved to be a butler,' Gregory later recalled. 'I drove to his home, and found that he was attending a whist drive at the village institute.' So nothing would do but that Gregory should rout the butler-cum-churchwarden out of the whist drive and obtain his consent, which the latter gave readily after hearing about the *douceur* which Gregory had attached to his strange request.

*   *   *

Gregory's mad chase up and down the Thames Valley was barely touched upon at the coroner's inquest, Walter Mann, the undertaker, skimmed over it in his testimony. Nor was this the only respect in which the inquest proved unsatisfactory. Key witnesses were not called to testify, promising lines of enquiry were not followed up. In fact, the inquest raised more questions than it answered.

To take but one example, Mrs Rosse in the midst of her illness was stricken by near blindness. Yet this all-important matter was never gone into by the coroner either in his questioning of Dr Plummer or of Dr George Blair, both of whom had attended Mrs Rosse. Mrs Eyres, however, had made a pointed reference to Mrs Rosse's troubled eyesight which could not have escaped the coroner's notice. After telling how Mrs Rosse had felt well enough on

September 1 to go for a drive with Gregory, the housekeeper declared, 'She came back from that drive complaining that she could hardly see.' Alkaloid, or plant, poisons such as morphine affect the eyesight; hence the condition of the eyes, whether pupils are contracted or expanded, becomes an important indication of the presence of such poisons in the body.

Independent confirmation of Mrs Rosse's eye affliction was forthcoming when I interviewed Leila MacKinlay, whose mother Dagny was Mrs Rosse's closest friend.

—Was your mother in contact with Mrs Rosse during her illness?—My mother talked to her on the telephone shortly before Mrs Rosse died. Mrs Rosse had to break off the conversation, saying she was about to be ill.

—You also mentioned that Mrs Rosse's eyes had been troubling her?—That's what Mrs Rosse said. She was wearing dark glasses when my mother went to see her. Then on the phone she complained to my mother that there was something off-colour with her sight.

—Did your mother see her again?—No, whether Gregory said that she was too ill to have visitors or not, I don't know.

Chief Inspector Askew must certainly have seen Mrs MacKinlay, as Mrs Rosse's closest friend, and have taken a statement from her. Mrs MacKinlay's evidence, therefore, was available. Why wasn't she called as an inquest witness?

Another who might have thrown light upon the proceedings was Ethel Davies. As early as February, it will be recalled, Miss Davies had been to Scotland Yard to see detectives about her aunt's death. It had taken her three days to make her statement, which in the end filled nearly sixty·foolscap pages. Whatever happened to those sixty foolscap pages, one wonders? If Miss Davies had been called it would have given the coroner the opportunity to assess how much, if any, spite had been the motive force behind the exhumation proceedings. He would have been able to question Miss Davies about the quarrels with her aunt, and about the 1928 will naming Ethel as chief beneficiary, which was destroyed. Ethel's testimony might have cleared up the question whether or not she was Mrs Rosse's natural daughter, which would explain her stormy relationship with the latter. That justice must not only be done, but be seen to be done is the cornerstone of English law, and this applies to an inquest in the coroner's court as well as to proceedings before the High Court of Justice.

The mind keeps returning to Gregory's frantic search for a Thames-side burial spot. If Mrs Rosse had really expressed a wish to be buried by the river, as Gregory maintained, why did he not try the parish church of St Nicholas at Thames Ditton? Here there would have been no question concerning Mrs Rosse's eligibility for burial; since 1910 she had been the lessee of the 'Vanity Fair' bungalow on Ditton Island, where she and Gregory spent most of their week-ends boating during the summer. So technically she qualified as a resident. Moreover there would have been ample room in the churchyard to accommodate Mrs Rosse's remains, as I have ascertained by personal inspection. Possibly the answer is that the St Nicholas churchyard lies back several hundred yards from the river.

Speaking of Ditton Island, Gregory's long occupancy of 'Vanity Fair' had made him thoroughly familiar with the Thames in spate, a point which appears to have been overlooked by all who have commented on his strange burial instructions for Mrs Rosse. 'Vanity Fair', like every other house on the island, had been flooded badly in 1928 and again in 1930. In particular the flood of January 7, 1928, which caused the death of fourteen Londoners trapped in basement rooms, had hit Ditton Island hard, the dirty river water slopping over the raised doorsills to stand several feet deep in every house. Across the river at Hampton Court the Tudor moat of Cardinal Wolsey's palace was flooded as was the Hurst Park racetrack. A group of revellers returning home at midnight from a ball at York House, Twickenham, found themselves cut off by the Thames near Richmond Bridge, where the river had overflowed its banks.

I have visited Mrs Rosse's grave which is located a few feet from the banks of the Thames in Bisham churchyard. The day I visited, which was in January, the Thames was high, perhaps 4 feet from the level of the cemetery, but nowhere near flood level, which usually occurs in March when the river spills over into the water meadows on the opposite side. Not since the great flood of 1894, when the water reached the church pulpit, has the river actually flooded the graveyard, I was told by the sexton. What happens, I was told, is that the water seeps through the gravel bank, rises and falls with the tides by capillary action, so to speak. The result is a continuous flushing action.

*　　*　　*

Did Maundy Gregory murder Edith Rosse? No cause of death having been ascertained, the coroner's open verdict at Mrs Rosse's inquest was the only possible one. No trace of poison was found in her body, but in this regard the testimony of Dr Roche Lynch is worth recalling. 'In view of the time that elapsed since death and the condition to which the body had been subjected,' Dr Lynch declared, 'it is quite possible that certain poisons could have become decomposed, thus rendering their detection impossible.' No doubt the type of poison Dr Lynch had in mind was an alkaloid extracted from a plant, which attacks the central nervous system, but which is difficult to detect. Aconitine is such a plant poison, and no sure method of detecting it has yet been devised. Digitalin, extracted from foxglove, is another poison which decomposes so rapidly it is almost impossible to detect. In this connection, Mrs. Maisie Saunders' story about her lunch with Gregory at the Ritz, when he boasted to her that he had obtained some curare, is worth recalling.

The motive for murder—inheritance of Mrs Rosse's £18,000 estate—was certainly present. Indeed, it could be described as a compelling one, in view of Maundy Gregory's dire financial circumstances. In this connection, Gregory's by-line article in the *Daily Express* is worth quoting. 'I had a shock,' he wrote, 'when I went through her papers. "Why! Goodness gracious," I said, "the little lady must have been holding out on me. There must be quite £6,000 here!" I looked through more of her papers and found another £1,000 here and another £1,000 there, until the sum total mounted up to £18,000 odd. I was never more astonished in my life.' This is Gregorian humbug at its worst. Thanks to the fact that they shared the same accountant Gregory knew the extent of Mrs Rosse's savings and investments down to the last farthing.

'The swindler is not, as a rule, a thug,' writes Judge Gerald Sparrow, who in his time has seen quite a few pass before him for sentencing. 'He will not murder. Your daughter is reasonably safe with him.'[1]

Was Maundy Gregory psychologically capable of a cold-blooded

[1] Gerald Sparrow. *The Great Swindlers*. London: John Long, 1959.

murder for gain? F. Tennyson Jesse, the crime writer, has defined the poisoner as the 'foulest' of all murderers. 'He must have the confidence of the person whom he is killing,' she writes; 'he must appear amiable, pleasant; he must be willing to give from his hand those drops that mean death . . .' 'Confidence has been established,' she adds, 'and a betrayal of confidence even in ordinary affairs of human life means the death of the heart.' Was Maundy Gregory's heart dead within him? Does this explain how he could leave the bedside where Mrs Rosse had just passed away to keep a luncheon appointment with the King of Greece?

In the absence of conclusive evidence either way one can only fall back on the opinions of those who either knew Gregory or who have written about him, after studying his behaviour. 'My parents were positive that Maundy Gregory had nothing to do with Mrs Rosse's death,' Leila MacKinlay tells me, adding, 'This was probably an emotional reaction first and foremost—they had received a great deal of kindness and hospitality from him.' Sir Colin Coote's relations with Gregory were slight; nevertheless he had opportunity to observe him at first hand. 'He was essentially kindly, not a killer,' Sir Colin writes; 'flamboyant but not ferocious; more of a leech than a lecher; more vulgar than vicious.' He was also inclined to panic in moments of stress, according to J. Rowland Sales, who was Gregory's secretary-manager when the latter was trying his wings as a theatrical impresario. 'Maundy was an awful coward—he could never face anything unpleasant,' declared Sales, who instanced the closing of *Dorothy* at the Waldorf Theatre when Gregory rushed to the basement, pulled the mains switch, and then pretended that there had been an electric failure. Poisoners are generally thought to be cold and calculating. Panic reactions such as exhibited by Gregory hardly square with the accepted notions of this category of killers.

Gerald Macmillan writes of 'the inherent improbability that a man of Gregory's birth, upbringing, and character would commit murder in any circumstances, let alone merely to save himself from financial ruin'.[1] However, three paragraphs later Macmillan forgets himself and writes that 'it is difficult to believe that he did not take advantage of the good fortune of Mrs Rosse's . . . making of a will in his favour . . . to extricate himself from his difficult financial position'. 'It may not have been the perfect murder,'

[1] Gerald Macmillan. *Honours for Sale.*

Macmillan concludes, '. . . but it was near enough to perfection for him to escape being brought to trial.'

Lastly, there remains the opinion of the man who played Porfiri Petrovich to Gregory's Raskolnikov—Chief Inspector Arthur Askew. As we have seen, Askew led both the investigation into the sale of honours, and that into the mysterious circumstances surrounding Edith Rosse's death, from which fact observers might conclude that he was biassed where Gregory was concerned. Indeed, some might hold that Askew's interest in Gregory went far beyond the call of duty. Impartial or not, there is not a shadow of doubt in Askew's mind but that Gregory was a killer, as I learned when I talked to the ex-detective at his home near Sevenoaks. 'I'm convinced that Gregory murdered Mrs Rosse,' Askew told me. 'Furthermore, if he had not skipped out of the country on his release from Wormwood Scrubs I would have re-arrested Maundy Gregory on the murder charge.'

PART FOUR

'He [Maundy Gregory] was a rather sinister Maecenas
. . . no novelist could have accurately described him.'

SIR SHANE LESLIE

'. . . it would have required a collaboration between
Balzac and Dumas to do him justice.'

MAURICE RICHARDSON

'Who, then, the public might ask, was this Maundy
Gregory . . . he never revealed anything of his real self
or activities.'

GERALD MACMILLAN

XVI

Sir Arthur

The Germans dropped their first bomb on Dieppe on the night of Saturday, May 18, 1940. 'I remember that it was a Saturday night,' Peter B. Taylor, who was then British Vice-Consul at Dieppe, recollects, 'because I was at the local cinema—we only had movies on Saturday night—and all during the film I could hear this lone reconnaissance plane droning overhead until finally the miserable ack-ack gun mounted on the western cliff near the château pooped off a couple of shots. Then the German plane, as if to express its contempt for this performance, dropped a single bomb on the town and flew off.'

This was merely the prelude to *Götterdämmerung*, for the following night the Heinkels came over, wave upon wave, to drop their bombs on the railway station and the port. A channel steamer which had been converted into a hospital ship sustained a direct hit and turned turtle in the harbour, while the railway station, where a canteen had been set up for Belgian refugees, was both bombed and strafed. 'In desperation we turned over some of the fishcarts we had been using for the canteen, and crawled under them for shelter,' Mrs Kathleen Tronson (then Kathleen Fairbanks, the daughter of the American Consul at Dieppe) recalls.

There were the usual spy scares which accompany such raids. Someone was reported to have lit a bonfire near the railway station as a beacon for the German bombers to guide on; someone else was said to have flashed a torch as a signal to the Germans. That night north of Dieppe a quarter of a million British troops dug themselves in on the beach at Dunkirk and prayed for deliverance; during the day their land escape routes had been cut off when Guderian's tanks had raced to the coast near Abbeville.

Among the houses in Dieppe's fashionable Rue du Général Chanzy hit by incendiaries on Sunday night was the Villa Graziella, a *pension* whose guests included two Englishmen, E. Mountjoy Griffiths, the British Consul at Dieppe, and 'Sir Arthur Gregory', the name Maundy Gregory used in his final avatar. None of the boarding-house's guests was hurt, as became apparent when they came tumbling out after the raid. As the fire began to burn out of control 'Sir Arthur', who had managed to rescue some of his clothing, could be seen on the sidewalk wringing his hands. 'My papers, my papers,' he cried, 'I must save my papers.' This was the cue for his fellow lodger Mountjoy Griffiths to dash back into the burning house, to haul to safety on the pavement a trunk containing Gregory's papers, and to be squirted on the back of his neck by a fireman's hose for his pains. Griffiths, a Welshman noted for his short temper, would have been even more livid had he known the contents of Gregory's trunk. His 'papers' consisted largely of a four-foot long scroll compiled by the College of Heralds tracing his pedigree back to King Edward III, and various armorials and phylacteries from the Papal Orders to which Gregory had belonged, and from which he had been expelled following his conviction in the honours case.

Until that moment the war had seemed remote to Gregory— something that affected other people, not himself. However, as he watched the Villa Graziella go up in flames his own predicament came vividly to mind. At the outbreak of the war his friend Captain Kelly had suggested that Gregory return to England. 'Come home, all is forgiven,' was Kelly's message in effect, meaning that Gregory's remittance would no longer be conditional upon his living abroad. Captain Kelly even offered Gregory the shelter of Hyde Manor, the Kelly family seat at Kingston-near-Lewes in East Sussex. But Gregory had asked for time to consider the offer. On August 24, 1939, the very eve of the war, Gregory had taken precautions by instructing his London solicitors, Messrs Kenneth Brown, Baker, Baker to hand over presumably for safe keeping 'about twelve bundles of papers' to Mrs Edith M. Stone, who was Captain Kelly's secretary.

As the war resolved itself into that period of stalemate and boredom known as the *drôle de guerre* so did all sense of urgency leave Gregory, and he politely but firmly refused Kelly's offer. Like the majority of his compatriots at Dieppe Gregory mentally took refuge behind the Maginot Line, nurturing himself on such crumbs of comfort as the fact that the Germans had never got as far as Dieppe in the 1914–18 war, forgetting that Dieppe had been occupied by the Boche in the Franco-Prussian war. Besides, if the worst came to the worst, Gregory could always return to Paris and seek out his friend Ronnie Russell, who was head barman at the Meurice, and the two of them could make their way south to the Spanish border. Russell had been after him to move back to Paris, which had seemed safe in comparison to Dieppe's exposed position as a port of disembarkation for British troops. (This, of course, was before the Nazis had overrun Holland and Belgium.) Now as he sat on the trunk containing what remained of his personal belongings Gregory realized that the time of indecision was past. His options rapidly were being taken away from him by events. Upon his ability to think clearly and to act quickly his very life depended.

* * *

'I remember the first time Maundy Gregory ever set foot inside this bar.' With a wave of the hand Ronnie Russell indicated the American Bar of the Hôtel Meurice, where we were sitting, and where he had been head barman for forty years until his retirement in 1965. His gesture encompassed the art-deco frieze of Diana the huntress, the marble-topped tables, the spindly gilt chairs upholstered in pale green velvet which, for the most part, were unoccupied, it being 3 o'clock in the afternoon. Russell is a small, slender man in his sixties, with lively black eyes and a humorous face framed by hair that had turned snow white during the years he spent in a Nazi prison camp at Vittel. British-born, Russell married a French girl before the war, and he has lived in France ever since.

'I recognized Gregory instantly from the photographs of him I had seen in the papers,' Russell declared. 'I had read all about his trial in the continental edition of the *Daily Mail*. But in the flesh he was plumper—or more portly, shall I say—and balder than the press photos had indicated. And more arrogant. He stood in the doorway with his friend Captain Phipps surveying the scene as though he were planning to buy the Meurice, and maybe Phipps was the estate agent. Not a detail escaped his eye. After inspecting the bar arrangements, including the clientele, he nodded approval to Phipps. "This will do, Bertie," I heard him say. "I think we'll make this our headquarters."'

And headquarters it became for Gregory during the long years of his exile in Paris. Thackeray in his *Paris Sketch Book* mentions the Meurice in the rue de Rivoli as a place where the English came to read the London newspapers. A century later it became a favourite stopping-off place for the Prince of Wales, which may have accounted for Gregory's decision to make the bar of the Meurice his 'home from home', according to Russell.

'On that first afternoon, Maundy waited until the last customer had drifted away,' Russell continued, 'then he introduced himself to me as "Sir Arthur Gregory", and startled me with a most unusual request. He said that he was planning to be in Paris for some time, and that he would like to run up a bar bill, explaining that he received his remittance from home once a month. The Meurice bar was no "Sloppy Joe's" where the customers got drinks on tick. On the other hand, I could think of no good reason for refusing Gregory credit.

'At the end of the first month when I presented him with his bar bill Maundy whipped out a little notebook from his waistcoat pocket and pretended to check the bill against figures he had noted down. Straightening up, he announced, "Yes, the total seems to be correct," and paid up promptly. But I thought to myself, This man must be crooked or he wouldn't suspect other people of being crooks.'

Gregory's manner of payment was in itself unique. 'Maundy would come in at the beginning of the month and slap down on the bar a brown paper parcel all done up with red sealing wax and sent from England by registered mail,' Russell explained. 'He would undo the parcel, extract a few banknotes to pay his bar bill, and stuff the rest of the money into his pockets.' The former head barman smiled wryly at the recollection. 'I used to worry about him going home alone late at night with banknotes sticking out of every pocket.'

*   *   *

Fortunately, Gregory did not have far to walk, for Captain Kelly had found him a tiny apartment at 8 Rue d'Anjou within easy walking distance of the Meurice. A *hôtel privé* where Lafayette had once lived, 8 Rue d'Anjou is set back in a courtyard protected by massive wooden doors with a concierge's lodge to the right as one enters. Gregory's apartment on the second floor consisted of a small entrance hall, one large room which Gregory divided into two by means of a wrought-iron screen, kitchen, and bath. It was located about equidistant from the British Embassy in the Rue du Faubourg St Honoré, and from the Madeleine where Gregory worshipped, and whose cold, italianate interior reminded him of the Brompton Oratory in London's South Kensington.

But Gregory spent very little time in his apartment. Mostly he was to be found in the American bar of the Meurice, his table—to the right of the door as one entered from the lobby—being so placed that he could beat a hasty retreat should he spot someone whom he wished to avoid. Gregory smoked Greys cigarettes, and drank only Hedges and Butler's Vat 250 whisky, which the bar stocked especially for his benefit. Curled at his feet was the companion of his exile, Monsieur le Beau, a brown Pomeranian dog.

'Monsieur le Beau was all that kept Maundy from going round the bend,' Captain Bertie Phipps told me. 'Maundy lavished all of his affection on that dog, which was a horrid little beast, always yapping at anyone who came too near it. But Maundy would spend hours grooming it, and he never ate himself until Monsieur le Beau had been fed, usually off the best Sèvres china.' Captain Phipps, himself, had had an adventurous career. Now in his eighties and retired, Captain Phipps, who spoke Russian fluently, was sent to Archangel in 1919 in advance of the Allied armies of occupation. Afterwards, in the backwash of the revolutionary tide that swept Europe, he had a habit of turning up at various trouble spots in Germany and Poland. In the thirties, Phipps, who was then living in Paris, was asked to keep an eye on Gregory, which he did, reporting to Captain Kelly from time to time. Phipps, who was thoroughly manly, disapproved of Gregory's effeminacy, but they became good friends.

Monsieur le Beau was responsible for Gregory making another friend at this time—Berry Wall, the American playboy, who stopped at the Meurice, and who owned a chow dog named 'Toi-toi'. Berry Wall, who ran through several fortunes in his lifetime to end up nearly penniless, had three loves—chow dogs, horses (he had his first bet on a horse at the age of ten), and pretty women. 'Never give a pretty woman anything she cannot eat or drink if you want to keep out of trouble,' Wall used to tell Gregory, on whom the advice, of course, was lost. Although he was in his early seventies when Gregory met him, Wall still gave evidence of that sartorial splendour which had earned him the title 'the last of the dandies' (he is credited with having invented the tuxedo). He thought nothing of appearing in the bar of the Meurice with three full-blown roses pinned to his lapel.

Thinking to impress him, Gregory once invited Wall to hear him play the baby grand piano Gregory had had installed in the Rue d'Anjou apartment. Having seated himself at the piano Gregory let his fingers ripple lightly over the keyboard as though he were warming up to tackle something by Debussy. 'You see,' he called out, 'I play as the inspiration takes me.' But the virtuoso performance was lost on the American who, his chin buried in his collar, was snoring gently.

In the early days of his exile Gregory was seldom in such a playful mood. He was, in fact, subject to spells of loneliness and depression during which he would complain to Captain Phipps that he didn't have a friend in the world. Sometimes he would give way to fits of weeping. 'If you've ever had a nervous breakdown you'll know what it was like,' Captain Phipps told me. Once Gregory came rushing into the bar from the dining-room of the Meurice, white-faced and obviously agitated. 'There's a horrid man in there,' he told Ronnie Russell. 'I must not be seen by him on any account.' Russell told me that later he recognized the man who had spoiled Gregory's lunch as an official of the Bank of England.

*   *   *

Gregory was wrong in supposing that all of his friends had deserted him. Peter Mazzina was to remain loyal to his employer until the end, which is perhaps not too remarkable in view of the fact that, as Gerald Macmillan points out, each was in a position to blackmail the other. However, Mazzina was much more than a friend. Armed with Gregory's power of attorney, Mazzina continued to represent Gregory's business interests in England, making frequent trips across the Channel to Paris to confer with the latter. 'What passed between these two men is known to God alone,' Mazzina's son, Peter, told me when I asked him about these business trips. What is known is that Gregory, although adjudicated bankrupt, continued to draw income from investments that had been made in Mazzina's name, such as the Deepdene Hotel in Dorking, and the Ambassador Club, which did not close its doors immediately. As these enterprises stood in Mazzina's name there was nothing Gregory's creditors could do about it.

Not only that, but Gregory had managed to salt away most of his personal assets before the bailiffs closed in. His offices in Parliament Street and his Hyde Park Terrace home had, in fact, been stripped bare of everything of value. Mazzina, acting on Gregory's behalf, was in no hurry to dispose of this loot, but gradually it began to appear in the auction salerooms. The pink diamond which had once belonged to Catherine the Great, and which Gregory had acquired, was offered for auction at Christie's in November, 1933, but bought in at £1,800 when it did not reach its reserve price. Booksellers with whom Gregory dealt had no sooner concluded that the so-called Venice Letters of Frederick Rolfe, alias the Baron Corvo, were lost for ever than they surfaced, being offered by Foyles. Gregory had paid £150 for them, it will be recalled.[1]

Unfortunately, Mazzina soon found himself in hot water as far as his own enterprises were concerned. The Bristol Grill, for example, which he bought in Cork Street, did not prosper, and in 1936 he lost both it and the Deepdene Hotel when he was adjudged bankrupt with liabilities of £8,000. He fared somewhat better with the Millionaires' Club, located likewise in Cork Street, which was a forerunner of the Playboy clubs, and which featured the 1930s equivalents of today's Bunny girls. One wall of the Millionaires' Club was covered by a mural showing Hitler, Mussolini, and Neville Chamberlain meeting appropriately sticky ends, which may have been designed to give the lie to rumours that Mazzina was pro-Mussolini. 'I always had the feeling that the club was a cover for something else,' says Donald McCormick, who visited it in order to do a piece for one of the Sunday papers.

Early in 1943, while London was being blitzed, Mazzina himself was the victim of a two-pronged offensive that had nothing to do with the war. First the police raided the Millionaires' Club for selling liquor after licensing hours. Unable to pay fines totalling £215, Mazzina was arrested and remanded on bail. Secondly, the

[1] The mildly erotic letters in which Rolfe extolls the beauties of certain gondoliers were purchased through an intermediary by Percy Muir, who in turn sold them to C. K. Ogden, the collector. After Ogden's death in 1957 Muir bought them from his estate and sold them to an American dealer. (Information supplied to me by Muir.)

Westminster County Council took out a summons against Mazzina for rate arrears amounting to £292 12s 5d. When Mazzina failed to answer this summons a warrant for his arrest was issued.

On March 17, 1943, with a policeman waiting in the front room of his Welbeck Street flat to arrest him, Mazzina locked himself in the bathroom, and hanged himself with the silken cord of his dressing gown. The irony was that at the very moment he took his life, Mazzina's wife, Josephina, and some of his friends were on their way to the Welbeck Street flat with the money to pay the rates. 'My father was the most generous man in the world,' Peter Mazzina, Jr told me. 'For instance, if he was dining in a restaurant and happened to notice that it was half-empty he would dig deep into his pockets and come out with a substantial contribution to the tronc, which was how the waiters pooled their tips. "We all have slack days," he would say apologetically.'

The sad story of Peter Mazzina and of how he met his end is however getting ahead of the story of Maundy Gregory, who was last seen in the Meurice Bar complaining about a ghost from his past whom he had encountered in the dining-room.

*　　*　　*

Maundy Gregory was safe so long as he did not move out of the Meurice bar. So long as he confined himself to buttonholing the Americans whom he met there, and to boring them with his stories of being a British Secret Service agent in the First World War, his bona fides were not challenged. But when Gregory discovered Dieppe on the Normandy coast, and took to spending his weekends there, it was a different story.

Dieppe had long had the reputation of being the most sinful seaside resort in France, which partly explains its attraction for Gregory. Some said that it was the bracing sea air that made for so much wickedness. Others blamed the influence of Le Pollet, the fishermen's quarter, whose brothels were notorious, and whose matelots were apt to be red-headed in token of the Venetian blood in their veins (their ancestors had brought home Venetian wives from their travels in the east). Whatever the cause of its moral disarray, Dieppe became popular with English trippers intent upon spending a 'dirty weekend'. ('It makes a change from Brighton,' was the usual comment.) It was no accident that Dr Crippen, once he had buried his wife Belle under the coal cellar, hastened to Dieppe to spend the Easter Bank Holiday with his paramour Ethel le Neve. It was no accident either that Oscar Wilde made a bee-line for Dieppe as soon as he was released from Reading Gaol, registering at the Sandwich Hotel as 'Sebastian Melmoth'. Un-happily from Wilde's viewpoint, Dieppe was full of hard-drinking English colonels who had stopped off on their way home from Cawnpore to 'dry out', and who, finding the brandy cheap, had never left this seaside Gomorrah. The colonels and their ladies now proceeded to cut Wilde, making it a point to leave the Café des Tribuneaux whenever the poet entered. Even his friend Aubrey Beardsley crossed the street when he saw Wilde coming. ('It was *lâche* of Aubrey,' was Wilde's only comment.)

Forty years later when Maundy Gregory began to frequent Dieppe the English colony, thanks to a tax which the French imposed on foreigners, had shrunk from two thousand to perhaps a hundred, but the hundred stalwarts exercised a potent social influence. These expatriates had read all about Gregory in the continental edition of the *Daily Mail*, and they took delight in ostracizing him, much as their parents had done in the case of Oscar Wilde. Not long after Gregory began to make Dieppe his week-end haunt, his friend Captain Phipps was summoned to tea at the home of Georgette Carpentier (she was the wife of Georges Carpentier, the boxer), where the leaders of the English colony were gathered in full war council. There he was questioned about his friendship with Gregory. 'How can you bear to associate with that wife-poisoner?' he was asked. Phipps tells me that he was astounded by the vehemence of the attack. 'What is this, I asked, a tea party or an inquisition?' 'Ironically,' Phipps adds, 'there was hardly a member of the English colony who wasn't being paid to keep out of England for one reason or another.'[1]

The English colony might even have reconciled itself to Greg-ory's presence eventually (who among them had not at one time or other contemplated doing in a spouse?) had it not been for Gregory's use of the title 'Sir' in front of his name. This was what

[1] Even Winston Churchill's mother-in-law, Lady Blanche Hozier, who was at one time doyenne of the colony, had come to Dieppe originally because as a divorced woman she could not be received at Queen Victoria's court.

made the teacups rattle Chez Grisch, the *pâtisserie* in the Grande Rue where the colonels' ladies foregathered every afternoon. '"Sir Arthur," indeed!' they would say, and the way they pronounced the name, it was as though they had clawed it with the sugar tongs. 'Have you tried looking up "Sir Arthur Gregory" in Burke's or Debrett lately?' one of the good ladies would begin. 'Don't bother,' she would add, 'because it isn't there. There is no such title.' 'It's a disgrace,' another would chime in, 'an insult to His Majesty the King.'

Did Gregory mind being snubbed, I asked his friend Phipps. 'Not a bit,' Phipps replied. 'Maundy considered these people to be beneath contempt.' The colonels and their ladies were small beer, indeed, to a man who had been the friend of kings. Besides, Maundy had his French friends the D'Roubaix family to fall back on. Marcel D'Roubaix and his family were the real reason why Gregory spent most of his week-ends at Dieppe, and why eventually early in 1939 he went there to live.

Marcel D'Roubaix had spent most of his youth in England, where he studied medicine, and when the First World War broke out he had volunteered for the Royal Horse Artillery, eventually attaining the rank of Captain (he was secretary of the Dieppe branch of the British Legion). D'Roubaix had married twice: his first wife, a Belgian girl, died in 1926, and his second wife and widow Nadine now lives just outside Brussels. It was in Brussels that I talked to Mickey D'Roubaix, the son of that first marriage, who is now the Belgian representative for an American firm, the Muzak Corporation of America.

'We were the only family in Dieppe that would receive Gregory,' Mickey D'Roubaix, who was nineteen when Gregory began frequenting their home, told me. 'People used to ask us, What do you see in that impostor? But father found him amusing. Besides, Gregory was extremely thoughtful in the way he repaid hospitality. For example, at Christmas he would leave an expensive gift beside the dinner plate of each member of the family. On another occasion we had a full house, and so my step-brother had to give up his room to Gregory. The next morning my step-brother found that Gregory had tucked a 10-franc note under every knick-knack on the mantelpiece.'

From Gregory's viewpoint undoubtedly one of the great attractions of the D'Roubaix family was the Villa La Case which they occupied on the west cliff overlooking Dieppe harbour, and which Gregory upgraded to 'Château La Case' whenever he referred to it. Villa or château, La Case had strong Proustian associations, it having been built by the Comte Henri Greffuhle. The yellow-bearded count and his wife (she was formerly Princess Elisabeth de Caraman-Chimay) served as models for the Prince and Princess de Guermantes in Proust's novel, while her cousin, Robert de Montesquiou, was the original Baron de Charlus. By the time La Case fell into Marcel D'Roubaix's hands it was considerably run-down, however; and the state of its drains made it all but unin-habitable during the hot summer months.

But the real bond between Gregory and the D'Roubaix family was Catholicism. The D'Roubaix family were devoutly Catholic, and always had priests staying at La Case; and Gregory himself seems to have been going through a religious phase. 'Gregory used to attend Mass daily at the Église de St Jacques,' Mickey D'Roubaix told me. 'I remember him returning from church one morning full of apologies. "I hardly dared show my face at the Communion rail as I hadn't shaved," he said.' D'Roubaix showed me a copy of a book entitled *Ave Maria in 400 Languages* which Gregory had inscribed in purple ink and presented to his father. 'Gregory oc-casionally showed up at La Case with a red-headed Irishman named Captain Jimmy Keenan, who was a terrible boozer. When-ever the priests who were staying at La Case saw this pair approach-ing they would flee in terror as from the presence of Beelzebub and his cohort.'

It was Mickey D'Roubaix who told me about Maundy Gregory's drinking habits towards the end of his life. 'Gregory was drinking so heavily that I have known him to bring a whisky bottle to the dinner table when he stayed with us. He would then sip whisky during the meal while the rest of us shuddered and drank our wine.' 'He kept a bottle of whisky on the night table, as well—"Just in case I wake in the night," he told me. He was never drunk, but then he was never sober,' D'Roubaix added, 'and as the evening wore on he would become a little incoherent.'

*　　*　　*

Paris must have seemed dreary to Gregory after a week-end at La Case, where he enjoyed his first real taste of family life since his own childhood in Southampton. In the capital his world was circumscribed by his apartment in the Rue d'Anjou, the Meurice bar, and the Madeleine, where he had his own *prie-Dieu* near the pulpit with his name-plate affixed to it. Occasionally he browsed among the bouquinistes along the Seine, where he picked up detective thrillers (E. Phillips Oppenheim was his favourite). His knowledge of the French language never having progressed beyond *'le petit nègre'* stage, French literature was closed to him, as was the French theatre. This left Le Cirque Medrano as a source of entertainment for Gregory, but even this was marred when Monsieur le Beau's barking upset the elephants.

When the Paris International Exposition opened in 1937, Maundy Gregory lunched in the British Pavilion, was instantly recognized by the waiters, who had been brought over from the Savoy in London especially for the occasion. Remembering the big tips Gregory used to leave them in the old days, they hovered around him like moths. A year later when King George VI and Queen Elizabeth paid a State visit to Paris as President Lebrun's guests, Gregory bought a pearl-grey topper for the occasion, and rode in an open car down the Champs Elysées so close behind the official procession that he was cheered by bystanders, who mistook him for a member of the royal entourage. (Did Gregory, one wonders, boast to his Paris friends that he had served as usher at the king's wedding, when the latter was still the Duke of York?) Gregory in passing the British Embassy near his apartment on occasions such as Trafalgar Day never failed to bring his right arm up smartly in salute to the Union Jack fluttering over the portico.

A combination of boredom and apprehension at the approach of war drove Gregory to move to Dieppe early in 1939. He did not give up his Paris apartment, which continued to serve as a *pied-à-terre* for his frequent visits to the capital, but he did take with him to the Villa Graziella in the Rue du Général Chanzy most of his personal belongings. Personal safety did not enter into Gregory's consideration, though Dieppe, of course, was close to England in case the Germans broke through the Maginot Line. Gregory's friendship with the D'Roubaix family, on the other hand, was very much in his mind in making the move. In time of crisis Gregory felt the need for human companionship, a need which the chance acquaintances of the Meurice bar could not satisfy.

*　　*　　*

The man in the fur coat tugging at the little brown Pomeranian as they made their way haltingly along the promenade became a familiar sight to the Dieppois in that twilight period known as the *drôle de guerre*. The fur coat was of a long-haired variety and reached down nearly to his ankles, giving Maundy Gregory the appearance of an ambulatory caterpillar. His progress along the promenade was not much more rapid than that of the above-mentioned larva, for Gregory, now in his early sixties, had developed gout in his right leg. In other ways, too, he had aged. He had lost weight so that the suits he had brought with him from England now hung on him in scarecrow fashion. Also his nose had acquired a crimson hue which an Elizabeth Arden beauty preparation called 'Shine Off' was only partially successful in toning down. At the casino end of the *plage* Gregory would gather Monsieur le Beau into his arms and turn inland, admonishing the dog, 'Come along, darling, or we shall be late for our din-dins.'

Dieppe itself had changed no less than Gregory's appearance, though the transformation in this case had been more abrupt. Overnight it had become a British hospital base, its big, balcony-hung Edwardian hotels on the promenade being requisitioned for this purpose. First to arrive from England had been the lorries, in such haste that the names of the towns they came from—Birmingham, Glasgow, Newcastle—had not been painted out. They were followed by a contingent from the Queen Alexandra Royal Army Nursing Corps.

Workmen suddenly appeared one morning and began making a huge Red Cross insignia out of red bricks and whitewash in front of the Metropole Hôtel for the benefit of the German bombers. Gregory went to Paris one week-end, and when he returned all of the unshuttered windows in Dieppe had been painted blue as a form of blackout protection. In the resultant murkiness Gregory now had difficulty groping his way home from Harris's Bar in the slightly befuddled condition in which he ended his evenings.[1] The other change he noticed was that pilots from the big Lysander reconnaissance planes whose base was near by now took to dropping into Harris's Bar in the evenings.

How the rumour got started that Maundy Gregory was a spy

[1] Harris, himself, was killed in the black-out later during the German occupation. Being hard of hearing, he did not hear the German sentry's command to halt, and was shot in the back.

[233]

is something of a mystery, but this accusation was added to the others that the English colony laid at his doorstep. 'Somehow military intelligence got wind of the fact that Mountjoy Griffiths and Gregory lived in the same boarding-house, and that they occasionally enjoyed a drink together, and the intelligence blokes weren't very happy about it,' Peter Taylor told me. The British consulate in those days was located in the Windsor Hotel, and was plastered with posters by Fougasse showing Hitler with his ear to the ground listening to loose talk. 'Every afternoon Griffiths and I would lock up the consulate and repair to Harris's Bar, where we had tea in front of a roaring fire,' Taylor recalled. 'Gregory would join us, but not for tea, mind you—Scotch and soda was his drink.'

'After Griffiths had been warned by military intelligence against Gregory as a possible security risk, he continued to drink with Maundy, but naturally there was a certain reserve when they talked. As for going near the consulate office Gregory was too smart for that. I think that he looked upon the consulate as British soil, and remembered that there was a warrant out for his arrest in connection with his bankruptcy proceedings. Anyway, he gave it a wide berth.'

Gregory had, in fact, been trying to interest a Lieutenant-Commander A. B. Shepherdcross, as the senior British naval officer in Dieppe, in a mine-detecting device which was the product of his friend Marcel D'Roubaix's fertile brain. The device operated on the principle of what the French call 'radiethésie', i.e., detecting the radiations emitted by a mine, and may well have been in advance of its time. At any rate, nothing came of Gregory's efforts on its behalf.

As had happened with Gregory before in times of stress, his paranoia now came to the forefront. He told Ronnie Russell on one of his week-end trips to Paris that the Germans had mentioned his name specifically in one of their short-wave broadcasts heard in Dieppe, to the effect: 'Maundy Gregory, we know where you are. At this moment you are sitting in the Café des Tribunaux at Dieppe sipping a Pernod. We want you to know that we are coming to get you.' (When I told this story to Phipps he took it seriously. He said that there were two German spies operating in Dieppe, and that they were known to communicate with Berlin via short-wave radio.) When the Villa Graziella was hit by incendiary bombs on the night of Sunday, May 19, Gregory was convinced (or said he was convinced) that they had been dropped on the boarding-house in an effort to get him personally.

*   *   *

After being made homeless by the Villa Graziella fire, Gregory moved in with the D'Roubaix family at La Case which from the clifftop afforded a dress circle view of the havoc wreaked by bombs on the town and harbour below. It was here that Captain Phipps sought Gregory out to beg him to accept Captain Kelly's offer of a home in East Sussex. There was no time to lose, Phipps reminded his friend. He, himself, was leading a small party of English to St Malo, where they hoped to get transport to England. Meanwhile, the Army base hospitals that had been set up in Dieppe were being evacuated. 'I told Maundy bluntly that if the bombing raids con-tinued it would soon be impossible for trains to get in or out of Dieppe, in which case he might find himself trapped,' Phipps recalled.

The offer to share Hyde Manor, Captain Kelly's home in East Sussex, must have been a tempting one for Gregory, but in his heart of hearts he knew that he could not accept it. His reasons for turning it down he summed up in one word, 'Tipstaff'. The warrant for Gregory's arrest in connection with his bankruptcy proceedings was still open. Regretfully he told Phipps that he would make for Paris, where he hoped to join up with Ronnie Russell.

'Maundy asked me to take back to England some of the papers and personal belongings he had managed to salvage with his trunk,' Phipps told me. 'But then he dithered, couldn't make up his mind what to part with, and I couldn't wait—trains weren't all that fre-quent—so we shook hands, joking about meeting in Paris in the bar of the Meurice. I never saw him again.'

Maundy Gregory left Dieppe on Sunday, May 26, by which time the trains had stopped running. He was in fact the next-to-last Englishman to leave Dieppe (Peter Taylor, who had burnt the British consulate records in the furnace of the Aguado Hôtel, remained behind a few days longer to tidy up his affairs). 'Maundy managed to get hold of a bicycle from somewhere,' Taylor told me, 'and had had it fitted up with a basket on the handlebars for his dog, Monsieur le Beau. I saw them start out on that Sunday morning on the road to Rouen, Maundy, with his fur coat flapping around him, and wobbling uncertainly as he tried to get his balance, the dog yapping furiously at the unaccustomed indignity of the basket. A more ludicrous pair it would be hard to imagine. I wondered if they would get beyond the outskirts of Dieppe—for Maundy had a game leg, remember—and then I promptly forgot about them, as I had too much else on my mind.' Gregory was to get far beyond the outskirts of Dieppe. In fact, a whole new chapter now opened for him, and it was to be one of the most picaresque in a life composed of picaresque adventures.

XVII

L'Anglais du Belle-Vue

Either Mme Yvinec or Maundy Gregory or both must have read Edgar Allan Poe's tale about the purloined letter, I reasoned, for that story had as its point that the art of concealment lies in disdaining to conceal. In seeking to recover the purloined letter, which was being used for purposes of blackmail, Poe's detective hero guesses correctly that he will find it deposited 'immediately beneath the nose of the whole world by way of best preventing any portion of that world from perceiving it'. And so it was with Maundy Gregory, whom I had traced to Châteauneuf-du-Faou after he had left Dieppe. Gregory had made himself invisible by hiding himself in the midst of the Germans, who had requisitioned the Hôtel Belle-Vue where he was staying. He had escaped their notice by planting himself in their very bosom, so to speak.

But this left unanswered the question why Gregory had taken refuge in Châteauneuf-du-Faou in the first place, a town which was located in the wilds of the Finisterre. The answer, I concluded, was that he had no choice. Maundy Gregory was tired of running —or perhaps I should say hobbling, bearing in mind his gouty leg; therefore he accepted the first ride that was offered to him. Pure chance decreed that the offer should come from M Fevrier, the Parisian dentist, who was fleeing to the Finisterre with his family. Thus Gregory found himself travelling due west when he should have been heading for Paris, where funds and possible shelter awaited him. The date was Saturday, June 8, when the first German tanks rolled into Dieppe.

It was not until I had had my breakfast on the morning after my arrival at Châteauneuf-du-Faou that I got around to asking Mme Yvinec why she had decided to hide 'Monsieur de Grégoire', as she called him, from the Germans. We were sitting in her parlour with its heavy oak chests carved with curious Breton designs, and Madame was crocheting. 'When did you first discuss the matter with Gregory?' I prompted her. Madame looked up from her work with an expression of mild surprise on her face. 'We never discussed it,' she said. 'It was something that was understood.' 'But surely you were conscious of the risk you were taking?' I persisted. 'Weren't you afraid of what the Germans might do to you and to your family if they found out?' (I had in mind Madame's husband, who remained very much in the background during my stay at the hotel, and her three daughters, then only children.) 'They could have arrested you and your husband, and sent your daughters away to an orphanage,' I pointed out. But Madame merely shrugged her shoulders. '*Les Boches, vous comprenez, ils ne sont pas astucieux comme les Bretons. Ils manquent l'esprit fin.*' On such judgments are wars won and lost.

*   *   *

The first armoured cars to come roaring into Châteauneuf-du-Faou on Tuesday, June 18, did not stop, but raced on towards Brest, which was their objective. They were preceded by motorcycle outriders wearing huge goggles and with scarves over their mouths to keep out the white dust which otherwise covered them from head to foot. Rommel's 7th Panzer Division had advanced 150 miles in a single day to justify the name 'Phantom Division' which the awestruck French peasants had bestowed upon it.

The second echelon of Germans included a unit of the *Gast*, or Customs service, headed by Oberst Hans Kluver, who requisitioned the Hôtel Belle-Vue as a billet for his men. (Located inland midway between Brest and Quimper, Châteauneuf-du-Faou was the logical place to set up a checkpoint for contraband coming from these two ports.) Oberst Kluver and his grey-uniformed men occupied thirteen of the hotel's rooms, leaving Mme Yvinec four rooms in which to house her family and her French lodger 'Monsieur de Grégoire'. Thus began a drama which at times resembled a Feydeau farce.

It was pure Feydeau in the morning when Mlle Susanne, the housemaid, knocked at Gregory's door with fresh *croissants* and *café au lait*. Mlle Susanne was an exceedingly pretty girl, according to Mme Yvinec, and as soon as she knocked doors all along the corridor would open, the closely cropped heads of the Master Race would pop out, and Heinrichs, Wilhelms, and Fritzes would whistle appreciatively at the maid as she stood balancing her tray and waiting for Gregory to unlock. On the other side of the door Gregory would listen terrified that if he opened he might have to greet his fellow lodgers in his pidgin French. It was at this point that *Occupe-Toi de Susanne* gave way to Molière and *Le Malade Imaginaire*, for among the other ruses which Gregory resorted to in order to avoid talking and thus betraying his ignorance of the French language, he would appear at the door his head swathed in a towel as though he were suffering from toothache. Or again, if he should chance to encounter one of the Germans on his way to the water closet, Gregory would pretend to be deaf and dumb.

It wasn't all comedy, of course. Gregory's life was in greatest danger whenever the town garrison was changed and new troops brought in, for this change-over was usually accompanied by a thorough inspection of all billets. It was then that Gregory, who had developed almost a sixth sense as far as his personal safety was concerned, took to the attic, having first gone over it thoroughly with a flit-gun to kill any spiders that might be lurking there. He slept on a broken-down *chaise-longue* which Mme Yvinec had placed there, and in the daytime he tiptoed around in felt slippers. ('He knew every floorboard that creaked,' Madame told me.) His only diversion was to watch through a chink in the roof the Yvinec girls playing below in the garden whose paths were neatly bordered by shells, the relics of countless Coquilles St Jacques consumed by the hotel's guests. At times M Yvinec would appear with lettuces to feed the rabbits he kept in hutches in the yard. However, once the new garrison had settled in and danger of sudden searches had passed, Gregory would come down from the attic to his room, and the Feydeau farce would begin again.

The Germans may have been unaware of Gregory's presence in their midst, but the inhabitants of Châteauneuf talked of little else. Soon Gregory's fame had spread throughout the Finisterre, from the fishing port of Concarneau in the south to Roscoff, home of the onion-sellers in the north, and not overlooking Châteaulin, the seat of the Sous-Préfecture. Overnight *l'anglais du Belle-Vue*, as Gregory was universally known, had been transformed by local gossip into a legendary character whose feats partook equally of *Fanfan la Tulipe* and *Les Pieds Nickelés*, a comic strip which was the Gallic equivalent of the Bash Street Kids in *Beano*, and which was popular reading in these parts. The women gossiped about him as, their starched coiffes perched high on their heads, they came from Mass at St Theilo's on Sunday morning. At the Bar des Sports their menfolk had their own saltier versions of the tricks *l'anglais du Belle-Vue* got up to with Mlle Susanne, and all under the noses of the Germans. Probably no one believed the stories about Gregory outwitting the *Boches*. Laughter was one of the ways these simple folk had of getting their own back at their conquerors.

*   *   *

Not everyone in Châteauneuf felt kindly disposed towards Gregory. The town had its share of fascist-minded individuals of the type who composed the *milice* in Vichy France, and who did the Nazis' dirty work for them. These individuals were always looking for an opportunity to ingratiate themselves with their conquerors. It was one of them, a shopkeeper, who was to prove Gregory's downfall.

It happened like this. Finding confinement to his hotel room unbearable, Gregory took to making quick sorties into town with Monsieur le Beau, usually at mid-morning or dusk when the German garrison was most likely to be on fatigue duty. He carefully avoided entering any of the shops, nor did he set foot inside the Bar des Sports where formerly he had taken an aperitif. It was during one of these furtive sorties that Gregory was spotted by the shop-keeper-milicien in question, who at the time was chatting with Feldwebel Engelhard, Kluver's assistant. '*Tiens,*' remarked the shopkeeper, as Gregory passed the window, '*c'est drôle comme cet anglais du Belle-Vue se promène en plein jour avec son chien sans qu'on lui demande de se présenter au Kommandatur, n'est-ce pas?*' Engelhard, whose French was letter perfect, assured the shopkeeper that he was mistaken, that Monsieur de Grégoire, the man who had just passed, was French, not English. 'After all, I should know,' the feldwebel continued good-humouredly, 'since he is my neighbour at the Belle-Vue.' '*Mais non, c'est un anglais,*' the shopkeeper insisted smilingly. '*Tout le monde le sait. Içi à Châteauneuf-du-Faou on ne parle que de ça.*'

Gregory was arrested the following morning just as Mlle Susanne brought him his breakfast. Visibly shaken, he made no effort to deny his nationality (perhaps he was relieved that the intolerable strain he had been living under had come to an end). Gregory finished his breakfast ('*Moi je n'aurai pas eu grand faim, vous savez, dans les circonstances pareilles,*' Mme Yvinec remarked), dressed, and accompanied the two soldiers who had arrested him to the Kommandatur. Here certain formalities had to be complied with— i.e. before Gregory's arrest could be completed a formal denunciation of him had to be made by the shopkeeper who had betrayed him to Engelhard. Gregory, for his part, asked and was denied permission to take his dog with him. (Monsieur le Beau was left behind with Mme Yvinec as security against the 10,000 francs worth of comestibles her star boarder had consumed during his four-month stay under her roof.) Gregory was then loaded on to the back of a lorry, and driven to the German prison camp at Drancy, near Paris. It was the first week in November, 1940.

*   *   *

The camp at Drancy originally had been built for the French *Garde Mobile*. An uncompleted section had been used by the French before their capitulation to intern captured Germans, so it was with a certain poetic justice that the Germans in turn used Frontstalag III, as it was now re-christened, to house their enemies. The British herded together in the barracks to which Gregory was assigned were a mixed bag. They ranged from Palestinians who held British passports to jockeys with Cockney accents who had been riding for French owners at Malmaison and Chantilly, and included a Cecil (one of the 4th Marquess of Salisbury's sons) and Jimmie Hale, who had been *aide-de-camp* to the Duke of Windsor. Those British subjects who had been born in France, or who like Gregory had lived there much of their lives, tended to look down their noses at those birds of passage who had been trapped in France by the war. 'Hundred Percenters' was the pejorative term for these latter, meaning that they were 100% British.

By pure luck I was able to trace one of the prisoners who had shared Gregory's barracks. He is Captain Leonard White, of West Hartlepool, Durham, who, as a captured 17-year-old merchant seaman, was sent to Drancy in December, 1940. 'Maundy's fur coat made him the envy of the rest of us who were freezing to death,' Captain White, who now skippers oil tankers in the Indian Ocean, told me during a recent trip home. 'That and his boots which were fur-lined, basket-work sabots with wooden soles—most of us would have given a month's pay to own those boots.' The captain also told me of Gregory's kindliness towards him. 'We used to have long conversations as we trudged slowly around the camp—Gregory had difficulty walking, even with a cane—and he helped me with my French which was of the school-boy variety,' Captain White reminisced.

White, who had been brought up in a strict Protestant home, was horrified, however, when Gregory told him that he had renounced Anglicanism for the Church of Rome. 'But when Maundy told me that he had been a friend of the late Pope my face must have reflected my incredulity for he burst out laughing. It was one of the rare times I ever heard Maundy laugh.'

'Gregory looked much older than 63, but perhaps this was be-cause I was only 17 at the time. I remember one of the crew from our ship, a tough lad of 19, ex-borstal, got hold of a loaf of bread, and was walking around with it stuffed up his jumper when he bumped into Maundy. One look at that woebegone figure and he pulled out the loaf and tossed it to Gregory with, "Gawd amighty, you need this worse than I do."' Not long afterwards Gregory was taken ill, according to White, and was admitted to the camp hospital under the care of a Canadian internee, Dr R. Rabinowitz, which is perhaps ironical in view of Gregory's anti-Semitism. This was early in 1941.

*   *   *

In mid-summer 1941 Ronnie Russell, who earlier had been picked up by the Gestapo in Paris while waiting for Maundy Gregory to show up, was acting as postmaster at the German internment camp at St Denis when he noticed the name of 'Arthur Gregory' on the list of new arrivals. 'I was certain that it was Maundy, so I went immediately in search of him,' Russell told me. 'I found him in the midst of some Benedictine monks, and I was shocked by his changed appearance. He was much thinner than when I had seen him last, partly due to the prison diet no doubt; he looked haggard and ill. And, strange to relate, he seemed embarrassed to see me. Whether he feared that he would lose face with the White Friars by associating with a bartender I do not know, but he took me aside and whispered, "Pretend that you don't know me all that well, and don't come to see me too often."'

Russell is of the opinion that Gregory was having withdrawal symptoms due to deprivation of alcohol. 'Still Maundy managed to get whisky smuggled to him in the camp,' Russell revealed. 'It came from a little Italian delicatessen in Paris where Maundy used to deal in the old days. Civilian internees, you understand, were treated much more leniently than prisoners of war; for example, we were allowed to receive Red Cross parcels at St Denis.' Unfortunately, the bottles of whisky were only miniatures, and didn't go far to satisfy Maundy's craving. Russell was to be separated from his friend sooner than either of them anticipated, for early in August, 1941, Gregory collapsed, and was taken to the Val de Grâce hospital in Paris, then a German military hospital.

A myth has sprung up that Maundy Gregory was asked to make 'Lord Haw-Haw' type broadcasts for the Germans, and that he refused. Certainly if Gregory had agreed to collaborate his revelations concerning political corruption as he had experienced it in Britain would have had immense propaganda value for the Germans. This partly explains the anxiety of Captain Kelly and of those connected with the British Secret Services concerning the fate of Maundy Gregory in Occupied France. However, there is no indication whatsoever that the Germans were ever aware of 'Arthur Gregory's' true identity. On top of that, the state of Gregory's health would have precluded such broadcasts, even had he been so inclined.

But he was not so inclined. Whatever else he may have been during his lifetime Gregory in 1941 was not a collaborator. All indications are that he stood up well to the Germans under the trying conditions of Drancy and St Denis. When the German authorities, seeing that he was dying, offered to release him in the autumn of 1941, he was reported to have replied, 'You arrested me, now you can jolly well keep me for the duration of the war, and what's more, we are going to win.'

On September 21, 1941, Gregory made his last will and testament, which read: 'I leave everything I possess in England, France, and any other else place to Marcel D'Roubaix-Bulger, my dearest friend.[1] This will cancels all other wills, codicils, and other docu-

[1] Marcel D'Roubaix's stepfather was an Irish doctor named Bulger, hence the hyphenated name which Gregory's friend sometimes used.

ments.' The will was witnessed by one Benzion Samuel Hormesky, who was apparently an orderly or a fellow patient, and signed by a Dr Le Bayon certifying that Gregory was of sound mind when he made the will. Gregory died one week later, the cause of death being given as 'progressive cardiac insufficiency'. The records of the Val de Grâce hospital, which are now kept in an archive at Limoges, note that when Gregory entered the hospital he was in a 'very bad general condition, absolutely fleshless with notable dwindling of the muscles and a swollen liver'. Ronnie Russell's verdict was more succinct. 'Maundy died from lack of booze,' Russell told me. 'The Germans had cut off his whisky supply.'

Gregory was given a cheap burial at the Ivry-Paris New Cemetery, his grave being paid up for five years. By the end of that time none of Gregory's friends—and this includes those who had been so solicitous of his welfare while he was living in exile—had forked out the 250-franc annual renewal charge, so Gregory's bones were dumped into an ossuary. Russell tells me that not long after Gregory's death a letter arrived from the Vatican expressing sorrow at the passing of 'Sir Arthur Gregory', and that the letter was pinned to the bulletin board at the St Denis camp. 'I can't recall the contents of the letter exactly,' says Russell, 'but it spoke of Maundy in glowing terms.'[1]

*   *   *

There remains the question of Gregory's last will and testament. His dear friend Marcel D'Roubaix was never to have the opportunity of offering the will for probate, for D'Roubaix was to die a hero in the French Resistance. Betrayed to the Gestapo and picked up outside the Gare Montparnasse in July, 1944, D'Roubaix was taken to Buchenwald, where he was executed by means of an injection of phenol into the bloodstream.[2]

[1] In response to my query the Vatican Secretariat of State informs me that no document referring to Maundy Gregory has been found in the archives of the Apostolic Chancery.

[2] D'Roubaix was part of the 'Mithradate' Resistance network which was based at Marseilles. Unfortunately, 'Mithradate' got entangled with the Soviet-sponsored *Rote Kapelle* (Red Orchestra), which had been penetrated by the Gestapo. The Médaille Militaire and the Légion d'Honneur were both awarded posthumously to D'Roubaix, whose name is incised on the Monument at Dieppe to those who gave their lives for France in both world wars.

But what of those possessions in 'England, France, and any other else place', to which Gregory had referred in his will? When he died all that had been found on him by way of personal possessions were some letters, a rosary, and an ocarina (Gregory presumably eased his solitude by learning to play this wind instrument). Did he have assets salted away in England or France or both? Was there a tidy fortune awaiting the day when he could reclaim it? At least three people thought this to be the case. Benzion Samuel Hormesky, who witnessed the will, Mickey D'Roubaix, who was the heir-presumptive, and Madame Yvinec, who now rates as one of Gregory's creditors—each at one time or another has had a go at finding the buried treasure.

Hormesky thought that Gregory had left considerable assets, including a £2,000 promissory note from 'an Italian princess', or so he told reporters. Incidentally, it was Hormesky, then an employee of the United Nations Relief and Rehabilitation Administration (UNRRA) in Germany, who broke the news of Gregory's death to the world in August, 1950, or nearly nine years after it had occurred. Why the news was withheld for so long is one more mystery, for the British Foreign Office must have known about Gregory's death soon after it occurred. The Foreign Office would have been notified by the Swiss, who looked after British interests in Occupied France.[1]

It will come as no surprise to readers who have followed the Gregorian saga thus far to learn that in the intervening years the will itself has disappeared. The original cannot be found filed either with the Probate Registry, at Somerset House, London, or with the Greffe Civil at the Palais de Justice in Paris. When I talked to Mickey D'Roubaix in Brussels, he told me that although he had seen the original will it was now no longer in his possession, nor did he have a true copy of it. D'Roubaix thought that the will might have been deposited with the solicitors' firm of Stonehams & Pumfreys of Great Marlborough Street, London, but they inform me that they hold no such document. D'Roubaix, inci-

---

[1] Captain Richard Kelly knew about Gregory's death as early as May 29, 1946, for on that date he wrote to a friend, 'It is very sad to think that his [Gregory's] end was so horrible and I only hope that he was not ill-treated.' Yet as late as February, 1950, Maurice Richardson wrote in *Lilliput*: 'Few people, to this day, know for certain whether he is alive or dead.'

dentally, has revised his views since the euphoric days of 1950 when he boasted to a *Daily Express* reporter, 'Maundy Gregory left a vast fortune. It belongs to me.' He now thinks that the cupboard is and always has been bare.

*   *   *

Not so Mme Yvinec—she has never lost hope that one day she will recoup the losses sustained by sheltering 'M de Grégoire'. ('All those bottles of St Émilion, those glasses of Bénédictine and Cointreau, not to mention the *cafés filtres, mon Dieu*, M. de Grégoire nearly ate and drank me out of my hotel.')

After Gregory had been discovered hiding in her hotel Madame had stood in imminent peril of being arrested for harbouring an enemy alien. Indeed, Oberst Kluver had threatened her with worse. 'Do you know what I am going to do to you, Madame Yvinec,' Kluver had blustered, and as she told me the story Madame's eyes shone with excitement. 'I'm going to have you lined up against a wall and shot.' Of course, neither of them took the threat seriously. Madame had, in fact, played dumb, insisting that her boarder was French, since he was registered at the Préfecture as 'M de Grégoire'. Besides, she was not a detective bureau; it was not her business to enquire into the antecedents of her guests. Herr Kluver had no choice but to accept Madame's explanation. Had he laid a hand on her he would have become the laughing-stock of the region, already convulsed by the exploits of 'l'anglais du Belle-Vue'. One sees what Madame meant when she described the Breton people as '*astucieux*'.

But Mme Yvinec was to prove even more astute, and in the process of doing so to give the Gregorian saga its final ironical twist. After the war Madame wrote to Gregory at his Paris address enclosing a bill for 10,000 francs as his expenses at the Belle-Vue (she had no way of knowing, of course, that he was dead). Getting no reply she took the train for Paris and presented herself at 8 Rue d'Anjou, where she learned from the concierge, Mme Fauberge, of 'M de Grégoire's' sad demise. After suitable expressions of respect for the deceased, Mme Yvinec next enquired about Gregory's furniture and personal effects—'M de Grégore' had spoken to her often about the '*beaux meubles*' including the piano with which he had furnished his apartment. Now she learned that everything

[246]

had been stolen. The apartment had been stripped bare of every object that was not nailed to the floor.

It seemed that in June, 1940 Mme Fauberge had received a visit from a friend of Gregory's whose calling card gave his profession as '*dentiste*', though the concierge could no longer remember his name. Gregory had asked his dentist friend to place all of his furniture and personal property in storage, according to the latter's story. Like most Parisian concierges, Mme Fauberge was suspicious of strangers, asked the dentist to produce a written authorization signed by Gregory before she would let him into the apartment. Not having such an authorization, the dentist '*a reculé pour mieux sauter*', as Mme Yvinec expressed it. A few days later while Mme Fauberge was out shopping the dentist returned with a removal van and two helpers, and proceeded to empty the apartment of its contents. (The dentist, it appeared, had a key to the apartment, and, in the absence of the concierge, none of the locataires thought that there was anything unusual in such a removal.)

I myself spoke to Mme Fauberge, who confirmed the story as Mme Yvinec had told it to me. The concierge remembered Maundy Gregory well. ('*Il était toujours aimable, avec son petit chien.*') However, she was under the mistaken impression that the dentist had denounced Gregory to the Gestapo in order to gain possession of his property (apparently denunciations of this sort were common at the time). Finally, I consulted Didot-Bottin, the commercial directory, where I found a '*M Fevrier, dentiste*', listed a t106 Avenue Kléber, which is near the Trocadero.

Either M Fevrier (for it could be no other), acting on Gregory's instructions, placed all of the latter's personal property in storage in which case no doubt it has long since been dispersed in default of payment, or M Fevrier was an '*escroc*' (swindler) which is Mme Yvinec's term for him. The latter theory admittedly is intriguing. For if Fevrier stole all in the world that Gregory possessed then to him must go the credit for out-conning the prince of con-men.

Acknowledgments

For permission to consult the papers of David Lloyd George and of Andrew Bonar Law and to quote from copyright material contained therein I would like to thank A. J. P. Taylor and the Trustees of the Beaverbrook Library. (The initials 'LG' used in the text refer to the Lloyd George Papers, while 'BL' refers to those of Bonar Law.)

Among those who either knew Maundy Gregory personally, or who had some sort of contact with him during his London years, and who have given most generously of their reminiscences, I am most grateful to ex-Superintendent Arthur Askew of Scotland Yard, J. Rowland Sales, Miss Leila MacKinlay, Sir Colin Coote, Percy Muir, John Baker White, Mrs Maisie H. Saunders, and Dr Karl A. Abshagen.

I am indebted as usual for their advice and encouragement while I was writing the book to Tom and Elizabeth Van Dycke, who read it in manuscript. Another who has been of great help to me is Gerald Moylan, who was the first to investigate Gregory's life in any depth.

For documentation on Gregory's life in exile my thanks are due to Ronald Russell, Marcel D'Roubaix, A. E. Kitts, Peter Taylor, and Captain Leonard R. White. To Raymond Drey I owe the discovery that Maundy Gregory hid out from the Germans for four months in Brittany, and to Mme Yvinec a detailed account of how those four months were spent.

It seems invidious to select for individual mention among the names of the remainder who have been so helpful to me, and I can do no better than to list them alphabetically, with the hope that I have left no one out. They are: J. Vassall Adams, A. R. K. Barnard, Miss Phyllis Barnes, Msgr Kamal Bathish, Mrs Barbara Benjamin, Mrs Muriel Billyard-Leake, the Earl of Birkenhead, William Camp, Mrs Doris C. Cotton, the Dowager Countess Davidson, D.B.E., Cmdr Arthur Dunhill, M.V.O., Father Francis Edwards, S.J., George F. Hannam-Clark, Percy Hoskins, Mrs Victoria F. Houghton, Gerald Howson, Mrs Noel Iliffe, Robert Rhodes James, J. W. R. Keen-Hargreaves, Mrs Bryn Kelly, James Laver, the late Sir Compton Mackenzie, Donald McCormick, Peter Mazzina, Sir Francis Meynell, G. Ellis Miles, Prof. Emilio Morelli, Cyril Norton, Miss Helena Nicholls, H. B. Perkis, L. G. Pine, W. R. J. Pullen, M.V.O., Maurice Richardson, Donald

Rumbelow, Gordon Sewell, Miss May Trelawny, J. C. Trewin, Mrs Kathleen Tronson, Dr James Walsh, K.G.C.S.G., and Mme Edith Yapon.

Libraries and institutions to whom I am indebted include the British Museum Newspaper Library, the Public Record Office, the Lord Chamberlain's Office, the *Daily Telegraph*, *The Times*, the *Observer*, the *New Statesman*, the *Southern Evening Echo* of Southampton, the *Surrey Advertiser*, the *Dorking Advertiser*, and B.B.C.'s Radio Solent.

I am grateful to the following authors and/or publishers for permission to quote from their books: Robert Rhodes James and Weidenfeld and Nicolson for *Memoirs of a Conservative: J. C. C. Davidson's Memoirs and Papers, 1910–37*; Gerald Macmillan and The Richards Press for *Honours for Sale: The Strange Story of Maundy Gregory*; Cassell & Company Ltd for *The Quest for Corvo* by A. J. A. Symons.

Among other printed sources I have consulted I would like to mention the following:

Aldington, Richard. *Frauds*. London: William Heinemann Ltd., 1957.

Balfour, Patrick. *Society Racket: A Critical Survey of Modern Social Life*. London: John Long, Ltd., 1933.

Beaverbrook, Lord. *The Decline and Fall of Lloyd George*. London: Collins, 1963.

Beaverbrook, Lord. *Men and Power*. London: Hutchinson, 1956.

Birkenhead, the Earl of, *F. E.: The Life of F. E. Smith, First Earl of Birkenhead*. London: Eyre & Spottiswoode, 1960.

Blythe, Ronald. *The Age of Illusion: England in the Twenties and Thirties*. London: Hamish Hamilton, 1963.

Coote, Colin R. *Editorial*. London: Eyre & Spottiswoode, 1965.

Coote, Colin R. 'Scandals of the Century: £12,000 a Knight.' The *Daily Telegraph Magazine Supplement*, February 27, 1970.

Donaldson, Francis. *Evelyn Waugh: Portrait of a Country Neighbour*. London: Weidenfeld and Nicolson, 1967.

Graves, Robert and Alan Hodge. *The Long Week-End: A Social History of Great Britain, 1918–1939*. London: Faber & Faber, 1940.

Hamilton, Gerald. *The Way It Was With Me*. London: Leslie Frewin, 1969.

Hanham, H. J. 'The Sale of Honours in Late Victorian England.' *Victorian Studies*, March, 1960.

Jones, Thomas. *Whitehall Diary, 1916–1930*, 2 vols. London: Oxford University Press, 1969.

Lloyd George, Earl. *Lloyd George*. London: Frederick Muller Ltd. 1960.

Meyrick, Mrs Kate. *Secrets of the 43*. London: John Long, Ltd., 1933.

Mowat, C. L. *Britain Between the Wars, 1918–1940*. London: Methuen & Co., 1955.

Nicolson, Harold. *King George V*. London: Constable & Co. Ltd., 1952.

Owen, Frank. *Tempestuous Journey: Lloyd George, His Life and Times*. London: Hutchinson, 1954.

Pakenham, Simona. *Pigtails and Pernod*. London: Macmillan & Co., 1962.

Pakenham, Simona. *60 Miles from England: The English at Dieppe, 1814–1914*. London: Macmillan, 1967.

Richardson, Maurice. 'Coronets for Sale.' *Lilliput*, February, 1950.

Sparrow, Gerald. *The Great Swindlers*. London: John Long, 1959.

Symons, Julian. *A. J. A. Symons: His Life and Speculations*. London: Eyre & Spottiswoode, 1950.

Taylor, A. J. P. *Beaverbrook*. London: Hamish Hamilton, 1972.

Trewin, J. C. *Benson and the Bensonians*. London: Barrie & Rockliff, 1960.

Werth, Alexander. *France in Ferment*. London: Jarrolds, 1934.

White, John Baker. *True Blue: An Autobiography, 1902–1939*. London: Frederick Muller, 1970.

Index